THE SCOPE AND METHOD

OF POLITICAL ECONOMY

THE

SCOPE AND METHOD

OF

POLITICAL ECONOMY

BY

JOHN NEVILLE KEYNES

[*Fourth Edition 1917*]

AUGUSTUS M. KELLEY • PUBLISHERS

CLIFTON 1973

First Edition 1890

Fourth Edition 1917

(*London*: Macmillan & Company, 1917)

Reprinted 1963 & 1973 by

Augustus M. Kelley Publishers

REPRINTS OF ECONOMIC CLASSICS

Clifton New Jersey 07012

PRINTED IN THE UNITED STATES OF AMERICA
by SENTRY PRESS, NEW YORK, N. Y. 10013

PREFACE TO THE FIRST EDITION.

THE nature of the topics discussed in the following pages is sufficiently indicated in the introductory chapter, and a lengthy preface is therefore unnecessary. The abstract discussion of methods may appear to some to have mainly an academic interest, since it does not directly extend our knowledge of economic phenomena. Whilst, however, we ought to be upon our guard against allowing any such discussion to obscure the greater importance of actual economic investigations, the subject is one to which all students of economics must necessarily give some attention in the course of their reading, and its indirect bearing on the solution of practical economic questions is very far indeed from being without importance. Unfortunately almost every problem connected with the scope and method of political economy has given rise to conflict of opinion; and the resulting controversies have sometimes been very bitter. Those readers, therefore, who already have any acquaintance with the literature of economic method, will be prepared to find that several of the chapters are more or less controversial in character. At the same time, I have endeavoured to avoid the tone of a partisan, and have sought, in the treatment of disputed questions, to represent both sides without prejudice. Whilst making no attempt to bring about a complete reconciliation between opposing views, I have been able to shew that the nature of the opposition between them has sometimes been misunderstood, and its extent consequently exaggerated.

Since the scope and method of a science can never be satisfactorily discussed at the commencement of its study, some knowledge of political economy in its general outlines is presupposed. As far as possible, however, illustrations of a fairly simple and familiar kind have been chosen. A good many illustrations that were included in the first draft of the book have been omitted, partly because they would have occupied too much space if given with any completeness, and partly in order to avoid points of controversy not essentially connected with the subject immediately under discussion. A certain amount of repetition has resulted from the frequent necessity of treating the same problem from more than one point of view, and from the fact that the different questions to which the consideration of economic method gives rise are in so many ways connected one with another. I have not hesitated to repeat the same thing several times in different connexions, if clearness seemed to be gained thereby.

By means of quotations and references I have endeavoured to make clear my indebtedness to other writers; and it is, therefore, for the most part unnecessary to specify here the various sources from which I have derived assistance. To the works both of Professor Marshall and Professor Sidgwick, however, I am indebted in ways that it is impossible to identify and separately indicate. I am further under obligation to Professor Marshall, and also to Mrs Marshall, Mr W. E. Johnson, and Professor Nicholson, for their great kindness in reading the proof-sheets of the book while it has been passing through the press. Their criticisms and suggestions have been most valuable, and have enabled me in many ways to improve my treatment of the subject.

J. N. KEYNES.

6, HARVEY ROAD, CAMBRIDGE.
12 *December* 1890.

CONTENTS.

CHAPTER I.

INTRODUCTORY.

CHAPTER II.

ON THE RELATION OF POLITICAL ECONOMY TO MORALITY AND PRACTICE.

CHAPTER III.

ON THE CHARACTER AND DEFINITION OF POLITICAL ECONOMY REGARDED AS A POSITIVE SCIENCE

NOTE TO CHAPTER III.

CHAPTER IV.

ON THE RELATION OF POLITICAL ECONOMY TO GENERAL SOCIOLOGY.

NOTES TO CHAPTER IV.

CHAPTER V.

ON DEFINITION IN POLITICAL ECONOMY.

CHAPTER VI.

ON THE METHOD OF SPECIFIC EXPERIENCE IN POLITICAL ECONOMY.

CHAPTER VII.

ON THE DEDUCTIVE METHOD IN POLITICAL ECONOMY.

CHAPTER VIII.

ON SYMBOLICAL AND DIAGRAMMATIC METHODS IN POLITICAL ECONOMY.

CHAPTER IX.

ON POLITICAL ECONOMY AND ECONOMIC HISTORY.

NOTES TO CHAPTER IX.

A. ON THE LIMITS OF THE VALIDITY OF ECONOMIC DOCTRINES.

B. ON THE CONCEPTION OF POLITICAL ECONOMY AS A DISTINCTIVELY HISTORICAL SCIENCE . . 314

CHAPTER X.

ON POLITICAL ECONOMY AND STATISTICS.

NOTE TO CHAPTER X.

ON SOME OF THE PRECAUTIONS REQUISITE IN THE USE OF STATISTICS IN ECONOMIC REASONINGS.

THE SCOPE AND METHOD OF POLITICAL ECONOMY.

CHAPTER I.

INTRODUCTORY.

§ 1. *Nature and importance of the enquiry into the scope and method of political economy.*—In the terms *economy* and *economic* there is an ambiguity that underlies much of the current confusion as to the nature of political economy. Any line of action is commonly termed *economic* when it attains its end with the least possible expenditure of money, time, and effort; and by *economy* is meant the employment of our resources with prudence and discretion, so that we may derive from them the maximum net return of utility.

But the words are also used in a sense not implying any specially reasonable adaptation of means to ends;

and in works on political economy the term *economic* is generally employed simply as an adjective corresponding to the substantive *wealth*. By an economic fact, accordingly, is understood any fact relating to the phenomena of wealth. By economic activities are meant those human activities that direct themselves towards the creation, appropriation, and accumulation of wealth; and by economic customs and institutions, the customs and institutions of human society in regard to wealth.

Political economy or *economics* is a body of doctrine relating to economic phenomena in the above sense; and the purpose of the following pages is to discuss the character and scope of this doctrine, and the logical method appropriate to its development. In seeking to define the *scope* of any department of study, the object in view is primarily to determine the distinguishing features of the phenomena with which it deals, and the kind of knowledge that it seeks concerning these phenomena. The enquiry also involves an examination of the relations between the study in question and cognate branches of study. In passing to the consideration of *method*, we are dealing with a branch of applied logic, the object being to determine the nature of the logical processes specially appropriate to the study—that is, the methods of investigation and proof of which it can avail itself—

and the logical character of its conclusions as affected thereby.

The discussion that follows belongs, then, to what may be called the philosophy or logic of political economy, and does not directly advance our knowledge of economic phenomena themselves. For this reason, a certain impatience is sometimes felt when any such discussion is proposed. What we want, it is said, is not any more talk about method, but rather useful applications of the right method; let us increase our actual stock of economic truths, instead of indulging in barren disputes about the way in which economic truths are to be attained. To this objection the logician might reply that the enquiry has at any rate a logical, even if it has not an economic, significance. But it has also an economic significance. A moment's consideration will shew that, from the point of view of political economy itself, it is of material importance that its scope and method should be rightly understood.

There is, to begin with, a widely current confusion as to the nature of economic laws; and for this reason, amongst others, it is imperative that the economist should seek to define as accurately as possible the nature and limits of his sphere of enquiry. There should be no vagueness on the question whether political economy is concerned with the actual or the

ideal, whether it treats merely of what is, or asks
further what ought to be, laying down rules for the
attainment of those ends that it pronounces desirable.
Even if theoretical and practical enquiries are both
to be included within its scope, still the distinction
between the two, and their mutual relations, need to be
clearly and unambiguously set forth. Misunderstanding
on these points has led to a misunderstanding of economic truths themselves, and has consequently impaired
the influence and authority of economic science.

Next as to method, it is said that instead of arguing
about what method of investigation is the right one,
it is better to exemplify the right method by employing
it in the actual attainment of new economic truths.
But are we then to beg the question of its rightness?
In the long run, time cannot but be saved by making
a preliminary study of the instruments of investigation
to be used, the proper way of using them, and the kind
of results that they are capable of yielding. For in so
far as methods of reasoning are employed without due
regard to the conditions of their validity, the results
gained must likewise be of uncertain validity, and the
progress of economic knowledge, instead of being
advanced, will be retarded.

The process, moreover, whereby a conclusion is
reached affects its character and value, and the qualifications and limitations subject to which it is to be

accepted. If it is purely empirical, then it will be established only with a more or less high degree of probability, and it cannot be extended far beyond the range of space or time over which the instances on which it is based were collected. If, on the other hand, it is obtained deductively, then it is hypothetical until it has been determined how far, and under what conditions, the assumptions on which it rests are realised in fact. It has been plausibly argued that Ricardo's chief weakness was that he did not clearly appreciate the true nature of his own method. At any rate he did not, in interpreting his results, take the precautions necessary to provide against misconception on the part of many of his readers.

It is true that it is one thing to establish the right method for building up a science, and quite another thing to succeed in building it up. It is also true, as the Austrian economist Menger has remarked, that sciences have been created and revolutionized by those who have not stopped to analyse their own method of enquiry. Still their success must be attributed to their having employed the right method, even if they have employed it unconsciously or without going out of their way to characterize it. Their method must, moreover, be subjected to careful analysis before the value of their contributions to the science can be properly estimated.

Economics is not in any way peculiar in requiring that its method should be discussed. The logic of other sciences is, however, for the most part sufficiently dealt with in general works on logic or methodology. There are special reasons, partly to be found in the nature of the subject itself, and partly due to extrinsic causes, why the logic of political economy needs a more detailed consideration.

In the first place, economic science deals with phenomena that are more complex and less uniform than those with which the natural sciences are concerned; and its conclusions, except in their most abstract form, lack both the certainty and the universality that pertain to physical laws. There is a corresponding difficulty in regard to the proper method of economic study; and the problem of defining the conditions and limits of the validity of economic reasonings becomes one of exceptional complexity. It is, moreover, impossible to establish the right of any one method to hold the field to the exclusion of others. Different methods are appropriate, according to the materials available, the stage of investigation reached, and the object in view; and hence arises 'the special task of assigning to each its legitimate place and relative importance.

Another reason for discussing the true principles of economic method in some detail is that fallacious reasonings are more common in political economy than in most other studies. This is due only in part to the difficulty and complexity of the subject-matter with which the science is concerned. It deals with phenomena which, while encompassed with difficulties, are matters of every-day observation; and it has few technical terms that are not also terms of every-day discourse. A not unnatural consequence is that people think themselves competent to reason about economic problems, however complex, without any such preparatory scientific training as would be universally considered essential in other departments of enquiry. This temptation to discuss economic questions without adequate scientific preparation is all the greater, because economic conditions exert so powerful an influence upon men's material interests. "Few men," says General Walker, "are presumptuous enough to dispute with the chemist or mechanician upon points connected with the studies and labours of his life; but almost any man who can read and write feels himself at liberty to form and maintain opinions of his own upon trade and money. The economic literature of every succeeding year embraces works conceived in the true scientific spirit, and works exhibiting the most vulgar ignorance of economic history, and the most flagrant contempt for the conditions of economic investigation. It is much as if astrology were being pursued side by side with astronomy, or alchemy with chemistry." Broadly speaking, the general tendency of popular economics is towards rash generalizations and fallacious arguments *post hoc ergo propter hoc.* This is frequently combined with an imperfect analysis of fundamental conceptions, leading to confusion of thought and the selection of false propositions as self-evident postulates; and where deductive reasoning is employed, its results are often applied without regard to the conditions requisite for their valid application.

To this it must be added that the sharp distinctions drawn by opposing schools, and their narrow dogmatism, have unnecessarily complicated the whole problem. The subject has become involved in heated controversies, that have not only made it wearisome to unprejudiced persons, but have also done injury to the credit of political economy itself. Outsiders are naturally suspicious of a science, in the treatment of which a new departure is so often and so loudly proclaimed essential. So far, it may be inferred, from economists having made progress in their science, they cannot even agree how to set about their work.

The besetting fallacy of writers on economic method has been justly said to be the fallacy of exclusiveness.

A single aspect or department of economic study is alone kept in view, and the method appropriate thereto aggrandized, while other methods, of equal importance in their proper place, are neglected or even explicitly rejected. Hence the disputants on both sides, while right positively, are wrong negatively. Their criticisms on rejected methods are, moreover, too often based on misapprehension or misrepresentation. Methods are attacked for not doing what those who advocate their use have never imagined they could do; and the qualifications and limitations, with which each side expounds its own method, are overlooked by the other side. Thus combined with the fallacy of exclusiveness, or rather in consequence of it, there is in these controversies a remarkable prevalence of *ignoratio elenchi*. In the following pages an attempt will be made to do justice to all the different instruments of investigation of which the economist can avail himself; while attention will also be drawn to the limitations to which each in turn is subject.

§ 2. *The conception of political economy as a positive, abstract, and deductive science.*—The main points involved in controversies about economic method may be indicated in outline by briefly contrasting two broadly distinguished schools, one of which describes political economy as positive, abstract, and deductive, while the other describes it as ethical,

realistic, and inductive. It should be distinctly understood that this sharp contrast is not to be found in
the actual economic writings of the best economists
of either school. In the methods that they employ—
when they are really discussing the same problems—
there is to a great extent substantial agreement.
They differ, however, in the relative importance that
they attach to different aspects of their work; and
in their formal statements about method these differences become exaggerated.

The question of the right method of economic
enquiry was not as such discussed by Adam Smith;
and his views on the subject have, therefore, to be
gathered from his way of dealing with actual economic
problems. As a matter of fact, the support of his
authority has been claimed on behalf of both the schools
above referred to. It has been said of him that he first
raised political economy to the dignity of a deductive
science. But he has also been regarded as the founder
of the historical method in political economy.

The reason for this apparent contradiction is not
far to seek. It is to be found in Adam Smith's freedom
from excess on the side either of _à priori_ or of _à
posteriori_ reasoning. He rejected no method of enquiry
that could in any way assist him in investigating the
phenomena of wealth. For argument or illustration
he had recourse, as the occasion might arise, either

to elementary facts of human nature, or to complex facts of industrial life. He believed in a "natural" order of events, which might be deduced *à priori* from general considerations; but he constantly checked his results by appeals to the actual course of history. He worked up from abstractions to the complex realities of the economic world in which he lived. Thus, if on deductive grounds he lays down a doctrine of the tendency of wages to equality, he combines it with an inductive enquiry into the causes that check or restrict the operation of this tendency. If he sets forth the "natural" progress of opulence, he enters also upon an historical investigation of what the actual progress of opulence has been. If he condemns the doctrine of protection to native industry mainly on abstract grounds, he enforces his views with concrete illustrations and arguments in the greatest variety.

As regards the inductive tendencies noticeable in Adam Smith, his successor is to be found in Malthus; for the continuation and development of the abstract deductive tendencies we turn to Ricardo. Subsequent economists of the English school assimilated what was most characteristic in both these writers; but it was Ricardo, rather than Malthus, who gave to their work a distinctive tone, particularly in their specific analysis of the method to be pursued.

Senior and J. S. Mill were the earliest English

economists who definitely formulated principles of
economic method. Senior's views are contained in his
introductory lectures before the University of Oxford,
and in his treatise on *Political Economy*; Mill's views
are to be found in his *Essays on some Unsettled Questions of Political Economy*, and in the sixth book of
his *Logic*. The problem is discussed in more detail
by Cairnes in his *Character and Logical Method of
Political Economy*, a work of admirable lucidity, which
was long considered the authoritative text-book of
English political economy, so far as concerned its logic.
Bagehot's essays on the postulates of English political
economy and on the preliminaries of political economy,
published in his *Economic Studies*, have also in some
respects a representative character.

There are minor differences in the principles laid
down by these four writers respectively, but fundamentally they are in agreement in regarding political
economy as a science that is in its scope positive as
distinguished from ethical or practical, and in its
method abstract and deductive. The following is a
very brief summary of their characteristic doctrines.

In the first place, a sharp line of distinction is
drawn between political economy itself and its applications to practice. The function of political economy
is to investigate facts and discover truths about
them, not to prescribe rules of life. Economic laws

are theorems of fact, not practical precepts. Political economy is, in other words, a science, not an art or a department of ethical enquiry. It is described as standing neutral between competing social schemes. It furnishes information as to the probable consequences of given lines of action, but does not itself pass moral judgments, or pronounce what ought or what ought not to be. At the same time, the greatest value is attached to the practical applications of economic science; and it is agreed that the economist ought himself to turn his attention to them—not, however, in his character as a pure economist, but rather as a social philosopher, who, because he is an economist, is in possession of the necessary theoretical knowledge. It is held that if this distinction is drawn, the social and ethical aspects of practical problems—which may be of vital importance—are less likely to be overlooked or subordinated.

As to its position amongst the sciences, political economy is not regarded as inseparably bound up with social philosophy in general. Economic facts are, it is allowed, influenced by social facts of very various kinds, and in their turn influence them; but it is nevertheless held to be possible up to a certain point to isolate the study of the phenomena of wealth from the study of other phenomena of society. Such isolation is, indeed, said to be necessitated by the requirements of science, which always proceeds by analysing concrete phenomena, so as to deal separately with their different aspects and the different elements of which they are composed. Economic science constitutes, therefore, a distinct, though not entirely independent, department of sociological speculation.

Passing to the means whereby the truths of the science are to be reached, it is held that on account of the variety and complexity of the influences to which economic phenomena are subject, the method of specific experience or direct induction is inadequate to yield more than empirical generalizations of uncertain validity. Experiment is, moreover, a resource from which the economist is debarred. It follows that we ought not to take as our starting point the analysis of concrete industrial facts. The right method of procedure is, on the contrary, deductive, or, as Mill puts it, à priori. The ultimate premisses upon which the deductive science is based are, moreover, limited in number, so that the more important of them admit of precise enunciation at the outset. For while the circumstances helping in some degree to mould economic phenomena are indefinitely numerous, there are a few whose influence is predominant, far outweighing that of all the rest. These predominating circumstances consist of a few simple and indisputable facts of human nature—as, for example, that in their economic dealings men are influenced by the desire for wealth—taken in connexion with the physical properties of the soil, and man's physiological constitution[1].

Political economy is accordingly spoken of as, in the main, an abstract science.   For in basing its conclusions on a limited number of fundamental assumptions, it has to leave out of account many circumstances, which are of importance in individual cases, but are nevertheless unimportant when instances are taken in the mass.   That other motives besides the desire for wealth do operate on various occasions in determining men's economic activities is recognised.   They are, however, to be neglected—at any rate in the first instance —since their influence is irregular, uncertain, and

[1] There is, however, some difference of view as to the extent to which the application of the resulting doctrines needs limitation. Bagehot regards the doctrines of English political economy as not applicable to all states of society, but only to those in which commerce has largely developed, and in particular taken the form of development which we find in England at the present time.   The relativity of economic investigations is also indicated incidentally by Cairnes.   Senior, on the other hand, remarks that those conclusions which relate to the nature and the production of wealth are universally true;   and although those which relate to the distribution of wealth are liable to be affected by the particular institutions of particular countries, still the natural state of things can be laid down as the general rule, and the anomalies produced by particular disturbing causes afterwards accounted for.   In other words, while Bagehot regards the premisses of political economy as relating only to the economic habits and institutions of a particular age and country, Senior regards them as "natural," and, with slight qualifications, as independent of age and country.

capricious. On these grounds, it is argued that the abstraction, whereby the science takes as its principal subject-matter an "economic man," whose activities are determined solely by the desire for wealth, is both legitimate and necessary; and, in further justification thereof, an analogy is drawn from mathematics and physics, which are said to be based upon corresponding abstractions[1].

On similar grounds, the science is spoken of by Mill and Cairnes as hypothetical. For inasmuch as its premisses do not exhaust all the causes affecting the result, its laws are only true hypothetically, that is, in the absence of counteracting agencies. The same point is expressed by saying that political economy is a science of tendencies only, not of matters of fact, its object being to work out and ascertain the result of certain great forces, as if these alone operated, and nothing. else exerted any modifying influence[2].

Senior sums up his views in the dictum that political economy "depends more on reasoning than on

[1] Mill and Bagehot specially insist upon the high degree of abstraction involved in economic reasonings. Bagehot more than once repeats that "English political economists are not speaking of real men, but of imaginary ones; not of men as we see them, but of men as it is convenient to us to suppose they are" (*Economic Studies*, p. 5).

[2] Senior, while affirming that the conclusions of political economy are true only in the absence of disturbing causes, still calls it a positive, as distinguished from a hypothetical, science. By this he means that its premisses are not arbitrarily assumed.

observation." Mill, Cairnes, and Bagehot, however, all insist that the appeal to observation and experience must come in, before the hypothetical laws of the science can be applied to the interpretation and explanation of concrete industrial facts. For it then has to be ascertained how far, as regards the particular cases under consideration, allowance needs to be made for the operation of disturbing causes—that is, for the peculiar modifications introduced by the minor influences affecting economic phenomena. Comparison with observed facts provides a test for conclusions deductively obtained, and enables the limits of their application to be determined. Accordingly, while the method of specific experience is regarded as altogether inefficacious for the discovery of economic laws, and as incapable of affording independent proof of their validity, it is nevertheless considered to form an indispensable supplement to the deductive reasoning that constitutes the framework of the science.

The above doctrines of economic method, which are those explicitly formulated by the writers referred to, need to be interpreted and in some respects qualified by reference to their actual economic writings. For if, from an examination of the latter, we seek to deduce their views on method, we find that their practice does not precisely correspond with their theory; and we are led to the conclusion that, judged by their own writings, they state their doctrines on method in too absolute a manner, in particular exaggerating the abstractness of political economy taken as a whole. They also speak as if the science had reached the deductive stage in a more definitive manner than is apparent from their own way of dealing with economic problems.

In treating of the production of wealth, for example, as is pointed out by Professor Sidgwick, Mill and other economists of his school have always employed an inductive and analytical method, the deductive element in their reasonings being in this part of their subject essentially subordinate. Mill is even more distinctly an inductive economist in his elaborate discussion of peasant proprietorship in its economic aspects. There is no doubt a deductive element, based on psychological data, in his argument as to the effect of ownership on the cultivator's industry and energy. But even on this point he brings a considerable amount of *à posteriori* evidence to bear; and his general argument depends mainly on an inductive and comparative investigation of the actual working of peasant proprietorship in France, Switzerland, and other countries, in which the operation of the system can be observed on a considerable scale. Cairnes, again, in his work on the *Slave Power*, where he analyses the general economic characteristics of slave labour, establishes some important economic doctrines by a careful inductive study of facts, comparatively little use being made of deductive reasoning.

It is true that the general theory of distribution and exchange, expounded by the school of Mill, is based on reasoning of an abstract character; but even here the writers, to whom reference has been made, tend to exaggerate the characteristics of their own method. They do not hold themselves aloof from the concrete realities of the actual economic world to anything like the extent that their description of the science would lead their readers to anticipate; and it is very far from the truth to say that their doctrines are wholly constructed out of a few elementary laws of human nature. At all events, in order to establish their consistency, a large portion of their best economic work must be regarded as concerned with the practical modifications of the truths of political economy, rather than with those truths themselves.

The contrast is specially marked between Mill's theory of method as contained in the *Essays*, and his practice as manifested in the *Principles*. In the former, the conception of the "economic man" occupies a position of central and all-pervading importance; in the latter, it plays a much humbler part. Moreover, in his *Principles of Political Economy*, Mill avowedly treats, not merely of these principles themselves, but also of "some of their applications to social philosophy." He states in his preface that while he desires to give an exposition of the abstract doctrines of political economy, he also desires to give something more than this; his object is to include "a much wider range of ideas and of topics, than are included in political economy, considered as a branch of abstract speculation." Moral and social considerations, in the widest sense, receive accordingly their due share of attention; and it would be difficult to find a better instance of an ethical treatment of economic problems than is contained in the chapter on "the probable future of the labouring classes."

§ 3. *The conception of political economy as an ethical, realistic, and inductive science.*—The emphasis with which the earlier systematic writers on economic method, especially in England, dwelt upon the abstract side of political economy led to a reaction, which took its rise in Germany, and is especially connected with the names of Roscher, Hildebrand, and Knies. The two schools, thus broadly distinguished, are sometimes spoken of as the English and the German respectively. These designations have the merit of brevity; and, taking into account what was actually written about method by English and German economists respectively during the middle part of the nineteenth century, they are not without justification. They must not, however.

be interpreted too literally. The doctrine of method set forth in the preceding section does not fairly represent the many-sidedness of English work in economics. In particular, it fails to assign a sufficiently important place to the mass of historical and statistical material that the labour of English economists has provided. The doctrine would, moreover, be accepted only in a modified and broadened form by those contemporary economists who avowedly carry on the traditions of the English school. Again, the so-called German doctrines, whatever may have been their origin, are no longer the peculiar possession of any one country. They are, for example, represented by a rising school of economists in the United States, who expressly repudiate the assertion that the new movement is exclusively a German movement. Even in England the spirit of the reaction was manifested long ago by Richard Jones, and in more recent years very forcible expression has been given to it by Cliffe Leslie and others. On the other hand, amongst distinguished economists who have employed a highly abstract method of treating economic problems, several Germans, *e.g.*, von Thünen, are to be included; and more recently there has sprung up in Austria a new school, which insists very emphatically on the necessity of an abstract treatment of the science[1].

---

[1] Professor Carl Menger of Vienna is one of the principal leaders

Subject to the foregoing explanation, it is convenient to speak of the school of Roscher and Knies as the German school. The explicit teaching of this school in regard to the scope and method of economics is briefly indicated in the following paragraphs[1].

In the first place, a more extended scope is given

in this later development of German opinion. Compare his *Untersuchungen über die Methode der Socialwissenschaften und der Politischen Oekonomie insbesondere*. He specially insists on the necessity of distinguishing theoretical political economy from economic history and statistics on the one hand, and from the practical sciences of political economy on the other; and he accuses the dominant German school both of misunderstanding the point of view of the abstract method, and of attributing an exaggerated importance to the historical. He further charges them with error in attempting to give an ethical direction to theoretical political economy. He speaks still more strongly in a very controversial series of letters specially directed against Schmoller, and published under the title *Die Irrthümer des Historismus in der Deutschen Nationalökonomie*. Professor Emil Sax of Prague is in agreement with Menger on fundamental points, but presents his views in a less controversial form. He insists strongly on the importance of pure theory. Compare his *Wesen und Aufgaben der Nationalökonomie*.

[1] On the points that follow compare Roscher, *Geschichte der National-Oekonomik in Deutschland*, especially pp. 1032—1036; Knies, *Die Politische Oekonomie vom Standpunkte der geschichtlichen Methode*; Schönberg's article on *Die Volkswirthschaft* (in his *Handbuch*), §§ 1—13; and Wagner, *Systematische Nationalökonomie* in the *Jahrbücher für Nationalökonomie und Statistik*, March, 1886 (translated in the *Quarterly Journal of Economics*, vol. i., p. 113). A good historical account of the new German political economy of which the foundations were laid in the years 1842—53, principally by Roscher, Hildebrand, and Knies, is given in Cohn's *System der Nationalökonomie, Grundlegung*, §§ 108—122. See also Professor Ashley's article on the *Historical School of Economists* in Mr Palgrave's *Dictionary of Political Economy*.

to the science than is usual with English economists; for it is avowedly made to treat of what ought to be as well as of what is. The possibility of drawing any clear line of separation between these enquiries is, indeed, practically denied. It is held that there can be no purely positive science of political economy, such as was contemplated by Cairnes.

The school explicitly calls itself ethical; it regards political economy as having a high ethical task, and as concerned with the most important problems of human life. The science is not merely to classify the motives that prompt to economic activity; it must also weigh and compare their moral merit. It must determine a standard of the right production and distribution of wealth, such that the demands of justice and morality may be satisfied. It must set forth an ideal of economic development, having in view the intellectual and moral, as well as the merely material, life; and it must discuss the ways and means—such as the strengthening of right motives, and the spread of sound customs and habits in industrial life, as well as the direct intervention of the State—by which that ideal is to be sought after[1].

[1] It should be observed that differences in regard to the scope of a science may be to a considerable extent merely verbal. One writer may include within the science itself enquiries which another writer regards as belonging only to its applications; but it does not follow that the latter neglects these enquiries, or even in the slightest degree attaches less importance to them.

Another characteristic of the German historical school is the manner in which its adherents insist upon the social side of political economy, and the interdependence of economic and other social phenomena. It is held that, because of this interdependence, political economy cannot be treated adequately except in close connexion with other branches of social science. The treatment adopted ought, accordingly, to be realistic. It is maintained that the economist should only very sparingly, if at all, abstract from the complex realities of actual economic life; and should consequently in most of his reasonings deal, not with an abstract "economic man," subject only to a single motive, the desire for wealth, but directly with men as they really are, moved by diverse motives, and influenced by the actual conditions of the age and society in which they live. Closely connected with this characteristic is the insistence upon the relativity of economic doctrines. The economic conditions of life are subject to variation; and subject to like variation are the laws by which men's economic activities are regulated.

As to the method of reasoning by which economic knowledge is to be extended, great stress is laid on the necessity of appealing constantly to specific observation of the actual economic world, and generalizing therefrom. Hence the school is spoken of as inductive and statistical. It is still more distinctively designated historical, from its special insistence on the importance of historical material in building up the science. Only by reference to the past, it is held, can the present be properly understood; and only by a comparison of the economic conditions of different periods and different countries can the limitations of economic doctrines be adequately realised, and economists saved from one-sided and narrow dogmatism. The importance of studying the course of economic evolution is, accordingly, emphasized.

It should be added that, independently of differences in regard to the scope and method of political economy, the dominant German school is distinguished from the older English economists by a difference of attitude towards *laisser faire* and government interference. This is, however, a point of contrast with which we are not directly concerned in the present treatise.

It will be observed that the above-mentioned characteristics are by no means independent of one another. In some cases the connexion is very close indeed. The more realistic our standpoint, for example, the more obvious becomes the necessity of direct appeals to history and statistics; the historical method leads perforce to the recognition of the relativity of economic doctrines; and the realistic and the social standpoints are also closely connected. In its turn, the ethical conception of the science emphasizes all the other points;

and in fact, if it be granted that political economy is directly concerned with what ought to be, then most of the rest may be said logically to follow[1]. It results from this dependence of characteristics that in discussing the various questions at issue a certain repetition is unavoidable. Accordingly, in the following pages, even when we are treating apparently distinct problems, there will not unfrequently be found a recurrence of the same fundamental points, viewed in different aspects.

Within the new school itself marked differences of tone and attitude are to be observed. The more advanced members of the school are not content with emphasizing the importance of the historical method, but go so far as to reject the aid of any other method except in extreme subordination to it. They are not simple reformers, but revolutionaries; for they advocate a complete reconstruction and transformation of political economy. In their view, the science in the past has been barren of valuable results; only by a radical change of method can it hope to be fruitful in the future. The old doctrines, and the old ways of reaching them, are to be put on one side and seen no more. Professor Schmoller and Dr Ingram may be taken as

---

[1] It will be shewn, however, that the converse does not hold good; that it is, in other words, possible to adopt a realistic treatment of economic problems without passing ethical judgments.

examples of this advanced wing of the new school.
The former would practically identify political economy
and economic history, or at any rate resolve political
economy into the philosophy of economic history. The
latter, whose aim is somewhat different, though he is
equally revolutionary in his tendency, would absorb
political economy into general sociology.

The position taken by the more moderate adherents
of the German school, including Roscher himself, is in
marked contrast to the above. They adopt a tone of
moderation and an attitude of compromise. While
insisting on the importance of historical investigation
in political economy, they admit the necessity of employing other methods in conjunction therewith; and
while taking a realistic view of the science as a whole,
they recognise the value of abstraction, at any rate in
certain preparatory stages. They accept many of the
most characteristic of the old conclusions, and on the
old grounds. According to Professor Adolph Wagner,
who may be taken as a leading representative of the
more moderate section of the new school, the inductive
and deductive methods both have their place in economics. "These, then," he says, "are the two methods:
on the one hand, deduction from psychological motives
—first and foremost, deduction from the motive of
individual advantage, then from other motives; on
the other hand, induction from history, from statistics,

and from the less exact and less certain, yet indispensable, process of common observation and experience.   With both methods we are to approach the
various problems of political economy, and to solve
them so far as we can.   Which method is most to be
used depends on the nature of the particular problems;
but it depends also on the turn of mind, very likely on
the accident of training and education, of the individual
investigator."[1]

[1] *Quarterly Journal of Economics*, vol. i., p. 124.   In his *Lehr- und
Handbuch der politischen Oekonomie*, vol. i., p. 17, Wagner writes further
in the same strain.   "It is not," he says, "a question of completely
changing the method of deduction, nor of entirely replacing it by the
method of induction.   It would not be possible to attain the latter
aim; and, if it were possible, it would be neither right nor desirable.
The problem is to obtain an improvement in deductive procedure, a
more refined and deeper psychological foundation and development
of it, and a more careful application, particularly in concrete practical questions.   To this must be added constant attention to the
hypotheses from which deductions are being made, and a keener
discernment of the necessary limits of the applicability of the method.
In short, the true solution of the contest about method is not to be
found in the selection of deduction *or* induction, but in the acceptance of deduction *and* induction.   Each must be employed in the
cases where it is specially adapted to the particular nature of the
problem to be solved, and as far as possible—for it is not always
possible—there must be a combination of both, although in concrete
cases one or the other will take precedence."   Dr von Scheel expresses himself similarly.   Different methods, he says, are serviceable for the solution of economic problems.   "We must use both
inductive and deductive methods.   The most suitable method will
continually vary with the particular nature of the problem to be
solved" (Schönberg's *Handbuch, Die politische Oekonomie als Wissenschaft*, § 3).   Professor Gustav Cohn may be quoted to the same
effect.   The idea, he says, that mere collections of historical or

§ 4. *The method of political economy cannot adequately be described by any single phrase.*—We must not then exaggerate the opposition between what may be called the classical English school and the new school. The former realise more vividly the abstract problems of the science, and in writing on method keep these problems mainly in view. The latter realise more vividly the concrete problems, and hence lay stress on all the points which the English school have tended to overlook. But the difference is strictly speaking one of degree only; and we find the opposition reduced to a minimum, when we compare the actual procedure in the solution of given problems adopted by the best contemporary economists, whether they profess to belong to the new school or are content to be classed with the old[1].

statistical material can be made available for science, without deductive aids, is just as much an extravagance, as the opposite idea that out of deductions from elementary hypotheses the whole science can be constructed (*Grundlegung der Nationalökonomie*, p. 35). Dr E. R. A. Seligman, again, writing on behalf of the American supporters of the new movement, remarks that the more extreme of the Germans "have themselves overshot the mark, have unduly undervalued the work of the English school, and have in their zeal too dogmatically denied the possibility of formulating any general laws" (*Science Economic Discussion*, p. 21).

[1] In 1890, when the first edition of this work was published, the controversies referred to in this chapter were gradually becoming less acute; and since 1890 there has been a further advance towards a mutual understanding on the part of economic theorists and economic historians. Compare Professor Ashley, *On the Study of Economic History* (*Surveys : Historic and Economic*, pp. 1—21).

As to the doctrine to be expounded in the following pages, it will suffice here to say that while great importance will be attached to the place of the deductive method in economic enquiry, and while a protest will be entered against the unhistorical spirit evinced by those adherents of the new movement who proclaim the necessity for a complete reorganization of the science, still no attempt will be made to justify the doctrines of the older school in the precise form in which they were laid down by Mill and Cairnes. The method of political economy cannot adequately be described by any single phrase; and accordingly no one method will be advocated to the entire exclusion of other methods. It will, on the contrary, be shewn that, according to the special department or aspect of the science under investigation, the appropriate method may be either abstract or realistic, deductive or inductive, mathematical or statistical, hypothetical or historical.

CHAPTER II.

ON THE RELATION OF POLITICAL ECONOMY TO MORALITY AND PRACTICE.

§ 1. *Distinction between economic uniformities, economic ideals, and economic precepts.*—As regards the scope of political economy, no question is more important, or in a way more difficult, than its true relation to practical problems. Does it treat of the actual or of the ideal? Is it a positive science concerned exclusively with the investigation of uniformities, or is it an art having for its object the determination of practical rules of action? What, for example, is the true problem of political economy in regard to the influence of competition on wages? Is it to investigate the precise nature of that influence, and to enquire how far and in what ways the operation of competition is or may be modified by other agencies? Or is it rather to determine how far the effects of competition can be morally approved, and to what extent it is desirable that its operation should be supplemented or superseded by combination or direct governmental interference?

The distinction here indicated is indeed threefold
rather than twofold as is usually implied. For when
we leave the enquiry into the veritable order of economic phenomena, their coexistences and sequences,
under existing or assumed conditions, we still have to
take account of a further subdivision of some significance. There is, on the one hand, the investigation
of economic ideals and the determination of a standard
by reference to which the social worth of economic
activities and conditions may be judged; and there is
also the investigation of economic rules, *i.e.*, the determination of maxims or precepts by obedience to
which given ends may best be attained[1]. Thus, in

---

[1] There is still another distinction, which need not, however, be
dwelt upon—namely, the distinction between economic maxims as
formulated by the student, and their practical outcome in the actual
legislation of different countries. Even this distinction is not always
clearly recognised. It seems, for instance, to be obscured in the
following passage in Lord Bramwell's address as President of Section F of the British Association: "What will be the best way to
add to the wealth of a society must be a subject of study by that
society, which will lay down rules—that is to say, make laws—for
the purpose; and this is political economy. Adam Smith was not
the first political economist, though well called the father of those
rules which now prevail. But rules for the purpose existed before
him, the great objection to them being that most of them were wrong.
There was a law that the dead should be buried in woollen. Laws
were made for fixing wages; laws were made against regrating and
forestalling. Then think of the usury laws. You cannot deny that
these were economical laws because you think them wrong." The laws
here referred to cannot in any proper sense be called laws of political
economy. Even if political economy is regarded as an art, the
precepts of that art must be distinguished from the actual practice

regard to the payment of interest, we have, first, the positive enquiries why, under certain conditions of industry, interest is paid at all, and what determines the rate paid. We have, secondly, the enquiries whether interest ought to be paid, and, if it ought, what constitutes a fair rate of interest. We have, thirdly, the enquiries whether any interference in regard to the payment of interest is desirable, and, if so, what are the best means whereby such payment may either be abolished or at least approximated to a fair standard.

Another illustration may be taken from the department of taxation. The investigation of the incidence of taxation is in itself a positive enquiry; so is the problem of the influence of different forms of taxation on relative values. These are, in other words, enquiries as to matters of fact. Passing to problems that belong to a different category, we may distinguish the determination of the ideal of taxation from that of rules of taxation in the narrower and stricter sense. It is one thing to ask in what sense, if any, and why, equality of taxation should be our aim; it is another thing to enquire by what rules, *e.g.*, the adoption of a system of progressive taxation or the judicious combination of direct and indirect taxation, such

of politicians and finance ministers, however much their acts may be the direct legislative embodiment of the precepts.

equality can with the nearest possible approximation be attained.

Intimate as are the connexions between the above kinds of enquiry, they are in themselves distinct in character, and belong to different departments in a classification of knowledge. The first belongs to positive science, the second to normative or regulative science (along with ethics, if indeed it be not a branch of ethics or of what may be called applied ethics), and the third not to science at all in the more modern use of the term, but to art as distinguished therefrom.

As the terms are here used, a *positive science* may be defined as a body of systematized knowledge concerning what is[1]; a *normative* or *regulative science* as a body of systematized knowledge relating to criteria of what ought to be, and concerned therefore with the ideal

[1] The use of the term *positive* to mark this kind of enquiry is not altogether satisfactory; for the same term is used by Cairnes and others in contrast to *hypothetical*, which is not the antithesis here intended. It is difficult, however, to find any word that is quite free from ambiguity. *Theoretical* is in some respects a good term and may sometimes be conveniently used. In certain connexions, however, it is to be avoided, inasmuch as it may be understood to imply an antithesis with *actual*, as when theory and fact are contrasted; it may also suggest that the enquiries referred to have little or no bearing on practical questions, which is of course far from being the case. Professor Sidgwick in his *Methods of Ethics* employs the term *speculative*; but this term, even more than the term *theoretical*, suggests something very much in the air, something remote from the common events of every-day life. It seems best, therefore, not to use it in the present connexion.

as distinguished from the actual[1]; an *art* as a system of rules for the attainment of a given end[2].   The object of a positive science is the establishment of *uniformities*, of a normative science the determination of *ideals*, of an art the formulation of *precepts*.

The problem whether political economy is to be regarded as a positive science, or as a normative science, or as an art, or as a combination of these, is to a certain extent a question merely of nomenclature and classification.   It is, nevertheless, important to distinguish economic enquiries according as they belong to the three departments respectively; and it is also important to make clear their mutual relations. Confusion between them is common and has been the source of many mischievous errors.

An endeavour will be made in the following pages

[1] It should be particularly observed that a department of knowledge does not necessarily belong to the category of art, as distinguished from science, simply because it is concerned with what ought to be.   Logic and ethics are both of them sciences, although they are concerned with *right* reasoning and *right* conduct respectively.   In the following pages, however, whenever science is contrasted with art without further qualification, positive science, and not normative science, is had in view.

[2] To avoid misunderstanding, it should be added that Adam Smith and his contemporaries, as well as some modern economists, use the term *science* without any reference to the distinction between science and art as above indicated.   They mean by a science any systematic body of knowledge, whether consisting of theoretical propositions, or of practical rules of action.   The best recent authorities, however, at any rate in this country, use the term in the narrower sense.

to shew that it is both possible and desirable to discuss economic uniformities independently of economic ideals, and without formulating economic precepts, although the converse proposition cannot be affirmed; and it follows that, if this view be correct, we ought at least to recognise as fundamental a positive *science of political economy* which is concerned purely with what is, and which seeks to determine *economic laws*[1]. It is a further question whether or not we should also recognise, as included under political economy in the widest sense—but distinct from the positive science—(a) a branch of ethics which may be called the *ethics of political economy*, and which seeks to determine *economic ideals*; and (b) an *art of political economy*, which seeks to formulate *economic precepts*.

---

[1] We here use the term *law*, as it will consistently be used in the following pages, in its scientific, and not in its jurisprudential, sense. We mean by a *law* a theorem, the statement of a uniformity, not a command enforced by sanctions. The law of supply and demand, the Ricardian law of rent, Gresham's law, and the like, may be given as examples of economic laws, in the above sense. The validity of such laws is a purely theoretical question, and our attitude towards them is not, or at any rate should not be, affected by our ethical or political views. It is otherwise as soon as we begin to lay down rules for the guidance of statesmen and legislators. When we argue for fair trade or for free trade, when we advocate the legislative restriction of hours of labour or the nationalization of the land, or when we contend for a general policy of *laisser faire*, we have advanced a stage further. Considerations based on political economy, conceived as a positive science, may still form the foundation of our argument, but such data have to be controlled by ethical and political considerations.

§ 2. *The possibility of studying economic laws or uniformities without passing ethical judgments or formulating economic precepts.*—It has been pointed out in the preceding chapter that the prevailing tendency amongst a certain school of economists is to widen the scope of political economy by giving it a distinctly ethical character and making little attempt to separate its treatment as a practical science from its treatment as a theoretical science. It is even maintained that such a separation is impossible. Thus Professor Wagner, while clearly distinguishing the positive and the ethical problems, denies that either of them admits of being treated apart from the other, although taken together their treatment may be separated from that of the dependent art. He gives the five following problems (of which the first two belong to positive science as above defined, the third and fourth to normative or ethical science, and the fifth to art) as between them constituting the great general problem of political economy : (1) the description of economic phenomena; (2) the explanation of the causes upon which they depend; (3) the determination of a standard by which their social merit may be measured; (4) the setting up of an aim for economic progress; (5) the examination of the ways and means for attaining this aim. Of these problems he regards the first four as too closely connected to permit

a separation. Only the fifth, he considers, where we
have to deal with the practical questions of an art, can
be clearly distinguished from the rest[1]. Others would
not even admit the degree of separation that Wagner
allows. Dr von Scheel, for instance, remarks that the
history, theory, and art of political economy form one
indivisible whole[2].

Yet on reflection it seems clear that there can be
no inherent reason why we should not both describe
and explain economic phenomena without either passing
a judgment on their moral worth or setting up an aim
for economic progress; although of course the converse
does not hold good. It is clear, for example, that
we cannot determine how nearly the results of free
competition approximate to our economic ideal until
we know what those results are. Nor can we say
how far it is desirable that the effects which would be

[1] *Quarterly Journal of Economics*, vol. I., pp. 124—128. In a
later edition (1892) of his *Grundlegung der politische Oekonomie*, §§ 57
—64, Wagner interpolates between (1) and (2) as given above a third
theoretical problem, namely, the discovery of types. This yields a
symmetrical and interesting scheme in which we have three theoretical
and three practical problems. It is to be observed that in the edition
of the *Grundlegung* to which reference is here made, Wagner seems
more willing to admit the possibility of a separate discussion of the
three theoretical problems, although he regards all six problems as
involved in a complete treatment of any economic question. This
must be granted; but we may at the same time clearly distinguish
between economic science in the strict sense, the ethics of political
economy, and applied economics.

[2] Schönberg's *Handbuch*, vol. I., pp. 71, 72.

brought about by unimpeded competition should be modified by governmental interference or voluntary combination, until we have also ascertained what kind of modification would ensue, and what would be the collateral effects of such interfering agencies. We can, however, successfully investigate the nature of economic phenomena under the *régime* of competition, without comparing them with any ideal standard; and we can also correctly ascertain the effects exerted, or capable of being exerted, by agencies other than competitive—such as law, public opinion, voluntary combination, and the like—without expressing an opinion on the practical question how far it is desirable that the operation of agencies such as these should be specially encouraged[1].

[1] In discussing the connexion between science and art, it is necessary to distinguish the *logical* order from what may be called the *historical* order. It has often been pointed out that while in the logical order science precedes art, the historical order is the reverse of this. The reason is that the demand for guidance arising from men's practical needs is recognised, and attempts are made to satisfy it, before bodies of speculative truth are systematically formulated. Thus an empirical art of medicine exists before there is any distinct science of physiology. Indeed, as is remarked by Sir George Cornewall Lewis, "the purely scientific treatment of any subject, without an attempt to lay down precepts or rules of practice, is in general one of the latest stages in the journey of knowledge" (*Methods of Observation and Reasoning in Politics*, Chapter 19, § 5). But, as we have said, in the logical order science precedes art, for we cannot satisfactorily lay down rules for practical guidance except on the basis of knowledge of facts. When, therefore, this knowledge is not to be found elsewhere, the art must seek it as best

The proposition that it is possible to study economic uniformities without passing ethical judgments or formulating economic precepts seems in fact so little to need proof, when the point at issue is clearly grasped, that it is difficult to say anything in support of it that shall go beyond mere truism.   We may, however, seek to explain away certain difficulties, based on misapprehension, that have tended to prevent its truth from being universally recognised.   The idea probably is that any attempt to treat economic laws, without passing ethical judgments, and without reference to an ideal to be aimed at, is certain to result in a practical denial that moral considerations have any bearing on economic

it can for itself, thus becoming at the same time both a science and an art, the two enquiries, however, not being definitely distinguished. Strictly speaking, instead of saying that historically art precedes science, it would for the above reason be more accurate to say that at the outset there is no clearly marked line of distinction between them. Accordingly in early treatises on any art we expect to find, and we do find, theorems of science more or less explicitly set forth, justifying the rules which it is the authors' main purpose to expound.   Herein is the explanation of the fact that, while Adam Smith conceives political economy as an art, the *Wealth of Nations* assumes for the most part the form of a science.   The system of political economy there advocated, being "the obvious and simple system of natural liberty," does not in itself consist of any elaborate code of rules. Adam Smith is chiefly concerned to confute on scientific grounds other systems, and to establish the scientific basis of his own.   His first three books, to a large extent his fourth, and to some extent his fifth, are thus taken up with discussions in which the actual relations of phenomena are discussed and expounded.   On this point, compare Sidgwick, *Principles of Political Economy*, Introduction, Chapter 2.

phenomena at all. It has indeed been made a specific charge against English economics of the middle part of the nineteenth century that, seeking to be purely theoretical, it became in the worst sense *unmoral*, its tendency being to claim for economic action a sphere altogether independent of moral laws.

Whilst it would be difficult to substantiate this charge by reference to the actual writings of English economists of the first rank at any period, a certain justification for it may be found in the tone and attitude of some popular interpreters of economic science at the time referred to; and it will be useful to seek to discover the source of the error into which they fell. That it was an error hardly needs to be insisted upon. Nothing can be more deplorable than that the economist should be understood to imply that, in his industrial dealings, a man is freed from the ordinary obligations of justice and humanity. To refer an injustice in the economic world to demand and supply may possibly account for it; but it cannot seriously be maintained that from the point of view of the moralist or the social reformer this settles the matter. It needs no proof that neither economic activities nor any other class of human activities can rightly be made independent of moral laws.

But it is far from being the case that the fallacious attitude of mind here combated is a necessary

consequence of the attempt to construct a purely positive science of economics. On the other hand, it is
rather the failure to recognise the fundamentally distinct character of enquiries into what is, and enquiries
into what ought to be, that is really responsible for
attempts to solve practical economic questions without
reference to their ethical aspects. And this danger will
certainly not be diminished by endeavouring systematically to fuse the two classes of problems. There is,
however, a further source of confusion, to which it is
necessary at this point specially to call attention, due
to the non-recognition of the fact that from the purely
positive standpoint the operation of moral forces may
need to be taken into account. It has too often been
implied, though it may not often have been expressly
stated, that—at any rate in regard to what can actually
happen, as distinguished from what one might desire
to see happen—the last word has been said when the
effects of competition have been correctly ascertained
and set forth[1]. As a matter of fact, although the

---

[1] In Kingsley's *Alton Locke* we are told how a member of Parlia-
ment—one that was reputed a philosopher, and a political economist,
and a Liberal—replied to a deputation of working men that however
glad he would be to help them, it was impossible—he could not alter
the laws of nature—wages were regulated by the amount of competition among the men themselves, that is, by the laws of political
economy, which it would be madness and suicide to oppose (ch. 10).
No doctrine so crude as this, however, is taught by leading English
exponents of the science. "The distribution of wealth," says

forces of competition may usually exert a preponderating influence in the economic world, they have not the universality and necessity which is here ascribed to them, nor are they incapable of being, as we may say, moralized. Economic phenomena depend upon the activity of free agents, whose customary behaviour may be modified not merely by legislative interference, but also by changes in their own moral standard, or in the social pressure brought to bear upon them by public opinion; and it follows that, in general, we are not justified in assuming finality in regard to concrete industrial facts, or in affirming that, in the economic world, what is must be. It is true that

J. S Mill emphatically, "depends on the laws and customs of society. The rules by which it is determined are what the opinions and feelings of the ruling portion of the community make them, and are very different in different ages and countries; and might be still more different, if mankind so chose" (*Political Economy*, ii. 1, § 1). By "the ruling portion of the community" we ought here to understand not merely those who have a voice in framing a country's laws, but also those who mould public opinion and exert an influence on the moral tone of a people. Compare further Mill's *Autobiography*, p. 246, where he speaks of the modes of the distribution of wealth as dependent on human will, and capable therefore of being modified by human effort. At the same time, a caution should be added against going too far in ascribing an optional or arbitrary character to the laws of the distribution of wealth. It must not, for instance, be supposed that the sovereign power, whether democratic or otherwise, can arbitrarily impose upon a people any principles of distribution it pleases, regardless of the operation of ordinary economic motives and of the economic habits and customs which have naturally grown up and established themselves in the community.

extra-regarding motives are not in economic affairs as powerful or as constant in their operation as motives of a self-regarding character. Still they none the less do exercise an appreciable influence, and as the sense of social responsibility grows stronger and becomes more diffused their importance is likely to be increased[1].

It involves confusion of thought, however, to suppose that economic phenomena are for the above reason incapable of being studied positively, or that in our investigation of them we are necessarily bound to pass a judgment upon their moral worth. To recognise the influence, actual or potential, exerted by the economic ideals that men may frame for themselves is not the same thing as to discuss the objective validity of those

[1] When people talk about supply and demand, they sometimes forget that these are themselves phenomena depending upon human will, and that among the changes which may lead to modifications in supply or demand are changes in moral conditions. This may be the case, for instance, if, because the public conscience has been touched, people will not purchase commodities which they believe to have been produced under what they regard as immoral conditions; or if they will not deal with shops where the employers have the reputation of treating their employees meanly or harshly. The fact that, at any rate in the estimation of traders themselves, causes of this kind may operate to a very appreciable extent is shewn by the anxious indignation with which some large London firms repudiated certain statements made before the Select Committee of the House of Lords on the Sweating System (1888) in regard to their manner of paying their workpeople. More than one firm specially called the attention of the Committee to the fact that they "were being damnified and injured in their business by reason of the statements which were being made before their lordships."

ideals; and our treatment of economic science may remain strictly positive (in the sense in which we are now using that term), while at the same time we enquire in detail in what ways economic phenomena are or may be affected by the pressure of public opinion, or by motives of justice, and kindliness, and concern for the general well-being.

It has been argued that the science cannot be separated from the art of economics, because of the influence exerted by the latter upon the actual course of economic development[1]. There is an element of truth in this argument, which has perhaps been sometimes overlooked; but it does not establish the desired conclusion. Men are influenced in what they actually do by what they think they ought to do; and economic precepts, when enforced by the agency of the law or public opinion, lead to modifications of economic facts. But all this may be taken into account without leaving the positive for the practical standpoint. Consider, for example, the influence exerted upon medieval trade by doctrines of the illegitimacy of usury and of what constitutes a reasonable price. It is one thing to study the nature and extent of this influence. It is another thing to enquire into the validity of the doctrines themselves. And although

[1] Compare Professor H. C. Adams in *Science Economic Discussion*, p. 102.

the historian may more or less combine the two discussions, they clearly admit of logical separation.

We may conclude the argument contained in this section by the remark that, just as the science of psychology recognises the existence and operation of moral motives, yet does not pass ethical judgments, so political economy may recognise the operation of moral motives in the economic world, and yet not become an ethical science.

§ 3. *Grounds for recognising a distinct positive science of political economy, the sole province of which is to establish economic uniformities.*—Granting that it is logically possible to separate the positive from the ethical and practical study of economic phenomena, there is still no absolute inconsistency in holding that such a separation is undesirable. It may be pointed out how enormous is the influence exerted upon the well-being of mankind by the modes in which wealth is produced and distributed ; and stress may be laid upon the fact that those human activities, which constitute the subject-matter of the economist's investigations, have an ethical significance, which is at least as worthy of consideration as their economic significance. It is indeed not strange that the idea of an essentially ethical treatment of political economy should have a strong fascination for earnest minds. Nor is it strange that as our social sympathies grow broader and stronger, the notion of stopping short at the purely positive enquiry should be viewed with an increasing degree of impatience.

But in all this the point really at issue is obscured. No one desires to stop short at the purely theoretical enquiry. It is universally agreed that in economics the positive investigation of facts is not an end in itself, but is to be used as the basis of a practical enquiry, in which ethical considerations are allowed their due weight. The question is not whether the positive enquiry shall complete as well as form the foundation of all economic discussion, but whether it shall be systematically combined with ethical and practical enquiries, or pursued in the first instance independently.

The latter of these alternatives is to be preferred on grounds of scientific expediency.· Our work will be done more thoroughly, and both our theoretical and our practical conclusions will be the more trustworthy, if we are content to do one thing at a time. The following are, in rather more detail, the reasons that may be given for explicitly recognising the independence of the positive enquiry[1].

[1] The question of combining positive and ethical enquiries is a somewhat different one from that of combining enquiries that belong respectively to the departments of science and art. The two questions have, however, a good deal in common, and we shall, therefore, in order to avoid unnecessary repetition, treat them together. The reader will observe that in the arguments that follow the undesirability

(1) The attempt to fuse together enquiries as to what is, and enquiries as to what ought to be, is likely to stand in the way of our giving clear and unbiassed answers to either set of questions. Our investigation, for instance, of the laws that determine competitive wages cannot but be seriously hampered, if the very same discussion is to serve for a solution of the problem whether wages so determined are fair wages. The value of economic theories is, indeed, rightly measured by their ultimate bearing on practical questions; and the economist should always seek to direct his theoretical investigations into the channels that will eventually prove most useful from the practical standpoint. But while the ultimate aim may be to guide human conduct, the immediate object to be kept in view is knowledge of positive facts. Such knowledge is not likely to be accurate and thorough, if, instead of pursuing his theoretical enquiries systematically, the economist works them out piecemeal, as they happen to rise into importance in connexion with particular practical issues. It may require an effort to keep the practical problems in the background even temporarily, but in the long run the guidance afforded will be the more trustworthy, if its scientific foundations are first made secure[1].

sometimes of the former, and sometimes of the latter, combination is chiefly had in view.

[1] Bacon, in an often quoted passage, comments on the hasty and untimely eagerness with which men are apt to turn aside from pure

It may be added that since purely economic data rarely by themselves suffice for the complete solution of practical problems, either our solution of the latter will be incomplete, or else the discussion that belongs to the positive science of economics will not improbably be overlaid by the introduction of considerations which, so far as it is concerned, are extraneous[1].

science to its practical applications. "Whence it comes that, like Atalanta, they go aside to take up the golden apple, so meanwhile interrupting their course and letting victory slip out of their hands. But in the true course of experiment, and the carrying it on to new effects, the Divine Wisdom and Order are entirely to be taken as our examples. Now God on the first day of Creation created only Light, and gave a whole day for that work, and on that day created no material object. Similarly, in experience of every kind, first the discovery of causes and true Axioms is to be made; and light-bringing not fruit-bringing experiments to be sought for. But Axioms rightly discovered and established supply practical uses not scantily but in crowds; and draw after themselves bands and troops of effects ' (Novum Organum, Book i., Aph. 70).

[1] The importance of maintaining the strictly scientific standpoint in the academic study of political economy is insisted upon by Professor Dunbar as follows: "The investigation of economic law is a strictly scientific enquiry, as much as the investigation of the law of gravitation and the determination of economic law falls within the competence of the university. Indeed, one of the great objects for which the university exists is to train minds for such enquiry and to further the advance of knowledge in precisely such obscure departments. But on the mixed questions of legislative policy and expediency, it is not the province of the university to pronounce. They indeed involve questions of science, as they involve much else; but their solution is not an act of the scientific judgment. It is, on the contrary, an act of the political judgment, enlightened by the aid of economic science, of jurisprudence, of the study of human nature itself, or whatever else may serve to clear up the matter in hand. The historical narratives in which the great questions of the past lie

(2) The attempt to combine theoretical and practical enquiries tends to confirm the popular confusion as to the nature of many economic truths. What are laid down as theorems of pure science are constantly interpreted as if they were maxims for practical guidance. In spite of repeated protests from economists themselves, there is an inveterate disposition on the part of the public to regard the principles of political economy as essentially rules of conduct, even when the sole intention of those who formulate them is to determine what is, and not to prescribe what ought to be. Thus, because in economic theory men's action in buying and selling is commonly assumed to be governed by self-interest, political economy is supposed to in-

embedded are no doubt objects of university study, and the unravelling of their tangled threads affords a valuable training, by means of a subject-matter of unfailing interest; but it is no part of the business of the university to pronounce *ex cathedrâ* upon the policies which may find in such narratives some illustration, but which must after all rest upon indeterminate and probably transitory conditions. So, too, the great financial and industrial questions of the day supply the best of material for practice in the analysis of complicated problems and in the collecting and weighing of evidence; but in all this it is the acquisition of power in the dealing with problems, and not the solution of any practical question, that is the real matter in hand. The university may, and if successful in its true functions will, supply scientific data for the use of all who are concerned in the settlement of legislative and administrative questions; but when to these data are added the many others which form a part of the basis for all practical decisions, the further declaration of opinion from the university chair becomes an *obiter dictum*, not necessary in the strict performance of duty, and raising some difficult questions of expediency " (*Quarterly Journal of Economics*, July 1891, p. 411).

culcate selfishness; because many economic truths are based on the postulate of competition, trades-unions are spoken of as violating economic laws; and because it is laid down that, in a perfect market, price is determined by supply and demand, the science is represented as teaching that price ought so to be determined. This kind of confusion is perhaps particularly common in England where, for reasons that are to be found in the historical development of the science, political economy has to a large extent become identified in the public mind with the policy of *laisser faire*[1].

In order to remove this prejudice, it is most desirable that care should be taken to distinguish economic precepts from the theorems of the positive science upon which they are based. But if theoretical and practical enquiries are systematically merged together, the distinction can never be made thoroughly clear. Moreover, if we profess that our treatment of the subject is throughout ethical, then where we do not blame we shall naturally be understood to approve, or at least to excuse. Actually to express on every occasion an ethical judgment, and in so doing to strike always the true note, is an impossibility. It may be added that the moral character of economic phenomena varies even when their scientific character is the same.

---

[1] The connexion between political economy and the doctrine of *laisser faire* is touched upon further n a note at the conclusion of this chapter.

(3) There is a further reason why a positive science of political economy should receive distinct and independent recognition. With the advance of knowledge, it may be possible to come to a general agreement in regard to what is or what may be in the economic world, sooner than any similar agreement is attainable in regard to the rules by which the economic activities of individuals and communities should be guided. The former requires only that there shall be unanimity as to facts; the latter may be prevented by conflicting ideals, as well as by divergent views as to the actual or the possible. Take, for instance, the problem of socialism *versus* individualism. Even if philosophers are agreed as to facts, they may still arrive at contrary solutions of this problem, because they differ as to the true ideal of human society, and as to the comparative importance to be assigned, say, to the realisation of individual freedom.

If political economy regarded from the theoretical standpoint is to make good progress, it is essential that all extrinsic or premature sources of controversy should be eliminated; and we may be sure that the more its principles are discussed independently of ethical and practical considerations, the sooner will the science emerge from the controversial stage. The intrusion of ethics into economics cannot but multiply and perpetuate sources of disagreement. For if an ethical treatment of economic problems is to be systematic and thorough, and not merely sentimental and superficial, fundamental ethical questions that have long been the subject of controversy cannot be excluded—such questions, for instance, as the determination of a standard of justice, and the relation of this standard to the ordinary utilitarian standard. However necessary it may be to face these questions at a later stage, there is no reason why we should not have a positive science of economics that is independent of them.

In the following pages, then, it is this positive science that is meant by *political economy* when that term is used without further qualification[1].

At the same time, it does not follow that in pursuing his theoretical investigations, the economist need

[1] As a designation for the positive science, *economics* or *economic science* may be preferred to *political economy*, as being less likely to be used ambiguously. The name *political economy* is, however, too firmly established to be altogether discarded; and we, therefore, use all three of the names more or less indiscriminately. It is to be added that whatever ambiguity attaches to *political economy* is beginning also to attach to the other terms. Dr Cunningham, for instance, in his *Economics and Politics* in the main understands by economics, and by economic science, a system of maxims. "Economic science," he says, "is wholly practical, it has no *raison d'être* except as directing conduct towards a given end," namely, the pursuit of wealth; and the principles of economics are accordingly described as practical principles (such as are embodied in the mercantile system or in the system of *laisser faire*) which state the means to be pursued with reference to this end. On the use of the term *economic politics*, and for some further observations on the general subject discussed in this section, compare the note on page 78.

consider himself altogether precluded from indicating the ethical or practical significance of the theorems of fact which it is his primary object to formulate. An isolation of this kind is generally speaking impracticable. There are, indeed, some practical questions, especially in currency and banking, in which economic considerations are of such paramount importance, and the connexion between theory and practice is so immediate and obvious, that the refusal to consider at once the practical bearing of the theoretical discussion might seem to be unnecessarily pedantic, and to involve needless repetition. All that is meant is that if moral judgments are expressed, or practical applications pointed out, they should be regarded as digressions, not as economic *dicta*, constituting integral and essential portions of economic science itself. In other words, the theoretical and practical enquiries should not be systematically combined, or merged in one another, as is maintained by those who declare that political economy is an indivisible whole of theoretical and practical investigations[1].

[1] Economists who take the stricter view of economic science have been criticised as inconsistent because after describing political economy as a positive science they generally go on to introduce into their own treatises a large number of ethical and practical pronouncements (compare Professor C. S. Devas on "The Restoration of Economics to Ethics" in the *International Journal of Ethics* for January 1897). There is, however, no inconsistency, if it is made clear that such pronouncements are merely introduced incidentally by way of illustration and application, and if the writer never forgets

§ 4.   *Applied economics.*—It is unnecessary to insist upon the enormous practical importance of the theoretical knowledge that economic science affords. Industrial and financial policy can be rightly directed, only if based upon such knowledge; and whether we seek to construct social ideals, or to decide upon adequate steps towards their attainment, an indispensable preliminary is a study of the economic consequences likely to result from varying economic conditions.

The question may, therefore, be raised whether, granting the existence of an independent economic science, economists should not supplement their treatment of this science by constructing a definite *art of political economy*, in which maxims for practical guidance are explicitly formulated.

In support of this view, it may be argued that if the economist is led to regard certain practical questions as definitely within his province, he is the more likely to direct his theoretical investigations into the most useful channels, so that they may ultimately become not only light-giving but also fruit-bearing.

It may further be urged that by explicitly recognising the twofold character of political economy, while at the same time carefully distinguishing the standpoints from which it becomes a science and an art that his primary object is the investigation of facts.   What we plead for is that there shall be no systematic combination of economics and ethics, and no ambiguity as to the nature of economic laws.

respectively, we shall best remedy the popular mis-conception as to the true nature of economic laws[1].

Granting, however, the desirability of treating systematically the practical applications of economic science, it may be doubted whether the phrase *art of political economy* does not suggest a body of doctrine, definite in scope and at the same time complete in itself, such as is really unattainable. The practical applications of economic theories are many and various; and the precepts based upon a study of the science may vary, according as we take the individual, or the national, or the cosmopolitan point of view. Leaving this point on one side, a more serious difficulty results from the universally recognised fact that but few practical problems admit of complete solution on economic grounds alone. It is true that in a few departments—such as those of currency and banking—we may meet with cases where, having determined the economic consequences of a given proposal, we practically have before us all the data requisite for a wise decision in regard to its adoption or rejection. But more usually—when we pass, for instance, to problems of taxation, or to problems that concern the relations of the State with trade and industry, or to the general discussion of communistic and socialistic schemes—it is far

[1] This is one of the main grounds given by Professor Sidgwick for recognising a distinct *art* as well as a *science* of political economy (*Principles of Political Economy*, 1901, p. 395).

from being the case that economic considerations hold the field exclusively. Account must also be taken of ethical, social, and political considerations that lie outside the sphere of political economy regarded as a science.

If, therefore, the art confines itself to the practical applications of the science, pure and simple, its precepts will necessarily lack finality. They cannot be more than conditional. At the same time, there is danger of their hypothetical character being forgotten, and of the idea consequently gaining currency, that the economist desires to subordinate all considerations that are not purely economic.

If, on the other hand, the art attempts a complete solution of practical problems, it must of necessity be to a large extent non-economic in its character, and its scope becomes vague and ill-defined. It may, accordingly, be objected that in attempting to formulate an economic art, that shall lay down absolute rules for the regulation of human conduct, economists are claiming to occupy too wide a range, and to frame a body of so-called economic doctrine, that is really much more than economic, and cannot with any advantage be separated from general political and social philosophy[1].

[1] The difficulty of assigning a definite scope to political economy, considered as an art, is discussed in further detail in a note at the conclusion of this chapter.

The question of recognising a definite *art of political economy* is to a certain extent a verbal one; and if all possible misunderstanding as to the scope of such an art and its relation to positive economic science can be removed, the way in which this question is decided is comparatively unimportant. On the whole, however, it seems likely to conduce to clearness of thought to regard the branch of enquiry under consideration as forming the economic side of political philosophy, or of the art of legislation, or of social philosophy, as the case may be, rather than as constituting a distinct art of political economy. In lieu of such an art, we should then recognise special departments of political and social philosophy, dealing with practical questions, in which economic considerations are of material importance, for the discussion of which, therefore, economic knowledge is essential, and to the treatment of which economists will naturally turn their attention. Adopting this alternative, we may still sum up the more important practical applications of economic science under the name *applied economics.* This term has the special merit that it does not suggest a definite body of principles with scientifically demarcated limits[1].

[1] It must be pointed out, however, that the name *applied economics* is also not altogether free from ambiguity. For a science may be applied in two ways: first, to the explanation of particular facts; secondly, to afford guidance in matters of conduct. The term applied economi s or applied political economy has indeed been

We may also, if we please, speak of certain of the practical enquiries under consideration, as the art of industrial legislation, the art of taxation or of State finance, and so on. To these phrases there seems to

employed in three different senses: (*a*) in the sense suggested in the text; (*b*) to designate the application of economic theory to the interpretation and explanation of particular economic phenomena, without any necessary reference, however, to the solution of practical questions; (*c*) to mark off the more concrete and specialized portions of economic doctrine from those more abstract doctrines that are held to pervade all economic reasoning. Compare the following:

(*a*) "*Applied* political economy studies economic phenomena with the immediate aim of providing safe rules for administration, or of directing economic institutions so that they may conduce to the general welfare. Its aim is therefore immediately *practical*, since it does not investigate the *how* or *why* of certain facts, but seeks rules for *doing* certain things well."—Cossa, *Guide to the Study of Political Economy*, First English Edition, Part i, Chapter 2. Compare also Cornewall Lewis's division of politics into *pure* and *applied* (*Methods of Observation and Reasoning in Politics*, Chapter 3, § 5).

(*b*) "The following essays consist in part of attempts to apply the principles of economic science to the solution of actual problems, of which those presented by the Californian and Australian gold discoveries, and by the state of land tenure in Ireland, are the most important. So much of the volume may not improperly be described as essays in applied political economy. The remaining essays deal mostly with topics of a theoretical kind."—Cairnes, *Essays in Political Economy theoretical and applied*, Preface. Under the name applied political economy, both kinds of applications noted above are here had in view.

(*c*) "Currency, banking, the relations of labour and capital, those of landlord and tenant, pauperism, taxation, and finance are some of the principal portions of applied political economy all involving the same ultimate laws, manifested in most different circumstances."—Jevons on *The Future of Political Economy*. Applied economics in this last sense constitutes what may be called the concrete, as distinguished from the abstract, portion of economic science itself.

be no objection. In each case we have a distinct and fairly compact body of doctrine, and there is no implication that our data are exclusively economic. For the notion of one supreme art of political economy, we should thus substitute a series of arts, in each of which there is a limitation to some particular sphere of economic activity.

§ 5. *Political economy and ethics.*—The relation between political economy and ethics may now be stated more explicitly, although this will involve little more than a repetition of what has been already indicated. We have seen that since men's economic activities are determined partly by moral considerations, it may be necessary in positive economic science to take account of the operation of moral motives. It is not, however, the function of the science to pass ethical judgments; and political economy, regarded as a positive science, may, therefore, be said to be independent of ethics.

But it is a different matter when we turn to the applications of economic science to practice, that is, to applied economics; for no solution of a practical problem, relating to human conduct, can be regarded as complete, until its ethical aspects have been considered. It is clear, accordingly, that practical discussions of an economic character cannot be isolated from ethics, except in so far as the aim is merely to point out the practical bearing of economic facts, without any attempt to lay down absolute rules of conduct. It may be added that although in the past there may have been a tendency with a certain school of economists to attempt the solution of practical economic questions without adequate recognition of their ethical aspects, there is, at the present time, no such tendency discernible amongst economists who have any claim to speak with authority.

Here, then, is the third of those subdivisions of economic enquiry in the widest sense, which we began by distinguishing from one another. In logical order, this division stands intermediate between the two others—between the positive science, that is to say, and the so-called art. It may be regarded as a branch of applied ethics, and may perhaps be called the ethics of political economy. In it the functions of the economist and the moralist are combined, the general principles of social morality being considered in their special bearing on economic activities[1].

In pursuing this enquiry, our object is scientifically to define men's duties in their economic relations

---

[1] A distinction may be drawn between the public and the private ethics of political economy. As an illustration of doctrines belonging to the latter category, attention may be called to a volume of sermons by Mr W. Richmond entitled *Christian Economics*. Compare also Dr Cunningham on the *Ethics of Money Investment* in the *Economic Review* for January 1891.

one with another, and, above all, the duties of society, in so far as it can by its action control or modify economic conditions. In other words, we seek to determine standards, whereby judgment may be passed on those economic activities, whose character and consequences have been established by our previous investigation of economic facts. We seek, moreover, to determine ideals in regard to the production and the distribution of wealth, so as best to satisfy the demands of justice and morality. It is subsequently the function of applied economics, or of the so-called art of political economy, to enquire how nearly the ideal is capable of being attained, and by what means; and to determine how, subject to the above condition, the greatest aggregate happiness may be made to result from the least expenditure of effort.

As an illustration, it may be pointed out that the many problems raised by medieval moralists, in connexion with the question as to what constitutes a *just price*, belong to the ethics of political economy. For instance,—Is it right to sell a thing for more than it is worth? Is it right to sell a thing which is not of the substance or measure or quality it professes to be? Is the seller bound to reveal a fault in an article? Is it right in trade to buy cheap and sell dear? The modern doctrine that, under a system of thoroughgoing competition, normal value is determined by cost of production is, on the other hand, a doctrine that belongs to positive science. The true solution of the ethical question, as to what constitutes a just price, may of course be held to be that competitive price will be a just price, if only it can be guaranteed that the competition is really free and effective on the part of all concerned. Or it may be held that, while this is not an ideally just price, no juster price is practically attainable. But these doctrines are in no way implied in the ordinary doctrine of cost of production as the regulator of normal value.

§ 6. *Methodological importance of the distinctions indicated in this chapter.*—We may conclude the present chapter by briefly pointing out the methodological importance of the distinctions that have been indicated. The main point to notice is that the endeavour to merge questions of what ought to be with questions of what is tends to confuse, not only economic discussions themselves, but also discussions about economic method. The relative value to be attached to different methods of investigation is very different, according as we take the ethical and practical standpoint, or the purely scientific standpoint. Thus it would be generally agreed that, in dealing with practical questions, an abstract method of treatment avails less and carries us much less far than when we are dealing with theoretical questions. In other words, in dealing with the former class of questions, we are to a greater extent dependent upon history and inductive generalization.

Again, while economic uniformities and economic precepts are both, in many cases, relative to particular states of society, the general relativity of the latter may be affirmed with less qualification than that of the former. "Political economy," says Sir James Steuart, and by this he means the art of political economy, "in each country must necessarily be different"; and, so far as practical questions are concerned, this is hardly too strong a statement. On such questions there is nearly always something to be said on both sides, so that practical decisions can be arrived at only by weighing counter-arguments one against another. But the relative force of these arguments is almost certain to vary with varying conditions. Hence, in general, a given economic policy can be definitely formulated only for nations having particular economic surroundings, and having reached a certain stage of economic development. Applied to nations not similarly situated, the policy is likely at least to require modification. It is even possible that what is excellent for a given nation at a given time may be actively mischievous and injurious for another nation, or for the same nation at a different period of its economic history. It follows, similarly, that the value of the economic institutions of the past cannot adequately be judged by reference to existing conditions alone. We are not here denying the relativity of economic theorems, but merely affirming the greater relativity of economic precepts. Unless the distinction between theorems and precepts is carefully borne in mind, the relativity of the former is likely to be over-stated.

It is because differences of this kind are often overlooked that divergences of view on questions of method become exaggerated. In the controversies that ensue, one set of disputants is thinking mainly of theoretical problems, while the other set is thinking mainly of practical problems; and hence each in turn is liable to commit the fallacy of *ignoratio elenchi*.

Again, because economics is regarded as wholly practical, some writers have been led erroneously to deny that any economic doctrines admit of definite or exact expression. It is implied that the study cannot yield anything more than a useful collection of rules, having a restricted validity and application, and subject to numerous limitations and exceptions. Even if it be granted that this description is not altogether inapplicable to political economy conceived as an art, it is obviously a fallacy to assume, without having made any clear distinction between them, that what is true of economic precepts is equally true of economic theorems.

The frequency of errors such as these must be our excuse for treating in so much detail the distinctions indicated in the present chapter. The chapters that follow relate almost exclusively to the scope of political economy conceived as a positive science, and to the methods whereby the theorems of this science are to be established.

NOTES TO CHAPTER II.

A. On Political Economy and *Laisser Faire*.

THE connexion between political economy and *laisser faire* may be discussed from two different points of view, which are not always as clearly distinguished as they should be. There is, first, the connexion between political economy and *laisser faire* considered as an assumption or basis of reasoning; there is, secondly, the connexion between political economy and *laisser faire* considered as a maxim or rule of conduct.

(1) Abstract economic doctrines are for the most part based upon the assumption of free competition and absence of government interference. This assumption may indeed be said to have occupied a central position in the development of economic theories during the last hundred and forty years. There are two reasons why this has been so. One is to be found in the general principle of reasoning that it is best to take the simplest cases first. If we can accurately determine what will ensue under conditions of economic freedom, we shall be the better able to deal subsequently with more complicated cases, and to estimate the influence exerted by various interfering agencies. The second reason is that in modern economic societies *laisser faire* has been

as a matter of fact the general rule. Conclusions, therefore, based on the assumption of non-interference have more nearly corresponded with the actual facts of modern industry than any conclusions obtained from other equally simple hypotheses could have done.

Beyond this, however, there is no essentially necessary connexion between political economy and *laisser faire* regarded as a basis of reasoning. Economists recognise that in certain states of society, actual or possible, the conditions are so different from those of modern industry that conclusions depending on the hypothesis of non-interference are not even approximately applicable. Moreover, in relation to modern economic phenomena themselves, it becomes necessary ultimately to deal with more complex problems in which various interferences with thorough-going competition have to be taken into account. The assumption of *laisser faire* represents, therefore, only a preliminary stage, and by its aid we traverse only a portion of the ground that has to be covered in the course of our economic reasonings.

A little reflection will shew that it is far from being the case that political economy always presupposes the absence of government interference. It investigates the effects of export and import duties, of bounties, and of state-created monopolies—such as the opium monopoly in Bengal. It seeks to determine the influence exerted on wages by the existence of poor relief guaranteed by the State. In nearly all modern currency discussions—as, for instance, those relating to bimetallism or the regulation of convertible paper currencies—the whole argument is so far from being based on the assumption of *laisser faire*, that everything turns on the supposition that some control over the currency is exercised by governments. In short, wherever government intervention becomes a prominent factor, the economist recognises and discusses the influence exerted by it; and if in the future the part played by the State in economic affairs is extended, account will have to be taken of the fact in current political economy.

A contrast is sometimes drawn between a socialistic and an economic state of society; but when the distinction is thus expressed, the term economic is not used in the sense given to it by economists themselves. It is true that in a purely communistic society a good deal of ordinary economic theory relating to distribution and exchange would be irrelevant or inapplicable. But although in such a society men's economic activities would be in certain directions controlled, they would clearly not be annihilated; and a scientific discussion of economic phenomena would, therefore, be by no means unnecessary. The functions of capital and the manner of its co-operation with labour would, for example, still require elucidation. Cost of production would still admit of analysis, and we should still have the phenomena of increasing and diminishing returns. We should indeed still have the phenomenon of rent, meaning thereby the difference between cost of production under more favourable and under less favourable circumstances.

Schemes of socialism, moreover, as distinguished from pure communism, do not necessarily involve the entire abolition of free exchange. Under such schemes, therefore, a theory of exchange would still be required. And unless our socialistic community were isolated from all others, there would still remain for discussion extremely complicated questions of foreign trade and international exchanges.

We may be sure, finally, that if some of the old economic phenomena were to become obsolete, new ones would arise demanding scientific treatment.

While then a contrast may be drawn between our current political economy in so far as it is specially designed to elucidate the existing economic order, and the form that the science would be likely to assume in so far as specially designed to elucidate the phenomena of a socialistic society, it is clearly erroneous to imagine that the triumph of socialism would mean the extinction of political economy as a science.

(2) We may pass to a consideration of the connexion between political economy and *laisser faire* regarded as a maxim of conduct. The question is quite distinct from that which we have just been discussing. For it is clear that we may on the one hand work out the consequences of *laisser faire* with the very object of discrediting it as a practical principle; or that we may on the other hand recognise the necessity of investigating the economic effects of government interference, while deploring the fact that instances of such interference are ever to be met with.

Nevertheless the questions are not unfrequently confused together, and because *laisser faire* is a common economic postulate it is supposed to be a necessary economic precept. This confusion of thought has been encouraged by the circumstance that, until comparatively recently, the leading modern writers on the science have in their practical teaching expressly advocated a general policy of non-interference with trade and industry. Hence, starting with the conception of political economy as the general art of legislation in matters relating to wealth, the public have come to identify it with the particular system of reducing government interference to a minimum; and the maxim of natural liberty—that everyone should be left free to use his mind, his body, and his property in the manner he deems best for himself—is often regarded as the fundamental economic axiom.

Political economy being thus transformed into a dogmatic creed, the worth of the study itself is measured by the degree of acceptance accorded to this creed. So common is the identification of political economy with the principle of non-interference that rarely do we find any professed attack on the former that does not on analysis resolve itself mainly into an attack on the latter. Compare, for instance, Dr Hutchison Stirling's vigorous diatribe in his *Secret of Hegel*[1]. Similarly, when people talk about political economy being exploded and becoming a thing of the past, all they mean is that *laisser faire* is ceasing to be an accepted maxim. On reflection it is clear that there is an inherent absurdity in attacking *political economy* as distinct from any particular system of political economy. For if particular systems are exploded, that only necessitates their being replaced by some other system.

Regarding political economy as a positive science, it is of course clear that neither *laisser faire* nor any other maxim of conduct can form an integral portion of its teaching. Hence the advocacy of a policy of *laisser faire*

[1] Volume 2, pp. 569, ff. Compare, also, Carlyle's various attacks upon political economy.

by individual economists, based though it may be on their interpretation of economic truths, belongs at any rate to *applied economics*. It has been said above that the leading English economists have in their practical writings been as a rule in favour of *laisser faire*. Looking a little closer, however, we find that their advocacy of the principle is at any rate accompanied by numerous qualifications and exceptions. They do not regard it as an axiomatic and inexorable formula by which all particular proposals may be finally tested, but as a practical conclusion whose validity in every case depends on particular circumstances[1].

Adam Smith, for example, holds that besides maintaining such public institutions as are necessary for defence and the administration of justice, it is the duty of governments to maintain certain institutions for facilitating commerce and promoting education. "The third and last duty of the sovereign or commonwealth," he remarks, "is that of erecting and maintaining those public institutions and those public works, which though they may be in the highest degree advantageous to a great society, are, however, of such a nature, that the profit could never repay the expense to any individual, or small number of individuals; and which it, therefore, cannot be expected that any individual, or small number of individuals, should erect or maintain." He moreover admits exceptions to a

---

[1] "Let us remember," says Cairnes, "that *laisser faire* is a *practical rule*, and not a doctrine of science; a rule in the main sound, but like most other sound practical rules, liable to numerous exceptions; above all, a rule which must never for a moment be allowed to stand in the way of the candid consideration of any promising proposal of social or industrial reform" (*Essays in Political Economy*, p. 251).

policy of free trade; for he explicitly recognises certain
cases in which protection to native industry is desirable,
and other cases in which it may rightly be a matter of
deliberation "how far it is proper to continue the free
importation of certain foreign goods," or "how far, or in
what manner, it may be proper to restore that free importation, after it has been for some time interrupted."
There are other instances in which he justifies interference.
"The law," he says, "which obliges the masters in several
different trades to pay their workmen in money, and not in
goods, is quite just and equitable."   Again, while allowing
that any regulations affecting the note issues of a country
may be regarded as "in some respect a violation of natural
liberty," he nevertheless considers that certain regulations
of the kind may be justified on the ground that "those
exertions of the natural liberty of a few individuals, which
might endanger the security of the whole society, are, and
ought to be, restrained by the laws of all governments; of
the most free, as well as of the most despotical."[1]

Turning to Malthus, we find in the ranks of leading
English economists a defender of the corn laws. Ricardo
indeed touched only to a small extent on the economic
functions of the State; but McCulloch, who is usually

---

[1] On Adam Smith's attitude towards *laisser faire*, compare Sidgwick, *Scope and Method of Economic Science*, pp. 5—7. "To attribute
to Adam Smith," says Dr Sidgwick, "a dogmatic theory of the natural
right of the individual to absolute industrial independence—as some
recent German writers are disposed to do—is to construct the history
of economic doctrines from one's inner consciousness." Compare,
also, Professor Nicholson's edition of the *Wealth of Nations*, Introductory Essay, pp. 14—18, and Rae, *Contemporary Socialism*, 1891,
pp. 353—359.

looked upon as one of the narrowest of Ricardo's disciples
definitely advocated government interference in certain
directions[1], and J. S. Mill's long list of exceptions to the rule
of *laisser faire* is well known.   Coming to quite recent writers
there is still less justification for the notion of an essential
and necessary connexion between political economy and the
principle of non-interference.   One of the distinguishing
marks of a powerful school of economists at the present
time is the definite repudiation of this principle; and even
those, who find in the study of economics most weighty
arguments against protective and against socialist legislation, would still never think of setting up the acceptance
of a policy of unrestricted freedom of trade and industry as
a test of economic orthodoxy.

B.   On the Scope of Political Economy
considered as an Art.

Some of the difficulties, which arise in the endeavour to
determine the scope of political economy considered as an
art, have been briefly indicated in the preceding chapter.
In this note they will be discussed in somewhat further
detail.   Questions may be raised in regard to, first, the
range of well-being contemplated by the art; and, secondly,
the precise nature of the ideal at which it aims.

(1)   Under the first of the above heads it may be asked
whether the aim of the economic art is individual or social;
and whether it is national or cosmopolitan.

---

[1] For an enumeration of instances in which McCulloch regarded
State intervention favourably, see Rae, *op. cit.*, pp. 360—372.

(a) It is clear that individuals as well as societies may in their own interests turn to account their study of economic science. The monopolist may derive practical guidance from the treatment of monopoly-value; the manufacturer from the discussion of over-production and industrial depression; the banker from the enquiry into the conditions under which crises tend to become periodic; the trades-unionist from the analysis of the conditions favourable to the success of a strike. We might, accordingly, recognise a branch of the economic art, concerned with the principles according to which private persons should be guided in the pursuit of their own economic interests. There are, moreover, technical arts, such as the art of banking, which are to some extent based on economic science, but whose aim cannot be described as social.

It is, however, generally agreed by those who advocate the recognition of an art of political economy that it aims at some result that is desirable, not merely from the point of view of any given individual, but from the point of view of society taken as a whole. It is not regarded as an art of getting rich, or as an art of speculation, or as an art of investment, or as professing to indicate how producers should organize and carry on their business, in order to make their profits as great as possible. The art of political economy is, in other words, not identified with the whole of the practical applications of economic science[1].

[1] A minor question may here be raised, namely, whether in so far as the aim of the economic art is social, it is concerned wholly with legislation. M. de Laveleye defines political economy as determining "what laws men ought to adopt in order that they may, with the least possible exertion, procure the greatest abundance of things useful for the satisfaction of their wants; may distribute them justly, and

(*b*) Assuming that the aim of the economic art is social, not individual, the further question may be asked, whether it aims merely at national prosperity and national greatness, or at some result that is desirable for the whole human race. This point is suggested by List's distinction between *political economy* and *cosmopolitical economy*. He regards the former as limiting its teaching to "the enquiry how a *given nation* can obtain (under the existing conditions of the world) prosperity, civilization, and power, by means of agriculture, industry, and commerce"; while the latter "teaches how the entire human race may attain prosperity."[1]

consume them rationally" (*Elements of Political Economy*, § 2). The departments of economic practice here had in view are clearly of the utmost importance; and there may be good grounds for giving a separate recognition to what may be called the art of State finance, and the art of industrial legislation. The former of these would include a discussion of the general principles of taxation and of national debts from the practical standpoint. The latter would enquire how far and in what manner any State regulation of trade and industry is to be recommended. The art of political economy is, however, more usually regarded as having a wider scope than either of these. It may, for instance, in the matter of private almsgiving claim in the interests of society to formulate maxims for individual guidance; or, with a view to the more equitable distribution of wealth, it may advocate the voluntary adoption of the co-operative principle or of profit-sharing; or, accepting as its function a high moral task, it may seek in various ways to influence the economic activities of individuals so as to bring them into harmony with sound economic morality and secure the supremacy of right habits and customs in industrial life.

[1] *The National System of Political Economy* (Sampson Lloyd's translation), p. 119. It is recognised by other economists besides List—including some distinctly free trade economists—that the general problem of free trade and protection needs to be handled somewhat differently according as the national or the cosmopolitan standpoint is adopted.

It is true that cases of conflict between the precepts of
the two arts here indicated are not likely to be frequent.
But if it is maintained that no real conflict can ever occur,
attention may be called to certain problems connected with
emigration and immigration, and with export and import
duties.   J. S. Mill points out cases in which it is possible for
a country to gain at the expense of other countries by the
imposition of export duties.   The opium trade between India
and China affords an actual instance in which a country
raises a large revenue from foreigners by means of what is
practically a tax on exports.   "It is certain, however,"
Mill adds, taking the cosmopolitan standpoint, "that whatever we gain is lost by somebody else, and there is the
expense of the collection besides: if international morality,
therefore, were rightly understood and acted upon, such
taxes, as being contrary to the universal weal, would not
exist."[1]   Further, in reference to the question of restricting
the exportation of machinery, Mill observes that even if
by such means a country might individually gain, the policy
would still in his opinion be unjustifiable on the score of
international morality.   "It is evidently," he says, "the
common interest of all nations that each of them should
abstain from every measure by which the aggregate wealth
of the commercial world would be diminished, although of
this smaller sum total it might thereby be enabled to attract
to itself a larger share."[2]

Since then a conflict is sometimes possible, it behoves
the exponent of the economic art to make clear his view as
to what the aim of the art really is.   Perhaps the most

[1] *Unsettled Questions of Political Economy*, p. 25
[2] *Op. cit.*, p. 31.

obvious solution is to recognise, as List suggests, two distinct
arts—an art of *cosmopolitan* economy, and an art of *national*
economy.   The precepts of the former might often require
modification to suit the special circumstances of different
nations, but it would be cosmopolitan in the sense that it
would have regard to the well-being of the greatest number,
irrespective of nationality.   The latter would deliberately
sacrifice the interests of other nations, if they happened
to be in conflict with those of the nation specially under
consideration.

(2)   A more fundamental question in regard to the
scope of political economy considered as an art relates to
the nature of the ideal at which it aims.   (*a*) Does it seek
merely to point out the laws, and institutions, and economic habits, that are most favourable to the production
and accumulation of wealth?   (*b*) Or does it enquire
further by what means an ideally just distribution of
wealth may be attained?   (*c*) Or does it widen its range
still further, and ask how all economic activities both of
the State and of individuals should be moulded, with a
view to the general well-being in the fullest and broadest
sense?   This last alternative represents the prevailing view
amongst German economists[1].

---

[1] The first of the three enquiries indicated in this paragraph is
sometimes spoken of as *economic politics*, and the third as *social
politics*.   Compare Pierson, *Principles of Economics*, Introduction, § 1.
Dr Pierson himself holds that a clear boundary line can be drawn
between economics and social politics, but not between economics and
economic politics.   Indeed he defines economics as "the science which
teaches us what rules mankind should observe in order to advance
in material prosperity."   His main grounds for refusing to recognise
any distinction between economic politics and economics itself are
that the object of the study of economics is to throw light on questions

(a) If the end at which the art of political economy aims is simply the increased production of wealth, its scope is certainly definite, and the data upon which its conclusions are based belong exclusively to economic science. Since, however, the production of wealth is not the sole or supreme end that a society will have in view in framing its laws and shaping its institutions, the economic art so conceived can lay down no absolute or final rules. It can only speak conditionally, and say that in so far as the increased production or accumulation of wealth is concerned, such and such a line of action should be adopted. Hence, before deciding to act upon the hypothetical precepts of political economy (so interpreted), it is necessary to enquire how far they are consistent with other social aims, and how

of a practical nature, and that the precepts of economic politics are nothing more than a recapitulation of the conclusions arrived at by economics conceived as a positive science. At the same time, Dr Pierson admits that the precepts of economics are always of a conditional nature. The argument in the preceding chapter has been partly directed against identifying economics with social politics, and so far we are in agreement with Dr Pierson. But we have also argued against his view of the scope of economics whereby economics and economic politics are identified. It may be added that although there are some cases in which the difference between the uniformities of economic science and the precepts of so-called economic politics may not unfairly be described as a mere difference between statements in the indicative mood and statements in the imperative, there are others in which the theoretical statements do not admit of being immediately transformed into corresponding imperatives. This applies to the most fundamental principles of economics, such as the laws determining market and normal value, the law of rent, the principles determining the value of money, and so on. Even in such an enquiry as the incidence of a given tax, the result cannot, generally speaking, be immediately made the basis of an imperative. This seems decisive as against defining economics as a system of rules of conduct.

far they satisfy the claims of justice. Wherever there is conflict, an appeal must be made to some other and higher authority. This authority must determine to what extent each set of considerations shall be subordinated to the others.

It seems a doubtful gain to construct a definite art of political economy in this sense. For inasmuch as the science of economics itself contains all the information that is requisite, it will suffice to call attention to the practical bearing of its theorems, without systematically converting them into precepts. To frame a definite system of precepts, having regard entirely to the increased production of wealth, can indeed hardly fail to give rise to misapprehension. As a matter of fact, political economy has not unfrequently been subjected to startling misrepresentations, because it has first been identified with the art of making wealth a maximum, and then the necessarily hypothetical character of such an art has been forgotten. It is of little use to protest that economic precepts are not necessarily to be acted upon. If we have once formulated maxims of policy, and proclaimed that economic principles are directly practical, the impression that economists desire to subordinate all considerations to the increase of wealth will certainly be encouraged. If, however, it can be made clear that economic principles are in themselves positive, and that, whilst economics shews, amongst other things, how laws and institutions influence the production and accumulation of wealth, still it does not itself base any rules of action upon such knowledge, but merely places the results of its investigations at the service of the legislator and the social reformer, to be by them duly weighed and considered, then the chance of such misapprehension will at any rate be reduced to a minimum.

(b) According to Professor Sidgwick, "we may take the subject of political economy considered as an art to include, besides the theory of provision for governmental expenditure, (1) the art of making the proportion of produce to population a maximum,...and (2) the art of rightly distributing produce among members of the community, whether on any principle of equity or justice, or on the economic principle of making the whole produce as useful as possible."[1] This conception of the economic art is broader than that discussed above. But it seems to go either too far or else not quite far enough. For we pass outside the boundary of economic considerations in the narrowest sense, taking account also of considerations of justice; and yet our maxims will still be, in some cases, only conditional. They cannot claim to be absolute, until we have taken into account all classes of considerations that may in any way be pertinent. In framing maxims of taxation and State finance, for example, political and social aims have to be borne in mind as well as equitable and strictly economic aims. The same may be said of free trade or protectionist maxims. Again, in seeking to determine what is the ideal distribution of wealth, we ought to consider not merely the relation of distribution to desert, but also the manner in which methods of distribution affect the various other elements of social well-being. The individualistic organization of industry is by some writers condemned on the ground of the anti-social spirit engendered by the competitive struggle. On the other hand, the

[1] *Principles of Political Economy*, 1901, p. 397.

socialistic organization of industry is by a different set of writers condemned on the ground that it hinders the realization of individual freedom, and the development of individual character. Both these arguments are independent of the effect of socialism and individualism on the production and distribution of wealth.

(c) According to the third conception of the economic art, its aim is to direct the economic activities of the State and of individuals, with a view to the completest realization of social well-being. "Political economy," says Professor Schönberg, representing the view of the dominant German school, as well as his own view, "does not ask primarily whether the greatest possible amount of wealth is produced, but rather how men live, how far through their economic activity the moral aims of life are fulfilled, and how far the demands of justice, humanity, and morality are satisfied."[1] Professor Ely, taking a similar view, and writing on behalf of the so-called "new school" of economists in the United States, describes the ideal of political economy as "the most perfect development of all human faculties in each individual, which can be attained." The aim, he goes on to say, is "such a production, and such a distribution, of economic goods as must in the highest practicable degree subserve the end and purpose of human existence for all members of society."[2] The end had in view is now the supreme end for which a society exists, and every question that arises is to be considered from all sides, and not from a single point of view. The rules laid down will accordingly be no longer conditional, but absolute, at any rate in

[1] *Handbuch der politischen Oekonomie, Die Volkswirthschaft*, § 9.
[2] *Science Economic Discussion*, p. 50.

relation to the particular country or state of civilization under discussion.

The above corresponds with the attitude that the great majority of economists of all schools have at least desired to take, so far as they have attempted a complete solution of practical problems for social purposes. The conception seems, moreover, to raise the economist to a position of greater importance than he can occupy, so long as he limits himself to purely theoretical investigations or merely conditional precepts. But does he not herein become a good deal more than an economist? He will certainly need for his scientific basis very much more than economic science can by itself afford, for he must be a student of political and social science in the widest sense. He must also solve fundamental problems of social morality. We have, in fact, no exception to the general rule that arts, claiming to lay down absolute rules, cannot be based exclusively on single theoretical sciences.

We are, accordingly, led to the conclusion, indicated in the preceding chapter, that a definitive art of political economy, which attempts to lay down absolute rules for the regulation of human conduct, will have vaguely defined limits, and be largely non-economic in character.

CHAPTER III.

ON THE CHARACTER AND DEFINITION OF POLITICAL ECONOMY REGARDED AS A POSITIVE SCIENCE.

§ 1. *Political economy and physical science.*— Inasmuch as the production of material wealth is dependent largely upon physical conditions, it may be asked whether political economy does not partake to some extent of the nature of physical science. This question is, however, to be answered in the negative, on the ground that while the science has to take account of the operation of physical laws, it is still concerned with them only indirectly; such laws do not constitute its subject-matter. It does not, for instance, seek to establish or explain the physical laws that are involved in agriculture or mining or manufacture. This is the function of such sciences as mechanics, chemistry, geology, and the science of agriculture. The only concern of political economy with these laws is that it assumes certain of them as premisses or data, and makes them the basis of its own reasonings, tracing the influence which they exert in moulding and modifying men's economic activities. Thus even the law of diminishing return from land, regarded as a bare physical fact, is hardly to be considered a true economic law, although it no doubt occupies a unique position amongst the physical prolegomena of economic science. Its economic importance consists in its relation to the productiveness of human labour as applied to land, and in its consequent influence upon the distribution and exchange of wealth. If economists are led into giving fuller details about agriculture than they usually give about processes of manufacture, it is because, from this point of view, the importance of the above law is exceptionally great.

The relation of political economy to the physical sciences is then simply this, that it presupposes them; it is sometimes concerned with physical laws as premisses, but never as conclusions.

Accordingly when the production of wealth is said to be one of the great departments of economic science, reference is made primarily to what may be called the social laws of the production of wealth (*i.e.*, to the various influences exerted on production by division of labour, foreign trade, methods of distribution, and so forth), rather than to the physical processes by whose aid production is carried on. The physical requisites of the production of wealth need to be summarised in their broadest outlines; but the science is not directly concerned with the technique of different trades and occupations. Again, whilst economists recognise the physical conditions affecting men's economic efficiency, the immediate effects of these conditions are accepted as facts from physiology and other sciences; it is only in so far as they indirectly affect or are affected by the social facts of wealth that economic science itself investigates them.

The differentia of economic laws, as contrasted with purely physical laws, consists in the fact that the former imply voluntary human action[1]. The forces of competition are, indeed, sometimes spoken of as if they were themselves mechanical and automatic in their operation. But, as we have already had occasion to remark, this is not the case. When, for instance, we speak of the price of a commodity as determined by supply and demand, we mean by supply not the total amount in existence, but the amount offered for sale by holders of the commodity; and it is clear that in

[1] "Various laws of nature have to be considered in connexion with human economy, but these are not economic laws. By the latter we understand laws of economic facts. An economic fact is not a phenomenon of the natural, material world. It originates when in some way man, as an intelligent being with free will, enters actively into co-operation with natural phenomena, for the purpose of satisfying human needs."—Schönberg, *Handbuch der politischen Oekonomie, Die Volkswirthschaft*, § 13.

this sense supply, equally with demand, is dependent upon human judgment and will.

§ 2. *Political economy and psychology.*—In order to mark off political economy from the physical sciences, it is spoken of sometimes as a moral science, sometimes as a social science. Of these descriptions, the latter is to be preferred. The term moral science is, to begin with, not free from ambiguity. This term is no doubt sometimes used in a broad sense as including all the separate sciences that treat of man in his subjective capacity, that is, as a being who feels, thinks, and wills. But more frequently it is used as a synonym for ethics; and hence to speak of economic science as a moral science is likely to obscure its positive character[1].

But the above is not the only reason why it is better not to describe political economy simply as a moral science. The sciences that relate to man fall into two subdivisions—those that are concerned with man in his purely individual capacity, and those that are concerned with him principally as a member of society. Political economy belongs to the latter of these subdivisions. It is true that some of the problems discussed by the science—those relating, for example, to the functions of capital—would arise in a more or less rudimentary form in relation to an isolated

[1] Compare what has been said in the preceding chapter as to the relation of political economy to ethics.

individual; and it is accordingly possible to illustrate certain elementary economic principles by reference to the conduct of a Robinson Crusoe. As soon, however, as we advance beyond the threshold of the science, it becomes necessary to regard human beings, not in isolation, but as members of associated communities including others besides themselves. The most prominent characteristic of actual economic life is the relation of mutual dependence that subsists between different individuals; and political economy may be said to be essentially concerned with economic life as a special aspect of social life.

Political economy should then be described as a social, rather than as a moral or psychological, science. It presupposes psychology just as it presupposes the physical sciences, and the natural starting point for the economist in his more abstract enquiries is a consideration of the motives by which individuals are usually influenced in their economic relations; but the science is not therefore a branch of psychology. The bare facts that other things being equal men prefer a greater to a smaller gain, that under certain conditions they will forego present for the sake of future gratifications, and the like, are psychological facts of great economic importance. But they are assumed by the economist, not established by him. He does not seek to explain or analyse them; nor does he investigate all the consequences to which they lead. Economic laws in the strict sense are different from the above. They are not simple laws of human nature, but laws of complex social facts resulting from simple laws of human nature. An illustration may be quoted from Cairnes. "Rent," he observes, "is a complex phenomenon, arising from the play of human interests when brought into contact with the actual physical conditions of the soil in relation to the physiological character of vegetable productions. The political economist does not attempt to explain the physical laws on which the qualities of the soil depend; and no more does he undertake to analyse the nature of those feelings of self-interest in the minds of the landlord and tenant which regulate the terms of the bargain. He regards them both as facts, not to be analysed and explained, but to be ascertained and taken account of; not as the subject-matter, but as the basis of his reasonings. If further information be desired, recourse must be had to other sciences: the physical fact he hands over to the chemist or the physiologist; the mental to the psychological or the ethical scholar."[1]

No doubt the relation of political economy to psychology is more intimate than its relation to the physical sciences, and this is perhaps not sufficiently realised in the passage just quoted from Cairnes. The

[1] *Logical Method of Political Economy*, pp. 37, 8.

fact that social, rather than purely psychological, phenomena constitute the subject-matter of political economy is, however, clear if we take any recognised work on the science, such as the *Wealth of Nations*. Adam Smith traces many of the phenomena of wealth to man's mental constitution, but it is not man's mental constitution that it is his purpose to analyse. This is not always sufficiently borne in mind when the *Wealth of Nations* is contrasted with the *Theory of Moral Sentiments*, and spoken of as forming its supplement.

J. S. Mill, indeed, in speaking of political economy uses the phrase "moral or psychological science"; and he goes on to define political economy as "the science relating to the moral or psychological laws of the production and distribution of wealth."[1] Take, however, the following laws as formulated by Mill himself in his *Principles of Political Economy*: rent does not enter into the cost of production of agricultural produce; the value of money depends, *ceteris paribus*, on its quantity together with the rapidity of circulation; a tax on all commodities would fall on profits. Such laws as these ought certainly not to be described as moral or psychological, even if it be granted that they rest ultimately upon a psychological basis.

Moreover, as will be shewn in the following chapter,

[1] *Unsettled Questions of Political Economy*, pp. 129 133

notwithstanding the importance of psychological premisses in certain departments of economic enquiry,
the phenomena of the industrial world cannot be explained in their entirety simply by deductive reasoning
from a few elementary laws of human nature. To
what purpose, and subject to what conditions, political
economy uses its psychological data will be considered
later on; it need only be said at this point that
reasoning from such data requires to be supplemented
in various ways by direct observation of the complex
social facts which constitute economic life[1].

[1] It may be remarked in passing that the description of economics
adopted by Jevons in his *Theory of Political Economy* seems to give
the science too much of a psychological, and too little of a social,
character. The theory of economics is described as "the mechanics
of utility and self-interest" (p. 23); it is "entirely based on a calculus
of pleasure and pain; and the object of economics is to maximise
happiness by purchasing pleasure, as it were, at the lowest cost of
pain" (p. 25). A few pages further on the same idea is expanded.
"Pleasure and pain are undoubtedly the ultimate objects of the calculus of economics. To satisfy our wants to the utmost with the
least effort—to procure the greatest amount of what is desirable
at the expense of the least that is undesirable—in other words, to
maximise pleasure, is the problem of economics" (p. 40). The outcome
of Jevons's conception of a calculus of pleasure and pain is a theory of
utility, whose economic importance it would be difficult to exaggerate.
Still this theory does not itself constitute the central theory of economics. It should indeed be regarded as an essential datum or basis
of economic reasonings, rather than as itself an integral portion of
the science at all. It seems more properly to belong to a branch of
applied psychology, to which the name hedonics may be given. At
the same time, because of its economic importance, the economist
must work out the theory for himself, if he does not find it worked
out independently. Thus accidentally as it were, it may occupy an

§ 3. *Political economy a social as distinguished from a political science.*—From whatever point of view we look at it, political economy is best described as a *social* science; and if a distinction is drawn between social and political sciences, it must, notwithstanding its name, be regarded as belonging to the former, and not to the latter, category[1]. For while the science has sometimes to take account of political and legal conditions, it is essentially concerned with man in his social as distinguished from his political relations. It is, in other words, only in certain departments of political economy that we are concerned with men in their special character as members of a State. As remarked by Knies, "a large preliminary division of political economy has to investigate only the social economic life of man independently of all political influences."[2] The laws of distribution and exchange under conditions of free contract may be taken as an example. These

important place in economic writings, and yet be a premiss rather than an ultimate conclusion of the science. Jevons himself, after laying down his theory of utility, goes on to consider its applications to what are economic phenomena in the strictest sense. He thus throws so much light upon these phenomena that his *Theory of Political Economy*, taken as a whole, may rightly be regarded as one of the most suggestive and valuable contributions to the science that have ever been made.

[1] Hence a further reason, besides the one given in the note on p. 53, why some recent writers prefer to speak of the science as *economics* rather than as *political economy*.

[2] *Die Politische Oekonomie vom geschichtlichen Standpunkte,* 1883, p. 3.

laws do not exhaust political economy, but at any rate they fill a large and fundamentally important place in the science. Again, whilst economic doctrines may be in some cases relative to particular political conditions, they are more frequently relative to particular stages of industrial organization that are to a considerable extent, if not altogether, independent of political influences.

The above remarks relate primarily to the positive science of economics. Regarding political economy in its practical aspect, the connexion with politics is more intimate. Applied economics may indeed be said to be mainly concerned with the economic activities of the State in its corporate capacity, or of individuals as controlled by the State. Still, as we have already had occasion to shew, economic maxims—having for their object the interests of society as a whole—may also be formulated for the guidance of individuals acting independently of external constraint[1].

§ 4. *Definitions of Wealth and Economic Activity.*— The point has now been reached at which it seems desirable to give a formal definition of political economy, regarded as a positive science; but before doing this, it is necessary briefly to discuss the meaning of certain terms of which we have already had occasion frequently to make use, namely, the terms wealth

[1] Compare Chapter 2, Note B.

and economic activity. Wealth is one of those words
that may without disadvantage be defined somewhat
differently from different points of view; and it must
be borne in mind that our present object is merely to
give a definition that shall suffice broadly to distinguish
economic enquiries from those relating to other human
interests. No attempt need, therefore, be made to
deal with the difficulties that arise in connexion with
the measurement of wealth.

Utility may be defined as the power of satisfying,
directly or indirectly, human needs and desires; and
the possession of utility is the one characteristic that all
writers are agreed in ascribing to wealth. It seems
clear, however, that we cannot from our present standpoint identify wealth with all sources of utility what-
soever, since there are many means of satisfying human
needs, such as family affection, the esteem of acquaintances, a good conscience, a cultured taste, which have
never been included within the scope of political economy, and the laws of whose production and distribution have hardly anything in common with the laws
that are as a matter of fact discussed by economists.
Some characteristic besides the possession of utility
must therefore be added, whereby such sources of utility
as consist in a man's own nature, or in the subjective
attitude of others towards him, may be excluded
from the wealth category. This further characteristic

may be found in the quality of being potentially exchangeable. It is not meant that nothing is wealth unless it is actually bought and sold. For a thing may be potentially exchangeable without being actually made the subject of exchange. Even in a communistic society the criterion would be applicable. It is true that with special reference to such a society, it might more naturally be expressed in another form, the essential characteristic of wealth being described as the capability of being distributed by fiat of government. The sources of utility capable of being thus distributed would, however, be identical with those that could in a state of economic freedom be acquired by purchase. In either case personal qualities, and such objects of desire as affection and esteem, would be excluded.

Wealth may then be defined as consisting of all potentially exchangeable means of satisfying human needs[1].

---

[1] Professor Marshall defines wealth as including "all those things, external to a man, which (i) belong to him, and do not belong equally to his neighbours, and therefore are distinctly his; and (ii) which are directly capable of a money measure,—a measure that represents on the one side the efforts and sacrifices by which they have been called into existence, and, on the other, the wants which they satisfy" (*Principles of Economics*, vol. I., 1895, p. 127). This definition corresponds broadly with that given in the text. For, on the one hand, things must be capable of appropriation, in order that they may be potentially exchangeable; and, on the other hand, potential exchangeability is a necessary and sufficient condition, in order that things may be directly capable of a money measure. It should be added

This definition brings within the category of wealth, in the first place, desirable material commodities that are capable of appropriation, such as food, books, buildings, machines; in the second place, rights and opportunities to use or receive or in any way derive benefit from material commodities, such as mortgages and other debts, shares in public and private companies, patents and copyrights, access to libraries and picture-galleries, and the like; in the third place, personal services not resulting in any material product, as, for example, those rendered by actors, soldiers, domestic servants, lawyers, physicians; and, lastly, the right to command or control the services of any person over a given period.

In regard to services it is to be observed that although the benefits they confer may be more or less permanent, they are in themselves merely transient phenomena. They are, however, the produce of labour; they admit of being made the subject of exchange; and they may possess exchange-value[1]. They give

that whilst emphasis may conveniently be laid on exchangeability for purposes of definition, other of the characteristics of wealth become more prominent in certain departments of economic science. For instance, in the department of production, the primary notion is that wealth is the result of labour and sacrifice. Again, in the department of distribution, the right of appropriation needs more explicit recognition. Compare Professor Nicholson's article on *Wealth* in the ninth edition of the *Encyclopaedia Britannica*.

[1] When a material commodity is sold or given away, its ownership is transferred from one person to another. When, however, a service

rise, therefore, to problems analogous to those which present themselves in connexion with material wealth; and they are accordingly rightly included under wealth from our present stand-point[1].

is rendered, nothing passes into the possession of one person that was previously in the possession of another; and hence it has been denied that services can possibly be exchanged. But it is a mistake to suppose that change of ownership either constitutes exchange or is essential to it. On the one hand, material commodities may change ownership gratuitously; and, on the other hand, we have all that is really essential to exchange, when A confers a benefit upon B on the understanding that B confers some other specified benefit upon him, and *vice versâ*. Either benefit thus conferred may consist in the possession of some material commodity; but it may also consist in a service rendered. that is in an expenditure of effort on the one side accompanied by the satisfaction of some actual or supposed need on the other. It is, therefore, quite correct to say that a service may be rendered in exchange for another service, or in exchange for a material commodity; and it is quite correct to speak of services as having exchange-value.

[1] It is sometimes considered essential to the idea of wealth that it shall be susceptible of accumulation; and in speaking of services as wealth there is no doubt some departure from the ordinary usage of language. It is also true that, in certain connexions, whatever is not susceptible of accumulation may be left out of account in the estimation of wealth. But, on the other hand, as Dr Sidgwick observes, "in ordinary estimates of the aggregate income of the inhabitants of a country, directly useful—or, as we might say, 'consumable'—services are commonly included: for as such services are reckoned as paid out of income, if we add the nominal incomes, estimated in money, of those who render such services as well as those who receive them, the result will only represent the aggregate *real* income of the country, if this latter notion is extended so as to include services" (*Principles of Political Economy*, 1901, p. 88). The following passage, from a journal of high standing specially devoted to economic questions, may serve as an example of the kind of inaccuracy to which the omission of services from the category of consumable wealth may

It will be noticed that the above definition excludes from the category of wealth personal abilities and attainments of all kinds. For abilities and attainments are not in themselves capable of being made the subject of exchange. We sometimes indeed speak of paying for the use of a man's skill; but in reality the payment is for services rendered by aid of the skill. The right to command the services of any one over a given period is included under wealth, as pointed out above.

The exclusion of human qualities and capacities from the wealth category is on the whole in accordance with scientific convenience, as well as with popular thought and speech, which—as Professor J. B. Clark observes—broadly distinguishes between the able man and the wealthy man, between what a man is and

give rise. "What comes out most strongly upon a review of the distribution of wealth is the smallness of the portion which is even theoretically available for redressing apparent inequality. It is only a small part of a wealthy man's riches which can actually be taken from himself, because it is after all but a small part which he actually consumes himself. The greater part is only his in so far as he directs the mode of spending or employing it. He directly maintains a number of persons who might conceivably be more usefully employed than in lounging in his hall, attending to his horses, or cultivating his flowers, but who are maintained, nevertheless, out of his wealth. Nearly the whole of his income goes in paying directly or indirectly for labour, and to take it from him means a general dislocation of the whole apparatus." This passage, if not actually erroneous, is at least very misleading. In addition to the material wealth that the rich man consumes, he enjoys a multiplicity of services which, under other conditions, might be distributed more equally through the community.

what he has[1]. At the same time, it is important to
recognise that labour expended in the acquirement
of skill is indirectly productive of wealth, in so far
as it ultimately results either in the production of
material commodities or in the performance of useful
services. Thus, labour expended in acquiring the skill
of the actor or the doctor is *productive*, as well as
that expended in acquiring the skill of the carpenter
or the shoemaker. Moreover, in any correct estimate
of the productive resources of a country, the natural
and acquired abilities of its inhabitants may occupy
a position of the greatest importance.

It may be added that the scope of political economy
is practically not affected by the question whether
wealth is limited to exchangeable sources of utility, as
in the above definition, or is used in a broader sense so
as to include under the title of *personal wealth* all those
capacities that enable men to be efficient producers of
exchangeable wealth. For although so-called personal
wealth does not, under the former alternative, directly
constitute part of the subject-matter of the science, it
still comes in for discussion as a source of wealth, and
as such has still to be recognised as an economic factor
of vital consequence.

Wealth being defined as above, *economic activity*
may be correspondingly defined as human activity which

[1] *Philosophy of Wealth*, pp. 5, 6.

directs itself towards the production and appropriation of such means of satisfying human needs as are capable of being made the subject of exchange. The economic life of a community is constituted by the economic activities of the members of which it is composed, acting either in their individual or in their corporate capacity. The term *economy* is sometimes used as equivalent to economic life, and by *national economy* is meant accordingly the economic life of a nation. It is to be observed that as civilisation advances, each individual becomes more and more dependent on others for the satisfaction of his needs; and hence economic life increases in complexity. In other words, with the progress of society, the organization of industry and the distribution of industrial functions grow increasingly complicated, and the phenomena resulting from men's economic activities become more and more varied in character.

§ 5. *Definition of Political Economy.*—Political economy, regarded as a positive science, is often briefly defined as the science of the phenomena of wealth; and this definition has the merit of directness and simplicity. There seems, however, some advantage in attempting so to define the study as explicitly to indicate that it is not primarily concerned with either physical or psychological or political phenomena as such, but with phenomena that originate in the activity of human beings in their social relations one with another.

With the object of making this clear, political economy may be defined as the science which treats of the phenomena arising out of the economic activities of mankind in society.

It is not pretended that this or any other definition can by itself suffice unambiguously to express the nature of economics. The proposed formula must, therefore, be taken subject to the various explanations that have been already given, or that may subsequently be given, in regard to the province of the science, and its relations to other branches of enquiry. It may be said of the definition of political economy, as of most other definitions, that the discussion leading up to it is of more importance than the particular formula ultimately selected.

NOTE TO CHAPTER III.

On the Interdependence of Economic Phenomena.

THE phenomena with which political economy is concerned are usually classified under the heads of the production, distribution, exchange, and consumption of wealth. This separation of the science into distinct departments should not, however, be regarded as absolute or essential. The object of the classification is convenience of exposition; but such is the action and reaction between the phenomena in question, that it is impossible satisfactorily and completely to discuss any one of the departments without having regard to the others also.

Taking, for instance, production and consumption, it is obvious that men's habitual consumption determines what kinds of wealth shall be produced; and, as indicated in the distinction between productive and unproductive consumption, the form in which wealth is consumed materially affects the amount produced. It is not quite so obvious, but it is equally true, that the production of wealth, both in kind and amount, is influenced by its distribution. The very rich consume luxuries, which, if wealth were more equally distributed, would in all probability not be produced at all or at any rate not to the same extent. Again, if wealth were more equally distributed, there would in all probability be an increase in the average efficiency of the previously worst paid classes of the community, either in consequence of their being better fed, housed, and clothed, or in consequence of a better education and training having been provided for them by their parents; on the other hand, the number of hours during which they would be willing to work might be diminished. That the amount of wealth produced would in some such ways as these be affected by changes in distribution seems practically certain; although it is impossible to say *à priori* in what direction the effect would predominate.

Turning to the connexion between production and exchange, it is to be observed that, as soon as division of labour is carried at all far, the former involves in some form or other the latter. Those whose function may *primâ facie* appear to be simply and entirely to facilitate the exchange of wealth—for example, bankers and bill-brokers, wholesale merchants and retail dealers—all play their part, and sometimes an important part, in assisting in the production of wealth. For without exchange in some form or other it is obvious that production could be carried but a very little way; and, strictly speaking, the work of production ought not to be considered complete, until commodities have found their way into the possession of those persons whose intention it is to consume them[1]. In the case of exchange

---

[1] J. S. Mill in his treatment of production introduces, under the head of capital, questions of distribution that might perhaps have been avoided. In his fundamental propositions respecting capital, and especially in the much criticized proposition that demand for commodities is not demand for labour, the truth of his conclusions

and consumption, there is a still more intimate connexion; for rates of exchange depend fundamentally upon laws of demand, and these in their turn depend directly upon laws of consumption.

The connexion between distribution and exchange may be discussed from more than one point of view. If it is asked how the distribution of wealth is effected under modern industrial conditions, the answer clearly is by means of exchange. As it has been well expressed, "the adjustment of rates of exchange constitutes, in the aggregate, the process of distribution."[1] We may go even further, and say that in an individualistic society the theory of distribution resolves itself immediately into a theory of exchange-value. Each share into which the net produce of a community is divided represents the price paid for a certain service or utility afforded by the recipient of that share. Wages may thus be regarded as the exchange-value of labour, interest as the exchange-value of the use of capital, rent as the exchange-value of the use of land[2].

From another point of view, the theory of the exchange-value of material commodities depends upon the theory of distribution. At any rate, as Cliffe Leslie insists, the theory of cost of production involves the whole theory of

depends partly upon the assumption of the perfect mobility of capital and labour. But that is a subject that comes in for explicit discussion only in connexion with distribution, and much later in Mill's work. Here is perhaps one reason why Mill's chapters on capital are by some readers found so difficult, and, it may be added, unsatisfactory.

[1] J. B. Clark, *Philosophy of Wealth*, p. 64.

[2] Compare Sidgwick, *Principles of Political Economy*, 1901, p. 176.

wages and profits; for unless we have already determined a law of normal wages and a law of normal profits, the doctrine of cost of production is meaningless.

It is, therefore, clear that theories of distribution and exchange cannot be divorced from one another, or discussed to any purpose in isolation.

In connexion with the interdependence of economic phenomena, we may touch briefly upon a controversy that has been raised as to whether the consumption of wealth should or should not be regarded as constituting a distinct department of political economy[1]. The question is to a large extent one of convenience of arrangement, rather than of actual divergence of view in regard to the scope of the science.

The following are among the topics, in addition to an analysis of the nature of economic consumption, that have been treated by different economists under the head of the consumption of wealth: the theory of utility, and the relation between utility and value[2]; the distinction between

[1] It may be observed that the consumption of wealth, in the sense in which the term is used by the economist, does not of necessity involve its destruction. We may say that by the consumption of wealth in political economy we mean its *utilization*, to which its destruction may or may not be incidental. Thus, in the economic sense, jewels are in process of consumption when they are being worn as ornaments; so are the houses in which we live, and the pictures that hang on our walls. A house in which no one lives, or a picture that is stowed away in a lumber room, lasts at any rate no longer than one that is being rationally "consumed." Compare Senior, *Political Economy*, p. 54; and Walker, *Political Economy*, § 328. Senior remarks that "it would be an improvement in the language of political economy if the expression 'to use' could be substituted for that 'to consume.'"

[2] Compare Jevons, *Theory of Political Economy*. General Walker is of opinion that what has led to the practical excision of the whole

different kinds of consumption, and in particular the
distinction between productive and unproductive consumption[1]; the effects of different kinds of consumption,
and in particular the effects of luxury[2]: the policy of

department of consumption from so many recent works is "the
fascination of the mathematical treatment of economical questions,
and the ambition to make political economy an exact science" (*Political Economy*, p. 298). We can hardly regard this view as correct;
for, if we take Jevons, who has insisted more strongly than any other
English economist on the mathematical nature of the science, we
find his most characteristic doctrines distinctly based on a theory of
utility, which theory of utility he himself rightly regards as a theory
of consumption. Indeed he lays it down explicitly that "the theory
of economics must begin with a correct theory of consumption"
(*Theory of Political Economy*, 1879, p. 43). Elsewhere he declares
that the doctrine of consumption is the most important branch of the
science, and he regards it as unaccountable and quite paradoxical
that English economists should, with few exceptions, have ignored
that doctrine. See *Fortnightly Review*, vol. 26, p. 625. Professor
Walras of Lausanne, who is another representative mathematical
economist, takes up practically the same position as Jevons. A consideration of the satisfaction of needs, which must involve a theory of
consumption is the basis of his doctrine of exchange-value. See his
Éléments d'Économie Politique Pure.

[1] Compare J.-B. Say, *Traité d'Économie Politique*; James Mill,
Elements of Political Economy; McCulloch, *Principles of Political
Economy*; Roscher, *Grundlagen der Nationalökonomie*; E. de Laveleye, *Éléments de l'Économie Politique*; Leroy-Beaulieu, *Précis
d'Économie Politique*; Lexis, *Die volkswirthschaftliche Consumtion*,
in Schönberg's *Handbuch der politischen Oekonomic*.

[2] Compare Say, McCulloch, Roscher, de Laveleye, Leroy-Beaulieu,
Lexis. McCulloch, in his treatment of the consumption of wealth,
brings out incidentally, but clearly, a point often supposed to be overlooked by economists, namely, that a taste for luxuries tends to increase, not to diminish, the amount of wealth produced. "The mere
necessaries of life may, in favourable situations, be obtained with
but little labour; and the uncivilised tribes that have no desire to
possess its comforts are proverbially indolent and poor, and are

sumptuary laws, and of other laws attempting to regulate consumption[1]; the causes of commercial depression, and the impossibility of general over-production[2]; insurance

exposed in bad years to the greatest privations. To make men industrious—to make them shake off that lethargy which benumbs their faculties when in a rude or degraded condition, they must be inspired with a taste for comforts, luxuries, and enjoyments" (*Principles of Political Economy*, p. 493). Cliffe Leslie goes a little too far in the same direction, when he remarks that unproductive expenditure and consumption "are the ultimate incentives to all production, and without habits of considerable superfluous expenditure a nation would be reduced to destitution" (*Essays*, 1888, p. 170). Men produce in the first place in order that they may live, and consumption which sustains a worker in efficient working condition is not usually spoken of as unproductive. Cournot (*Principes de la Théorie des Richesses*, § 31) points out that we can conceive a state of society in which there would be no such thing as strictly unproductive consumption; for every satisfaction given to animal appetites might tend either to the preservation of health, the increase of strength, the prolongation of existence, or the propagation of the species. General Walker under the head of consumption exposes the fallacy that the mere destruction of wealth in some way increases production. This fallacy may be regarded as in a way the complementary error of the true theory that a taste for luxuries and a high standard of comfort do, under certain conditions, tend to increase productive efficiency.

[1] Compare McCulloch, Roscher, and Lexis. Professor Lexis discusses the danger of the supply of certain commodities becoming exhausted (*e.g.*, coal, petroleum, quicksilver), and touches on the policy of restraining in some way their consumption with the object of protecting the interests of future generations. He touches also upon interferences with consumption based on climatic, sanitary, and moral considerations; *e.g.*, restrictions upon the destruction of forests, regulations in regard to house accommodation for the labouring classes, restrictions upon the consumption of alcohol.

[2] Compare James Mill, Roscher, Lexis, and Walker. This topic is treated under the head of consumption, because it relates to the equilibrium between production and consumption. Professor Lexis

and its economic advantages[1]; government expenditure and the theory of taxation[2]; the doctrine of population, and in particular the existence of economic wants and a standard of comfort as affecting the increase of population[3].

It is easy to shew that most of the above topics may quite naturally be dealt with in other departments of the science, as in fact they are by those economists who do not profess to treat explicitly of the consumption of wealth. The distinction, for instance, between productive and unproductive consumption, and the effects generally of different forms of consumption on production, are not inappropriately discussed under the head of production itself; while the phenomena of (actual or apparent) over-production may be taken in connexion with the theory of exchange, since only

goes on to touch upon possible remedies or palliatives for trade crises, such as State undertakings of which the main object is to provide work for the unemployed, and emigration.

[1] Compare Roscher, and de Laveleye.

[2] This topic is brought under the head of the consumption of wealth by Say, James Mill, de Laveleye, and others, on the ground that taxation is the means whereby the consumption of government is provided for.

[3] Compare Part v. of General Walker's *Political Economy*; also Part iv., Chapter 3, of Leroy-Beaulieu's *Précis d'Économie Politique*. It will be observed that even among those economists who recognise a distinct doctrine of consumption, there is far from being complete agreement as to what problems should be included within this department. The theory of population, for example, which General Walker introduces in this connexion, is treated by James Mill under distribution, and by McCulloch under production, while Roscher makes it a fifth department of political economy, distinct from production, circulation, distribution, and consumption. There is, again, a divergence of view in regard to the place of commercial depression, and the theory of taxation; and the theory of consumption of Jevons and Walras is quite different from that of any of the other writers above referred to.

under a system of exchange can these phenomena arise. Again, the incidence of taxation is directly connected with the phenomena and laws of the distribution of wealth; and the remainder of the theory of taxation, except in so far as it relates to the effect of different forms of taxation on production, belongs to applied economics, rather than to the positive science of economics, with which alone we are here concerned. This last remark applies also to the discussion of sumptuary laws, and to all enquiries how far and in what directions the increase of consumption should be encouraged or discouraged. Insurance may fairly be regarded as a question of distribution. As to the theory of population, since labour is one of the requisites of production, the law of its increase may be discussed in connexion with production; or it may be included in the theory of distribution, in connexion with the laws regulating, through the supply of labour, the normal rate of wages. The theory of utility occupies, as we go on to shew, a unique position. It is, however, intimately connected with the determination of laws of exchange-value.

The truth is that the phenomena of production, distribution, exchange, and consumption, respectively, all so act and react upon one another, that if any one of these classes of facts is given no independent treatment, it must nevertheless come in for a large share of discussion in connexion with the others. Whether all propositions relating to consumption should be arranged by themselves or discussed as they arise in relation to other topics is, therefore, to a certain extent a mere question of convenience of exposition[1].

[1] Thus, Dr Sidgwick, while explicitly admitting the fundamental importance of certain propositions relating to consumption, thinks

On the whole, it appears that the distinction between productive and unproductive consumption, the phenomena of over-production, the principles of taxation, &c., discussed under the head of consumption by James Mill and others, fall quite naturally and conveniently into other departments of economic science. The theory of utility, as discussed by Jevons, stands on a different footing. For unlike theories of taxation, population, and so on, it relates in itself purely to the consumption of wealth, and hence has a much stronger claim to be considered a distinct theory of consumption. At the same time, for reasons that have been already briefly indicated in connexion with Jevons's description of economics, this theory may be regarded as constituting part of the necessary prolegomena of economic science, rather than one division of completed economic doctrine. The consumption of wealth is not so much an economic

that in such a treatise as his own, it is more convenient to introduce these propositions in dealing with the questions of production, distribution, and exchange, which they help to elucidate, rather than to bring them together under a separate head (*Principles of Political Economy*, 1901, p. 34). J. S. Mill (*Unsettled Questions*, p. 132, note), and Cherbuliez (*Précis de la Science Économique*, p. 5) are somewhat less guarded in their rejection of consumption as a special topic for discussion. "Political economy," says Mill, "has nothing to do with the consumption of wealth, further than as the consideration of it is inseparable from that of production, or from that of distribution. We know not of any *laws* of the *consumption* of wealth as the subject of a distinct science: they can be no other than the laws of human enjoyment." "The consumption of wealth," says Cherbuliez, "is in its only important form a phenomenon which cannot be separated from the production of wealth. Unproductive consumption is the application of wealth to the needs for which it was produced. It requires no further discussion. When wealth gets into the hands of the unproductive consumer, economic activity is at an end."

activity in the sense in which that term has been above defined, as itself the end and aim of all economic activity. Wealth is produced, distributed, exchanged, in order that it may be consumed. The satisfaction of human needs is the motive power throughout. Thus, a true theory of consumption is the keystone of political economy; but it may, nevertheless, be regarded as occupying the position of a fundamental datum or premiss of the science, rather than as constituting in itself an economic law or laws on a par with the laws of production, distribution, and exchange.

CHAPTER IV.

ON THE RELATION OF POLITICAL ECONOMY TO GENERAL SOCIOLOGY.

§ 1. *Conflicting views of the relation between economic science and the general science of society.*— Before proceeding further, it is necessary to enquire explicitly whether political economy is really entitled to rank as a distinct department of study at all. It is maintained by Comte and his followers that on account of the extremely intimate connexion between the phenomena of wealth and other aspects of social life, any attempt to separate economic science from social philosophy in general must necessarily end in failure. The phenomena of society, it is said, being the most complicated of all phenomena, and the various general aspects of the subject being scientifically one and inseparable, it is irrational to attempt the economic or industrial analysis of society, apart from its intellectual, moral, and political analysis, past and present. It is admitted that certain of the facts of wealth may by a scientific artifice be studied separately, but it is denied that their investigation can constitute a distinct science[1].

In striking contrast to the above is the view of those economists who regard political economy as an independent abstract science, dealing with the phenomena of wealth in isolation, and having no concern whatever with other social phenomena. While on the former view the relation of economics to sociology is properly one of entire subordination or rather inclusion, on this view it is one of absolute independence; the facts of wealth are to be studied in and by themselves; they are to be treated as having no relation to other social facts; man is to be considered as a being who is occupied solely in acquiring and consuming wealth.

The truth lies between these two extreme views. What may be called the extreme separatist doctrine

[1] Compare Miss Martineau's *Positive Philosophy of Auguste Comte*, vol. 2, pp. 51—54; also Mr Frederic Harrison's essay entitled *Professor Cairnes on M. Comte and Political Economy* in the *Fortnightly Review* for July, 1870. Comte's views have more recently been given fresh prominence in this country by Dr Ingram's article on *Political Economy* in the ninth edition of the *Encyclopaedia Britannica* (republished as a *History of Political Economy*). Dr Ingram combines his history with an elaborate attack on the manner in which the science has been for the most part studied in England, and arrives at the conclusion that political economy cannot any longer command attention as a fruitful branch of speculation unless it is subsumed under and absorbed into general sociology. "The one thing needful," he says, "is not merely a reform of political economy, but its fusion in a complete science of society."

affirms of political economy as a whole what is true only of a certain portion or aspect of it, and hence would leave the science incomplete. Comte's view, on the other hand, overlooks the fact that only by specialization within proper limits can scientific thoroughness and exactness be attained in any department of knowledge. Students of economics may, moreover, naturally and fairly ask to have the province of sociology itself more explicitly defined, and to see its own fundamental doctrines more clearly formulated, before they can be expected to shew a willingness to have political economy subsumed under and absorbed into it.

It will be our endeavour to shew that whilst the study of economic phenomena cannot be completed without taking account of the influence exerted on the industrial world by social facts of very various kinds, it is nevertheless both practicable and desirable to recognise a distinct systematized body of knowledge, which is primarily and directly concerned with economic phenomena alone. On this view, economics is regarded as constituting one division of the general philosophy of society, of which other divisions are jurisprudence, the science of political organization, and the philosophy of religious, moral, and intellectual development; but it is allowed its own set of specialists, and the necessity of systematically combining the study of economic phenomena with that of other aspects of human existence is denied. It is, in other words, held to be possible for the economist to steer a middle course, neither assuming throughout the whole range of his investigations an entirely unreal simplicity, nor, through the neglect of that specialization which has been found indispensable in the physical sciences, allowing himself to be hopelessly baffled by the complexity of the actual phenomena.

It should be carefully borne in mind that throughout this chapter, as in the chapters that follow, political economy is regarded as a positive science. Similarly by sociology is understood a body of theoretical truth, not a system of practical maxims. The separate existence of economic theory is not imperilled, when it is admitted that practical arguments based on economic grounds alone are rarely in themselves decisive. The two questions are often not clearly distinguished from one another. It is, however, important to recognise that those who stand out most strongly for the recognition of a separate economic science may hold equally strongly that no true guidance in matters of conduct is to be obtained by appealing simply to economic considerations, all social consequences of a non-economic character being disregarded.

§ 2. *The place of abstraction in economic reasoning.*— According to what has been above called the extreme separatist view, political economy takes one aspect of human society and action, and considers it absolutely alone and apart, the science being concerned with man solely as a being who desires to possess wealth. Just as the geometer considers the dimensions of bodies apart from their physical properties, and the physicist their physical properties apart from their chemical constitution, so the economist is said to regard man simply as a being who, in all his economic relations, is actuated by an enlightened self-interest, and who is also free to act accordingly, so far as he does not interfere with a like freedom on the part of others.

This view of political economy is taken by J. S. Mill in his *Essays*, although, as we have previously had occasion to remark, his constructive treatise on the science is worked out on different and much broader lines[1]. He describes economics as treating of the laws of the

[1] Professor Marshall puts the contrast very clearly and forcibly. "In 1830," he says, "John Mill wrote an essay on economic method, in which he proposed to give increased sharpness of outline to the abstractions of the science. He faced Ricardo's tacit assumption that no motive of action except the desire for wealth need be much considered by the economist; he held that it was dangerous so long as it was not distinctly stated, but no longer; and he half promised a treatise, which should be deliberately and openly based on it. But he did not redeem the promise. A change had come over his tone of thought and of feeling before he published in 1848 his great economic work. He called it *Principles of Political Economy with some of their Applications to Social Philosophy*; and he made in it no attempt to mark off by a rigid line those reasonings which assume that man's sole motive is the pursuit of wealth from those which do not."

production and distribution of wealth, not so far as these laws depend upon all the phenomena of human nature, but only so far as they depend upon the pursuit of wealth, or upon the perpetually antagonizing principles to this pursuit, namely, aversion to labour, and desire of the present enjoyment of costly indulgences. Entire abstraction is to be made from every other human passion or motive. In other words, the economist is supposed to take as his subject of study, not the entire real man, as we know him in all the complexity of actual life, but an abstraction—usually spoken of as the *economic man*—a being, who, in the pursuit of wealth, moves along the lines of least resistance, and does not turn aside towards other ends.

In accordance with this view, political economy is defined as "the science which traces the laws of such of the phenomena of society as arise from the combined operations of mankind for the production of wealth, in so far as those phenomena are not modified by the pursuit of any other object."[1] It is admitted that the

---

[1] *Unsettled Questions of Political Economy*, p. 140. Bagehot, in his *Economic Studies*, expresses himself similarly. "Political economy in its complete form, and as we now have it, is an abstract science, just as statics and dynamics are deductive sciences. And, in consequence, it deals with an unreal and imaginary subject" (p. 73). It "deals not with the entire real man as we know him in fact, but with a simpler, imaginary man—a man answering to a pure definition from which all impairing and conflicting elements have been fined away. The abstract man of this science is engrossed with one

economist must allow for the interference of other impulses in applying his results, and that he ought, even in the formal exposition of his doctrines, to introduce many practical modifications; but the recognition of these other impulses is excluded from the science itself.

The single error involved in the above view 'is that of mistaking a part for the whole, and imagining political economy to end as well as begin with mere abstractions. The practical modifications, of which Mill speaks, themselves demand a scientific treatment, and should, therefore, have a place accorded to them within the science itself. For in many cases they are not mere isolated modifications, admitting of application to individual instances only. It is often possible to generalize on other foundations than that of the economic man; and, at any rate, the various inter-

desire only—the desire of possessing wealth" (p. 74). This view of political economy is justified by Bagehot on the ground that "the maxim of science is simply that of common sense—simple cases first; begin with seeing how the main force acts when there is as little as possible to impede it, and when you thoroughly comprehend that, add to it in succession the separate effects of each of the encumbering and interfering agencies" (p. 74). The maxim here cited may be accepted without hesitation; but it seems hardly consistent with the previous statement that political economy *in its complete form* is an abstract science, &c. Our contention is that while economics rightly begins with abstractions, in its complete form it has as good a claim to be called a realistic as to be called an abstract science. What appears to be the correct doctrine is clearly laid down by Cairnes in his *Logical Method of Political Economy*, pp. 42—45.

ferences with free competition admit of scientific enumeration and classification.

The abstraction by which men are supposed in their economic dealings to act exclusively with a view to a certain proximate end[1], namely, the attainment of a maximum value with a minimum of effort and sacrifice, has nevertheless its place, and a very important place, in political economy. For while it is true that our economic activities are subject to the influence of a variety of motives, which sometimes strengthen and sometimes counteract one another, it is also true that in economic affairs the desire for wealth exerts a more uniform and an indefinitely stronger influence amongst men taken in the mass than any other immediate aim. Hence, in order to introduce the simplicity that is requisite in a scientifically exact treatment of the subject, it is legitimate and even indispensable to begin by tracing the results of this desire under the supposition that it operates without check. By thus ignoring at the outset all other motives and circumstances, except those implied in the notion of free and thoroughgoing competition,

---

[1] It will help to prevent misunderstanding to regard the "economic man" as aiming at the attainment of a certain proximate end, rather than as acting from purely egoistic motives. From what ulterior motives, and with a view to what ultimate ends, men desire wealth is immaterial as affecting their conduct so far as the economist is concerned with it. We go on to shew that the ulterior motives which impel men to seek wealth may be far other than egoistic. Compare Sigwart, *Logic*, § 99 (English translation, volume 2, pp. 455—457).

we may, at any rate in certain departments of enquiry, determine the more constant and permanent tendencies in operation, and hence reach a first approximation towards the truth.

As a matter of fact, this approximation is in some cases a very near approximation indeed. In dealing, for instance, with prices on the Stock Exchange, or in the great wholesale markets, under modern industrial conditions, we are for the most part concerned with the economic activities of persons who practically realise in actual life the notion of the economic man. This by no means implies that the persons referred to are what we should ordinarily call selfish. For men of the most unselfish character are, in many of their commercial dealings, influenced directly by what may be termed strictly commercial aims— subject only to the restraints of law and of ordinary commercial custom and morality. They may desire wealth in order to educate and bring up their children with a view to their children's best interests, or in order that they may devote their wealth to particular philanthropic objects, or to the general well-being of the community to which they belong. Still the desire for wealth is in its immediate economic effects the same, whatever its ultimate object may be[1].

[1] Cliffe Leslie criticizes the conception of the desire of wealth as a barren abstraction, in which are confounded together many different desires whose actual consequences are indefinitely various. "No

There are cases, then, where ends other than pecuniary exert so little immediate influence that they

other branch of philosophy," he remarks, "is still so deeply tinctured with the realism of the schools as economic science. A host of different things resemble each other in a single aspect, and a common name is given to them in reference to the single feature which they have in common. It is, properly speaking, only an indication of this common feature, but it puts their essential differences out of mind, and they come to be thought of in the lump as one sort of thing. The desire of wealth is a general name for a great variety of wants, desires, and sentiments, widely differing in their economical character and effect, undergoing fundamental changes in some respects, while preserving an historical continuity in others. Moralists have fallen into a similar error, though from an opposite point of view, and, in their horror of an abstraction, have denounced, under the common name of love of wealth, the love of life, health, cleanliness, decency, knowledge, and art, along with sensuality, avarice, and vanity. So all the needs, appetites, passions, tastes, aims, and ideas, which the various things comprehended in the word 'wealth' satisfy, are lumped together in political economy as a principle of human nature, which is the source of industry and the moving principle of the economic world....The division of labour, the process of exchange, and the intervention of money have made abstract wealth or money appear to be the motive to production, and veiled the truth that the real motives are the wants and desires of consumers; the demands of consumers determining the commodities supplied by producers. After all the reproach cast on the Mercantile School, modern economists have themselves lapsed into the error they have imputed to it. If every man produced for himself what he desires to use or possess, it would be patent and palpable how diverse are the motives summed up in the phrase 'desire for wealth'—motives which vary in different individuals, different classes, different nations, different sexes, and different states of society....The desire for wealth is by no means necessarily an incentive to industry, and still less to abstinence. War, conquest, plunder, piracy, theft, fraud are all modes of acquisition to which it leads. The robber baron in the reign of Stephen, and the merchant and the Jew whom he tortured, may have been influenced by the same motives. The prodigal son who wastes his may, without serious risk of error, be neglected even in the concrete applications of economic doctrines. More usually, however, this abstraction from other substance in riotous living is influenced by the same motives—the love of sport, sensual pleasure, luxury, and ostentatious display— which impel many other men to strenuous exertion in business" (*Essays*, pp. 166—170). The whole of the above argument is very persuasively put, but it does not establish the conclusion that Cliffe Leslie desires to establish. By the desire of wealth is meant the desire of *general purchasing power*, that is, the desire to increase one's command over the necessaries and conveniences of life in general; and nothing that Cliffe Leslie says proves it to be either an illegitimate or a barren assumption that in their ordinary economic dealings men are in the main influenced by this desire, and that, in consequence, a greater gain is preferred to a smaller. That there are enormous variations in men's ideas, as to the particular things that constitute the necessaries and conveniences of life, is nothing to the point. For, as observed in the text, the immediate effects of the desire of wealth may be the same, although the ulterior objects had in view are very different. A man may desire general purchasing power in order that he may be assisted towards the attainment of the noblest and most unselfish ends, but it does not follow that he will therefore sell his services or his goods at less than their market value. Granting that the objects of men's desires are very various, still, as Dr Sidgwick puts it, so far as they are exchangeable and commensurable in value. they "admit of being regarded as definite quantities of one thing— wealth; and it is just because the 'desire of wealth' may, for this reason, be used to include 'all the needs, appetites, passions, tastes, aims, and ideas, which the various things comprehended under the word wealth satisfy,' that we are able to assume, to the extent required in deductive political economy, its practical universality and unlimitedness" (*Political Economy*, 1891, pp. 41, 2). We may add that it is also not to the point that, under different conditions, the desire of wealth may lead to very different lines of conduct. The assumption that men are actuated by this desire is, in economic reasonings, combined with other assumptions—as, for example, the absence of force and fraud—which circumscribe within certain limits the modes in which the desire can operate.

influences yields only an approximation towards the actual truth, which approximation needs subsequently to be developed and corrected.

Even the above degree of validity is denied to the postulate in question by some economists. They hold that if the abstraction whereby we suppose men to act solely with a view to their own advantage is not condemned as leading to positive error, it should at least be rejected as practically useless. It is in manifest contradiction, they say, to the facts of life. Knies, for example, rejects it on the ground that a society of men actuated solely and continuously by self-interest, and allowed absolute freedom of action, has never actually existed. He admits the possibility of hypothetically working out the laws of price, &c., that would arise in such a society were it to exist, but he denies that such a hypothetical enquiry has any utility or practical justification. One might just as well, he says, base an enquiry on the hypothesis that all men are inspired by altruism, or that they all have an equally strong impulse towards charity; and he implies that such enquiries as these would be in all respects equally serviceable—or unserviceable— in enabling the economist to understand and explain the phenomena of the actual economic world[1].

[1] *Die Politische Oekonomie vom geschichtlichen Standpunkte*, 1883, p. 504.

The first point in the above argument—that no society of pure egoists has ever actually existed—is, strictly speaking, irrelevant. For the economists, whom Knies is criticizing, have always insisted that they are dealing with abstractions, with imaginary beings of a simpler type than are to be met with in real life. They have never posited the actual existence of a society of men, guided in all their actions by pure self-interest. The gist of their argument is not even that, in the one sphere of life with which they as economists are concerned, the desire for wealth operates by itself and subject to no interference from the operation of other motives. All they affirm is that, taking a broad survey of the economic sphere, the desire of each man to increase his command over wealth is far more powerful, and far more uniform in its operation, than the other motives, which sometimes act as a drag upon it. They hence argue that by calculating the consequences of this desire, they will be materially assisted towards determining what will happen on the average or in the long run[1].

The latter part of Knies's criticism cannot be ruled out as irrelevant, but it breaks down on the

[1] Menger specially insists that the use of the so-called dogma of self-interest is misunderstood by the historical school of German economists, when they regard it as forming such a disturbing contrast to "full empirical actuality." See his *Methode der Socialwissenschaften*, p. 79.

score of invalidity. It amounts to this—that a doctrine, based on the hypothesis of pure altruism, would be just as near the concrete reality, as one based on the hypothesis of pure egoism; in other words, that, in their economic dealings with one another, men are as uniformly and as powerfully influenced by an immediate desire to augment their neighbour's wealth as by a desire to augment their own[1]. But this argument is certainly contradicted by all the facts of actual economic life. Look where we will in the industrial world, do we not find self-interest —controlled though it may be by moral, legal, and social considerations—the main force determining men's actions? Is it not a patent fact that in buying and selling, in agreeing to pay or to accept a certain rate of wages, in letting and hiring, in lending and borrowing, the average man aims at making as good a bargain for himself as he can? He may be restrained within certain limits by law, morality, and public opinion; and the influence exerted by restraining forces such as

[1] Theoretically an attempt might be made to work out deductively the consequences of the sole operation of altruistic motives, all interferences due to the operation of other motives being ignored. The contention in the text is, however, that this would not in any case have any practical value. Sir Henry Maine rightly urges that "the practical value of all sciences founded on abstractions depends on the relative importance of the elements rejected and the elements retained in the process of abstraction" (*Early History of Institutions*, p. 361). The question at issue turns therefore on the relative importance of egoistic and altruistic motives in economic affairs.

these must ultimately be taken into account. Still the desire for wealth is, under normal conditions, the active impelling force; and the immediate economic consequences of this desire are the same, however unselfishly the wealth gained may ultimately be expended. It is this fact of common experience that justifies economists in starting from the conception of the economic man, as approximately typical of actual men considered in their economic relations. Conclusions based on this conception contain a hypothetical element; but they are nevertheless, at any rate in certain departments of the science, within measurable distance of the concrete realities of the actual economic world[1].

[1] The above is freely allowed by some writers who on other grounds criticize the English school of political economy. "No economist," says Professor R. Mayo-Smith, "would venture on the solution of an economic problem without taking into consideration the fact that men are ordinarily moved by self-interest" (*Science Economic Discussion*, p. 113). "Hypothetically," says Wagner, "the use of the theory of self-interest is always proper; and, for the isolation of causes, it has proved the best of methodological tools. For we have here an element common to all men. We have an element founded on a law which is in truth a 'natural' and universal law. It is based on the physical nature of man, on his mental nature (which depends primarily on his physical nature), and on his relations to the external world. As it affects the individual, so, also, it represents the interest of the species, since the species exists and is continued only through the individual. The objections of historical economists are obscure, and are carried too far, when, instead of admitting the hypothetical value of deduction from self-interest, they deny that it has any value whatever. They make a mistake which is the reverse of the mistake of the advocates of pure deduction; and their mistake is the greater. In considering the modifications of industrial self-interest in different

At the same time, in so far as it can be shewn that in certain spheres of economic action men are normally moved by altruistic motives, this can be more or less recognised in the abstractions upon which the economist's more general reasonings are based. It is, however, doubtful whether it would be possible, in any case, to base upon the hypothesis of general altruism an exact science corresponding to English political economy. For the desire for the general welfare is not a motive capable of being measured in the same way as the desire for wealth can be measured[1].

We have in the above argument accepted the description which Knies gives of the economic man

individuals, different peoples, at different times, and its various combinations with other motives, they forget that there is, after all, a universal element of humanity in this selfishness" (*Jahrbücher für Nationalökonomie und Statistik*, March, 1886, p. 231; *Quarterly Journal of Economics*, October, 1886, p. 118). Wagner goes on to point out, what we have already insisted upon, that "self-interest, when spoken of as the motive of industrial action, often does not mean one's individual interest alone, but includes the interest of others; to be sure, of others in whose welfare the person who acts takes an interest. Consider the family, the acquisition of property for transmission to descendants. Here the egoistic action passes over into altruistic action. But it may nevertheless be said that, although there is a widening of the egoistic motive beyond the individual, it still remains egoistic." There may seem contradiction here; but there is no real contradiction. An individual action may form one link in a series of actions which, considered in their totality, are altruistic; and yet considered by itself, and in relation to its immediate consequences, it may be undistinguishable from an action that is purely egoistic.

[1] Compare Marshall, *Present Position of Economics.* §§ 8—11.

as being actuated solely by self-interest. But it must be remembered that, as we have shewn, the economic man need not be conceived as a pure egoist. All we assume is that in his economic activities his immediate aim is the attainment of a maximum of wealth with a minimum of effort and sacrifice; and it is only with reference to this immediate aim that we can describe him as actuated by self-interest alone.

But it is time now to turn to the other side of the picture. Whilst the process of abstraction from the full empirical actuality is an instrument of the greatest possible utility in economic investigations, the economist cannot by this means alone explain all industrial facts. Neither the conception of the economic man nor any other abstraction can suffice as an adequate basis upon which to construct the whole science of economics. In completing our investigations we have generally speaking to deal with something far more complex. As Roscher puts it, we must in our finished theory "turn to the infinite variety of real life."[1]

---

[1] "The abstraction according to which all men are by nature the same, different only in consequence of a difference of education, position in life, &c., all equally well equipped, skilful, and free in the matter of economic production and consumption, is one which, as Ricardo and von Thünen have shewn, must pass as an indispensable stage in the preparatory labours of political economists. It would be especially well, when an economic fact is produced by the co-operation of many different factors, for the investigator to mentally isolate the factor of which, for the time being, he wishes to examine

§ 3. *Examples of economic problems requiring for their complete solution a realistic treatment.*—It is in attempting the final solution of problems, relating to the distribution of wealth, that it is most obviously insufficient to regard mankind as simply and entirely concerned in the pursuit of gain, irrespective of social surroundings, and the operation of other than pecuniary motives[1]. The love of a certain country or a certain

the peculiar nature. All other factors should, for a time, be considered as not operating, and as unchangeable, and then the question asked, What would be the effect of a change in the factor to be examined, whether the change be occasioned by enlarging or diminishing it? But it never should be lost sight of, that such a one is only an abstraction after all, from which, not only in the transition to practice, but even in finished theory, we must turn to the infinite variety of real life" (*Principles of Political Economy*, § 22).

[1] If by an economic motive is meant any motive that influences men's economic activities, it is clear that the desire of wealth is not the only economic motive. Wagner gives a five-fold classification of economic motives in the above sense: four egoistic, and one non-egoistic. (1) The wish for gain, and the fear of want. (2) The hope of reward of a non-economic kind (*e.g.*, approval), and the fear of disadvantages of a non-economic kind (*e.g.*, punishment). The operation of such motives as these is important in connexion with slave labour. (3) The sense of honour, and the fear of disgrace. The gild system under ideal conditions is an example of the operation of these motives. Another example is to be found in the pride which every good workman takes in the quality of his work. (4) The impulse to activity and to the exercise of power, and the fear of the results of inactivity. "Sometimes, in the restless activity of men who carry on industry on a great scale, the wish to accumulate property is the immediate aim—but not so much for the sake of material advantage, as for the sake of the power which a fortune confers." The motive of rivalry, which may also under certain conditions exert an appreciable influence, is closely akin to the

locality[1], inertia, habit, the desire for personal esteem, love of power.   (5) The non-egoistic motive is the sense of duty and the fear of conscience.   "Because of it, competition is not pressed to the utmost, prices do not reach the highest or lowest limits which the pursuit of individual advantage would fix, and would fix without encountering an effective check in the mere sense of honour and propriety.   Under this head, we are to class not only all charitable action, but the cases where an industrial or social superior purposely refrains from making his own interest the exclusive ground of his economic conduct."   See Wagner's *Grundlegung der politischen Oekonomie*, §§ 33—46; and *Quarterly Journal of Economics*, vol. 1, pp. 118—121.

[1] "Political economists," said Mr Chamberlain in a speech at Inverness in September, 1885, "find it difficult, perhaps, to understand how such unpractical considerations as the traditions and the history of a race, the love of home and of country, religious enthusiasm, and political sentiments, should absolutely prevent a Highlander from accepting with complacency a proposal to exile himself from the land, which his forefathers have possessed and cultivated, for which they have shed their blood, and in which they lie buried. But human nature is a greater force even than the laws of political economy, and the Almighty Himself has implanted in the human breast that passionate love of country, which rivets with irresistible attraction the Esquimaux to his eternal snows, the Arab to his sandy desert, and the Highlander to his rugged mountains."   None of our leading economists are really open to this reproach.   In the applications of political economy, if not as an integral portion of the science itself, they recognise the necessity of investigating inductively the operation of all the forces that affect the movement of labour from country to country, and from place to place within the same country; and amongst such forces they do not overlook those here referred to by Mr Chamberlain.   The above quotation may serve to illustrate how narrow and one-sided is the political economist in the general estimation; and how common it is to substitute for the views of economists themselves, the opinions of superficial readers who have separated fragments of economic doctrine from their proper context.   Because of misunderstandings of this sort it becomes the more necessary to insist that the abstract theory does not exhaust the whole of the science.

the love of independence or power, a preference for country life, class prejudice, obstinacy and feelings of personal ill-will[1], public spirit, sympathy, public opinion, the feeling of duty with regard to accepted obligations, current notions as to what is just and fair, are amongst the forces exerting an influence upon the distribution of wealth, which the economist may find it necessary to recognise, though the precise weight to be attached to them varies enormously under different conditions. The special influence that may be exerted by ethical motives has been referred to in rather more detail in an earlier chapter. It is to be remarked that even in the abstract theory the economist assumes that the rules of conventional morality in matters of business are generally accepted and obeyed. The standard of such conventional morality is, however, subject to variations, as also the extent to which departures from it are common; and variations of this kind should not be overlooked by the economist in his more concrete investigations. As a special case, attention may be called to the extent to which the conventional morality of the market pushes the rule of *caveat emptor*. Even in the same society at the same time this varies in different classes of transactions.

Amongst important circumstances affecting wages are qualities of co-operativeness and habits of combi-

[1] These forces may exert an important influence in trade disputes.

nation amongst the labouring classes, as well as the social forces and legal regulations which determine how far these qualities and habits shall have free play. Again, in discussing the labour question, it is obvious that differences of enterprise and knowledge as affecting a man's willingness or ability to change his condition must not be overlooked. Regard must also be had to legislation of every kind in so far as it directly or indirectly affects the mobility of labour. To take a special case,—the economist has to discuss the circumstances determining the wages of women, and to enquire whether these are in any way different from those determining the wages of men; but only by investigating the operation of various social influences can he obtain anything like an adequate solution[1].

Turning to the more general problem of the causes of variations in the supply of labour, we find it to be one that depends materially on the social, intellectual, and moral circumstances that determine men's standard of comfort, as well as on such conditions as the price of food and other necessaries. This point may be illustrated by reference to Mill's treatment of the argument that under socialism, "the prudential restraint on the multiplication of mankind would be at an end, and

---

[1] Compare the treatment of this problem in Walker's *Wages Question*, pp. 372—384; and in Professor and Mrs Marshall's *Economics of Industry*, pp. 175—177.

population would start forward at a rate which would reduce the community, through successive stages of increasing discomfort, to actual starvation."[1] He says that "there would certainly be much ground for this apprehension," if socialism "provided no motives to restraint, equivalent to those which it would take away"; but he then goes on to speak of the force of public opinion as possibly supplying a new motive, to which, in accordance with the general tenour of his remarks, might be added that of public spirit and care for the general well-being. It is easy to exaggerate the probable efficacy of these forces; but the illustration will at least serve to shew how, in arguing from one state of society to another, there is need to investigate and allow for the effects which different surroundings may have on human action.

When we pass to the production and accumulation of wealth, we find again that the motives in operation vary in different instances[2]. Work, for instance, that

---

[1] *Principles of Political Economy*, ii. 1, § 3.

[2] "In vast permanent societies, in long ages of history, populations such as the Egyptian and the Indian, under a strict caste system, have shewn an astonishing degree of industry, directly stimulated by habit, social feeling, and religious duty, and, in a very slight degree, by personal desire of gain. In religious societies under very different kinds of faith, very active industry, on a scale quite decisive as an experiment, has been stimulated by purely religious motives. Some of the most splendid results of industry ever recorded—the clearing of wildernesses; vast public works, such as bridges, monuments, and

is inspired by mere love of routine, and saving that has become a mere habit, are not so uncommon as *à priori* we might be inclined to imagine. One consequence of the latter fact is that we cannot discover the laws determining the accumulation of capital, or the precise way in which a fall in the rate of interest will affect saving, by considering exclusively the effect of the desire of wealth.

Even in the case of a purely monetary question, such as the circumstances determining the amount of the depreciation of an inconvertible currency, an important consideration may be the extent to which a people's distrust is aroused, and this in its turn may depend partly on their political sympathies, or on their knowledge and intelligence, or on the extent to which their power of moral restraint prevents them from giving way to unreasoning panic. This last point is still more clearly important in connexion with the phenomena that constitute a financial crisis. The theory, for example, of the recurrence of such crises at regular intervals, so far as it does not involve the operation of physical causes (as in Jevons's sun-spot theory), may require

temples; the training of whole races of savages into habits of toil—have been accomplished by purely religious bodies on purely religious motives, by monks, missionaries, and priests."—Frederic Harrison on the *Limits of Political Economy* in the *Fortnightly Review*, 15 June 1865.

to be modified according to the stage of a nation's intellectual and moral development.

Further illustrations might be added, bringing out in particular the influence exerted on industrial phenomena by legal conditions[1], and by political and social institutions; but enough has been said to shew that, while the pursuit of wealth may be the main force of which account has to be taken, still—if economic science is to succeed in affording an adequate explanation and elucidation of the facts of economic life—it is necessary also to have regard to social surroundings, and the operation of diverse other motives.

§ 4. *Distinction between political economy and other social enquiries.*—Since a realistic treatment of economic problems is usually essential to their complete solution, it is necessary that economists should keep in view all the various aspects of social life; and it is clearly mischievous to aim at an entire isolation of economics from other social sciences. But political economy does not, therefore, lose its individuality. For the recognition that the various forms of social activity are in many ways interdependent does not destroy the significance of the differences between them; and to do away with the boundaries, that now separate the different social

[1] It is pointed out by Schönberg that the legal factor is one that must always operate, however much the maxim of *laisser faire* is allowed to exert an influence. There must be laws relating to property, &c.

sciences, would be to sacrifice all the gain resulting from scientific division of labour. Political economy has necessarily to take account of facts that belong primarily to other subdivisions of social enquiry; but its study of them is confined to one particular point of view; it is concerned with them only in so far as they have a direct economic bearing. Hence the economist rightly neglects, or passes over very lightly, many phenomena, and relations between phenomena, that are of central importance from the standpoint of other social philosophers, *e.g.*, the jurist, the moralist, or the student of political science. "The tendency of scientific progress," as Cherbuliez has well remarked, "has always been to separate the sciences, not to confuse them; to divide and subdivide the domain of their investigations, not to make of them a single field, cultivated by the same hands, following the same methods."[1]

It may be observed in passing that physical, as well as social, conditions have to be taken into account in political economy. If, for instance, a rise in wages takes place, the possibility of its being maintained may depend on the effect of better food upon the efficiency of the workers. The law of diminishing return, again, has a direct physical basis; and it is impossible properly to investigate the effects of free

[1] *Précis de la Science Économique,* vol. i. p. 9.

trade apart from the assumption of physical differences between different countries. But no one therefore regards political economy as having no existence independently of the physical sciences. We may argue further from the analogy of the physical sciences themselves. For it is also true that phenomena in the physical world are in various ways interdependent. Geological phenomena, for instance, are dependent upon physical and chemical phenomena. But no one therefore denies the right of geology to be recognised as a distinct science. It has been truly said that in a sense everything includes everything else, and no doubt on the problem of the rent of land it might be possible to build up an encyclopaedia of the sciences. Nevertheless, subdivision and specialization are necessary, if we are to advance in accurate knowledge.

Granting, then, that political economy is not a wholly independent and isolated science, it is still to be regarded as a distinct division of speculative truth; and it may rightly take rank as a social science marked off by special characteristics from other social sciences. It is, in other words, a science in which a form of social activity of a distinctive character is singled out for distinctive treatment[1].

---

[1] It is to be observed that Dr Schönberg—who may be taken as representing the prevailing view of German economists—whilst fully recognising, and indeed insisting upon, the interdependence of

Even if we recognise in the most unreserved way that political economy is only one division or department of social science, there is a special reason why, in the present state of sociological knowledge, we should not seek to give economic doctrine an entirely new form with a view to its absorption into general

economic and other social phenomena, still speaks of political economy as a special independent science ("*eine eigene selbständige Wissenschaft*"). He gives the following as the great fundamental life spheres of every people, constituting, in their totality, national life: justice, art, science and education, family life, social life and morality, religious life, political life, and economic life. The last of these spheres, he remarks, stands in the closest causal connexion with the others; it influences them, and is influenced by them. In studying it therefore, we must recognise these causal relations. But at the same time economic life is a distinct sphere of national life; in it men pursue peculiar ends; in it peculiar forces are developed; it depends on special institutions; into it enter peculiar problems; and it is consequently the subject of an independent science. See Schönberg's *Handbuch*, vol. I., pp. 3, 16, 17. Compare, also, Dr von Scheel in the same volume of the *Handbuch*, p. 69. "It has been proposed," he says, "that political economy should be enlarged into the science of society, while it ought only to be said of it that it should be enlarged into one of the social sciences—in opposition to the too narrow conceptions which were held formerly." Knies expresses himself similarly,—"One may take into consideration a science which, under the name of sociology or any other name, would have to set forth the underlying universal theory for all state and social sciences. But with all that, the just claim and unavoidable requirement of a special care for political and social economy, in the sense in which it is known to us, is still not in the least affected. If this branch of science, which has grown up with the development of the scientific division of labour for the special investigation of a very large and important sphere of human social life, were not there already, then it would have to be immediately invented" (*Die Politische Oekonomie vom geschichtlichen Standpunkte*, 1883, p. 9).

sociology.   Comte charged political economy with being
radically sterile as regards results.   But what results
has sociology, conceived as a master-science dealing
with man's social life as a whole, yet to shew?   It has
been well said by Lord Sherbrooke that sociology, as
distinct from the special social sciences, has yet its
spurs to win.   The time may come when in the domain
of social science wide generalizations are established,
from which each special science that deals with man in
society may learn.   There may thus be constituted a
body of general sociological doctrine, to which political
economy is subordinated.   But economics cannot wait
for sociology in this sense to be built up.   "It is
vain," says Professor Marshall, "to speak of the higher
authority of a unified social science.   No doubt if that
existed, economics would gladly find shelter under its
wing.   But it does not exist; it shews no signs of
coming into existence.   There is no use in waiting
idly for it; we must do what we can with our present
resources."[1]

[1] *Present Position of Economics*, p. 35.   Dr Sidgwick in his *Scope
and Method of Economic Science* expresses himself to a similar effect.
He discusses in some detail the claims of sociology to be regarded as
a positive or established science, taking Comte's own tests of (1) con-
sensus or continuity, and (2) prevision (p. 46); and on both grounds
he decides the question in the negative.   "There is no reason," he
says in conclusion, "to despair of the progress of general sociology;
but I do not think that its development can be really promoted
by shutting our eyes to its present very rudimentary condition.
When the general science of society has solved the problems which it

It may be added, partly by way of qualification, that there is one particular department of economic enquiry, in which the connexion with the general philosophy of society is closer than in other departments. It seems clear that in seeking a theory of economic progress, the method of specialization can be carried less far than when we are discussing laws that presuppose given conditions of industry. It is indeed possible to trace historically the actual course of progress from the specifically economic standpoint; and generalizations relating to points of detail in economic development are attainable apart from any general theory of social progress. But since it is admitted that the economic conditions of any given stage in the progress of society are determined not merely by the economic conditions, but by the general social characteristics, of the preceding stage, no theory of the tendencies of economic evolution as a whole seems likely to be reached independently of some theory of the general tendencies of social development.

has as yet only managed to define more or less clearly—when for positive knowledge it can offer us something better than a mixture of vague and variously applied physiological analogies, imperfectly verified historical generalisations, and unwarranted political predictions—when it has succeeded in establishing on the basis of a really scientific induction its forecasts of social evolution—its existence will be irresistibly felt throughout the range of the more special enquiries into different departments of social fact" (pp. 55, 56).

It is from the department of economic progress that those who attack the old political economy draw their most forcible illustrations; and it is further to be observed that, as general sociology is frequently conceived, its one fundamental problem is "to find the laws according to which any state of society produces the state which succeeds it and takes its place."[1] When sociology, as thus interpreted, can lay down propositions that are definitely formulated and clearly established, then the theory of economic progress may with advantage be specially subordinated to it.

[1] J. S. Mill, *Logic*, vol. 2, p. 510.

NOTES TO CHAPTER IV.

A. On the Distinction between Abstract and Concrete Political Economy.

THE discussion in the preceding chapter naturally leads to the recognition of two stages in economic doctrine, which may be called the abstract and the concrete stage respectively[1]. In the abstract or pure theory of political economy we concern ourselves entirely with certain broad general principles irrespective of particular economic conditions; or, as Jevons puts it, with "those general laws which are so simple in nature, and so deeply grounded in the constitution of man and the outer world, that they remain the same throughout all those ages which are within our consideration." The method of the abstract theory is almost wholly deductive and hypothetical; for though based ultimately on observation, it works from artificially simplified data. The results obtained are in one sense of universal application, since they are ready to be modified to suit particular circumstances as the occasion may arise; but they are in themselves always incomplete, since we cannot by their aid alone adequately understand the economic phenomena of actual life.

[1] Compare Jevons on *The Future of Political Economy* in the *Fortnightly Review* for November, 1876, p. 625.

Concrete economics comes in to supplement the pure theory, and is not content with merely hypothetical results. Its laws are obtained either by direct generalization from experience, or by the aid of the deductive method. In the latter case, however, the premisses are adapted to suit special circumstances, and both premisses and conclusions are constantly tested by direct appeals to experience. In formulating concrete economic doctrines we seek to lay down laws that are operative over a given period or in a given state of society. Such laws are for the most part relative, not universal, in their application[1].

We have the pure theory *par excellence*, when we concern ourselves with economic men, supposed to deal exclusively with one another in a state of economic freedom. On this basis the laws of competitive values, wages, rent, interest, &c. are worked out in their most general and abstract forms. Jevons's *Theory of Political Economy* may be given as a typical example of an abstract treatment of the subject, as contrasted with such a work as Walker's *Wages Question*, where the treatment is in the main concrete.

The line between abstract and concrete political economy hardly admits, however, of being rigidly determined; for the extent to which we have in view special circumstances and conditions of society may sometimes be a matter of degree. Even the same doctrine (*e.g.*, the doctrine of cost of production as the regulator of value) may be regarded

---

[1] What is here spoken of as concrete economics has sometimes been called applied economics. As already pointed out, however, the latter designation is ambiguous; and on the whole it seems best to keep it for what is also called the art of political economy.

as having an abstract or a concrete character according to the mode in which it is treated; and in some cases the concrete doctrines are just the abstract doctrines *plus* something more, namely, an enquiry into the special conditions under which alone the latter can be applied to existing facts, and an investigation of the modifications of doctrine needed in consequence thereof. Instead, therefore, of attempting to draw any hard and fast line between the two sets of doctrines, it may be better to say simply that political economy is abstract in so far as it neglects special conditions of time, place, and circumstance; while it becomes more and more concrete as it takes such conditions into account. This relativity does not detract from the importance of the distinction, which is of special utility in relation to problems of method.

It should be added that the manner in which the distinction is here expressed, and even the distinction itself, would not be universally accepted. For, as we have seen, some economists practically deny the possibility, or at any rate the utility, of any abstract or hypothetical treatment of economics at all, while others seem to regard the pure theory as exhausting economic science. An endeavour has been made in the preceding chapter to controvert both these views. The pure theory may rightly be regarded as of great and even indispensable value as the general basis of economic reasoning, while it is at the same time held to be only part of a larger whole.

It may, indeed, sometimes be possible to pass immediately from the pure theory to the interpretation of individual phenomena of the actual economic world; but more usually there is required the intervention of a body of doctrine, which, while possessing a certain generality of form, is still not purely abstract in character, or capable of being worked out merely by the aid of those simple and general data, which alone are recognised by the abstract theory. It is this body of doctrine that constitutes concrete political economy, as broadly distinguished from the pure theory of the science.

The reasoning of the abstract theory has a logical precision which concrete economics for the most part lacks. Being hypothetical it can be made demonstrative and necessary, so that among properly trained persons there should be no room for differences of opinion in regard to its conclusions. Concrete economic doctrines are in comparison contingent and indeterminate. But it does not follow that they therefore form no part of the science, or that they are essentially unscientific and untheoretical. It ought frankly to be recognised that not all science is of the demonstrative type; and it would be a great mistake to narrow our conception of political economy to the pure theory alone, simply in order to attain perfection of logical form.

B. ON THE DISTINCTION BETWEEN THE STATICS AND THE DYNAMICS OF POLITICAL ECONOMY.

IN speaking in the preceding chapter of the laws of economic progress, another subdivision of political economy has been indicated, about which a few more words may here be added. Economic doctrines may treat (a) of the phenomena of wealth as they present themselves under given economic conditions; or (b) of the manner in which these conditions themselves vary over long periods of time, together with the economic changes that ensue thereupon.

The former of these branches of enquiry constitutes the main body of economic science. To it belongs, for example, the investigation of the laws which in any given society regulate the division of what is produced into the shares of rent, interest, and earnings. The latter branch of enquiry may be distinguished as the study of economic progress; and the resulting doctrines constitute in their totality a general theory of economic development or evolution. The laws of the movement from *status* to contract, and of the transition from collective to individual property, may be given as examples of special doctrines belonging to this division of the subject.

Using terms which Comte introduced into the nomenclature of social science, Mill and some other economists speak of these two branches as the *statics* and *dynamics* of political economy respectively. These terms are not, as a matter of fact, specially appropriate; they may even be misleading. In so-called economic statics we are frequently engaged in examining the effects of particular changes, *e.g.*, changes in demand, in cost of production, in the amount of currency in circulation, and the like. The economic world, even in a given state of society, is in perpetual movement; prices, wages, profits, systems of currency, tariffs, &c. are continually changing; and it is the business of political economy, independently of any theory of economic progress, to investigate the mutual relations of these changes.

Apart, however, from the use of these particular terms, there can be no doubt of the importance of the distinction itself, especially in the discussion of economic method. The theory of economic progress is exceptional in its almost entire dependence upon an historical method of treatment; and, as pointed out in the preceding chapter, it is more distinctly subordinate than are other portions of economic doctrine to general sociology. Some members of the historical school consciously or unconsciously identify the study of economic development with political economy as a whole, or at any rate regard it as the only portion of political economy worthy of scientific treatment. The relative value that they attach to the historical method in economic investigations is consequently very great, and the nature of their disagreement with other economists is somewhat apt to be misunderstood.

It should be added that the expressions *statics* and *dynamics* of political economy are also used to indicate a distinction of a somewhat less thoroughgoing character than that described above. An economic theory is termed *static* if it is based on the assumption of what has been called a *stationary state*, that is to say, a state in which there occurs no essential modification of the general conditions under which production and consumption, distribution and exchange, are carried on. In other words, in a static enquiry, the effects of changes of a certain specific kind are considered, but the general social and economic conditions are supposed fixed; it is assumed that no fundamental changes take place in the general character of social wants, that no inventions lead to the introduction on a large scale of new methods of production, that no sudden diminution of population is caused by war or famine, that there is no progressive exhaustion of sources of supply, and so forth.

At a later stage it becomes necessary to consider the effects of such changes as these, and we then pass on to the *dynamics* of the subject. It will be observed that what is here meant by the dynamics of political economy amounts to something less than a general theory of economic evolution.

The distinction between statical and dynamical theories as here drawn is a relative rather than an absolute one. Still what lies at the root of the distinction is of considerable importance, especially from the methodological point of view; and it is also important to recognise the true nature of the relation between the two kinds of enquiry. The static, as distinguished from the dynamic, treatment of any problem involves a higher degree of abstraction; and the justification for such a treatment is to be found in the gain in clearness and precision that results from commencing our study of the operation of economic forces by considering them as far as possible in isolation and not in combination. Our problems are thus simplified and we take them first of all in a form in which they admit of a definite and precise solution. As in other cases, however, where we make use of abstraction, the statical treatment is not final; and it should be supplemented by a less abstract treatment wherever this is possible.

Professor Marshall has some interesting observations on the importation of the terms statics and dynamics from physics into economics. He allows that there is a fairly close analogy between the earlier stages of economic reasoning and the devices of physical statics; but he considers that dynamical solutions, in the physical sense, of economic problems are unattainable. He thinks that in the later stages of economics biological analogies are more serviceable than mechanical ones; and hence that while economic reasoning should start on methods analogous to those of physical statics, it should gradually become more biological in tone. In other words, economic problems as they grow more complex are less concerned with the interaction of forces, regarded as merely mechanical in their operation, and are more concerned with organic life and growth[1]. This accords with the view that we have elsewhere expressed that when we come to deal with problems of economic growth and progress the appropriate method becomes less and less deductive and more and more inductive. For it is to be observed that mechanical analogies (dynamical as well as statical) naturally suggest deductive methods of investigation, while biological and evolutionary analogies suggest inductive methods.

C. On Political Economy and Common Sense.

The point of view of Comte and his school is not the only one from which the claims of political economy to be regarded as a science have been denied. For the paradox is sometimes maintained that economic problems can best be solved by common sense, that is, by the natural untrained

---

[1] Thus, "in the earlier stages of economics, we think of demand and supply as crude forces pressing against one another, and tending towards a mechanical equilibrium; but in the later stages, the balance or equilibrium is conceived not as between crude mechanical forces, but as between the organic forces of life and decay....Again, with every spring the leaves of a tree grow, attain full strength, and after passing their zenith decay; while the tree itself is rising year by year to its zenith, after which it also will decay. And here we find a biological analogy to oscillations in the values of commodities or of services about centres which are progressing, or perhaps themselves oscillating in longer periods" (*Economic Journal*, March, 1898, p. 43).

intelligence and sagacity of the plain unscientific man; and it is accordingly considered a mistake even to attempt to give economic reasonings a scientific form[1].

The question at issue resolves itself to a certain extent into what is meant by *science* and *scientific*. Even those, who deny that political economy is a science, admit that it proceeds by systematic observation and analysis, and that it results in a body of ascertained and reasoned truth. But this is little different from what others mean by calling it a science. A science may be defined as a connected and systematized body of truths possessing generality of form. Truth lacking generality cannot constitute a science; nor can even general laws so long as they remain detached and disconnected. In maintaining, then, the possibility of a science of political economy, nothing more is meant than that it is possible to discover general laws of economic phenomena, to co-ordinate these laws, and to explain particular economic facts by means of them.

In so far as the possibility of an economic science in this sense is not denied, the question resolves itself into one of ways and means of attaining the desired end; and we may here consider very briefly one or two of the arguments put forward in favour of having recourse to what is called a practical as opposed to a scientific method.

A scientific treatment of political economy is deprecated, because political economy addresses an unscientific audience and is bound to make itself easy to be understood. "Its

---

[1] See Professor Bonamy Price's *Practical Political Economy*, Chapter I.; also his address as President of the Department of Economy and Trade, Social Science Congress, 1878, published in the *Journal of the Statistical Society*, December, 1878.

aim is to make common sense the supreme ruler of industry and trade. The test of a true political economy is that its teaching, its principles, its arguments, and above all its language, shall be intelligible to all." It is, in other words, maintained that the economist must not be scientific, because if he is he will be over the heads of his audience. Of course abstruse reasoning is out of place if simpler reasoning will serve the purpose equally well; and technicalities, that can without loss of precision be avoided, condemn themselves. But to make intelligibility to the ordinary untrained understanding the actual test of truth is simply to pave the way to error.

It is needless to say that in dealing with economic problems there is ample scope within legitimate limits for the exercise of sound common sense. Common sense, or at any rate common experience, supplies the economist with many of his ultimate premisses; and, in regard to practical questions where there is much to be said on both sides, common sense is often in the last resort the supreme arbiter to be appealed to[1]. In dealing with subject-matter so complex as that of political economy, however, it shews the reverse of true common sense to reject any of the aids that systematic methods of observation and reasoning can afford; and, all things considered, it is not an unqualified disadvantage that the use and proper appreciation of such methods should necessitate some preliminary training of a scientific sort. The concrete facts of economic life are

---

[1] It may be said that common sense of the kind here had in view is of a somewhat rare type; still it is entitled to the name of common sense, in so far as it is hardly amenable to scientific rule, and is not to be acquired by scientific training.

so familiar, that men are only too ready to imagine themselves competent to form sound judgments in regard to them. It is, therefore, the more important that the need of scientific training in methods of economic analysis and reasoning should receive general recognition. It has been said that political economy is losing its influence because it is becoming too scientific. It should rather be said that its scientific pretensions have sometimes been misunderstood and exaggerated, because the limitations to which it is subject, when treated as an exact science, have been overlooked. But however much the credit of political economy may have suffered from this cause, it has certainly suffered a good deal more from the crude dogmatism of those who have professed to speak in its name, although they have received no adequate scientific training in its study.

A further reason assigned for holding that political economy should not arrogate to itself the name of science is that "the truths proclaimed by it are ultimately truisms, which have always been known to all the world." In so far as this statement is true, it is a statement that does not apply to political economy alone. Most scientific laws include facts that have been known all through the ages; but they are far from being a bare restatement of these facts. The relation of science to everyday truths is that it examines their logical foundations and gives them a precise form, corrects and supplements them, explains them by means of higher generalizations, and so systematizes and co-ordinates them. To do all this for such economic truths as are already the common property of mankind is one of the aims of political economy.

CHAPTER V.

ON DEFINITION IN POLITICAL ECONOMY.

§ 1. *The problem of definition in political economy.*—
All writers on the method of science, from Bacon down-
wards, have in some form or other called attention to
the importance of the part played by the explication
of conceptions in the building up of any science; and
it is certainly not less essential in economics than in
other sciences that our fundamental notions should be
made clear. This end is effected chiefly by discussions
concerning definitions.

There are some writers who decry all attempts to
frame accurate definitions of economic terms. Such
attempts are viewed with suspicion; they are regarded
as throwing dust in the eyes of the student, and as
diverting his attention from more important points.
Political economy is said to have strangled itself with
definitions. Richard Jones, for example, who is known
chiefly as one of the earliest critics of the Ricardian
school, and who was also one of the first to emphasize
the relativity of economic doctrines, speaks with much

scorn of those who would spend time in discussing definitions. "I have been reproached," he says, "with giving no regular definition of rent. The omission was not accidental. To begin, or indeed to end, an enquiry into the nature of any subject, a circumstance existing before us, by a definition, is to shew how little we know how to set about our task—how little of the inductive spirit is within us."[1] Comte writes in a similar strain, and so do some members of the modern historical school. They regard disquisitions on the meaning of terms as pedantic and useless, even if not positively misleading[2]. In all this, there is an element of truth. Mere definition carries us a very little way; and to bind ourselves by rigid definitions, or even to attempt perfect consistency in the use of terms, may sometimes—for reasons that will presently be stated— hinder rather than advance scientific knowledge. Still, while excessive wrangling as to the meaning of words is to be avoided, the fundamental importance of discussing definitions in a really scientific way remains.

It may be observed, in the first place, that if some economists waste time by treating problems of definition

[1] *Literary Remains of Richard Jones*, edited by Whewell, p. 598.

[2] "Word-splitting and definition-extending," says Professor Thorold Rogers, "is a most agreeable occupation. It does not require knowledge. It is sufficient to be acute. Persons can spin out their definitions from their inner consciousness by the dozen, aye, and catch the unwary in the web" (*Economic Interpretation of History*, p. viii).

in too great detail, others waste more time in verbal disputes unrecognised as such. Failing to give precision to their own use of terms, and failing also to appreciate the sense in which the same terms are used by other writers, they fall easily a prey to the fallacy of *ignoratio elenchi*. Much controversy in economics might be avoided by a clear understanding of the different senses in which terms are used, and the relation of the different meanings one to another.

But it should always be remembered that the problem of definition, properly understood, is something more than a mere question of language. "Definitions," says Mill, "though of names only, must be grounded on knowledge of the corresponding things." In the discussion of a definition, insight is often gained into matters of fact; and, as Dr Sidgwick has insisted in a highly philosophic passage in his *Principles of Political Economy*, the discussion itself may be of much greater importance than the particular definition finally selected. Economists, Dr Sidgwick observes, have been apt to "underrate the importance of *seeking* for the best definition of each cardinal term, and to overrate the importance of *finding* it. The truth is— as most readers of Plato know, only it is a truth difficult to retain and apply—that what we gain by discussing a definition is often but slightly represented in the superior fitness of the formula that we ultimately adopt; it consists chiefly in the greater clearness and fulness in which the characteristics of the matter to which the formula refers have been brought before the mind in the process of seeking for it."[1]   In choosing one definition of a term rather than another, there is not unfrequently something arbitrary; and so long as all sources of ambiguity and vagueness are cleared away, it may not, within certain limits, be of essential importance which of two or more alternatives is adopted.   But there is nothing arbitrary or unessential in analysing the precise content of a notion in the various con- nexions in which it is involved.   In such an analysis, it is generally assumed either that the extension of the notion is more or less agreed upon, or else that some proposition into which the notion enters is true. In analysing, for instance, the conception of capital it is usually taken as granted that capital is one of the co-operating factors in the production of wealth.   Our economic notions are thus no mere fictions of the imagination, but are drawn from the facts of industry and commerce that have come under our notice; and their analysis fixes our attention on distinctions and relations of fact.

It is unnecessary to insist on the impossibility of gaining, without clear notions, an accurate knowledge of the things themselves to which the notions relate.

[1] *Principles of Political Economy,* 1901, p. 59.

In economics, numerous errors have been the result of vague and ill-defined notions; and in consequence of the complexity of economic phenomena, the attainment of clear ideas in this department of knowledge is undoubtedly attended with peculiar difficulty[1]. This is one reason why the problem of definition assumes a greater relative importance in economics than in some other studies. It is, as we have said, by discussing definitions that we are aided in making our ideas clear; and our success in framing satisfactory definitions may also be taken as a test of their clearness[2].

The assistance afforded by the discussion of definitions towards the explication of fundamental

---

[1] Fallacious theories of wages—to take but one example—may be at least partly ascribed to the difficulty that has always been found in precisely analysing the conception of capital, and keeping clearly before the mind the result of that analysis.

[2] Whewell remarks that "though definition may be subservient to a right explication of our conceptions, it is not essential to that process. It is absolutely necessary to every advance in our knowledge, that those by whom such advances are made should possess clearly the conceptions which they employ: but it is by no means necessary that they should unfold these conceptions in the words of a formal definition" (*Novum Organon Renovatum*, p. 38). It is quite true that it is possible to have clear notions without definitions clothed in definite language. We have, for example, a clear conception of *capital*, if we can analyse with precision and accuracy the functions of capital in industry; and it is not absolutely essential to this, that an exact definition of capital should be constructed. At the same time, the ultimate test of the clearness of any conception would seem to be the ability to express in clear and definite language the corresponding definition.

conceptions is not, however, the only reason why the problem of definition is important. All definition involves classification. By giving a name to phenomena of a certain description we thereby constitute them a class by themselves; and it is of great scientific moment that we should bring together into the same category those things which have from the economic standpoint the closest affinity one to another, and that we should not class together those things whose resemblance is only superficial and unimportant. For this reason, it is after all only within certain limits that it can be said to matter little what precise definitions of economic terms are ultimately selected. Our aim should always be to render our terms significant of those distinctions that are from the economic point of view of principal importance. Only by the aid of an appropriate nomenclature will it be possible without circumlocution to formulate exact general statements concerning the phenomena of wealth.

From this point of view the problem of definition resolves itself into one of classification; and it is again made clear that definition is not a mere question of words, but a question of things. The truth is that the discussion of definitions in political economy— so far from requiring, as Professor Thorold Rogers says, no knowledge, but only acuteness—requires, if it is to be carried on to any useful purpose, wide experience and a thorough knowledge of economic phenomena and their mutual relations. In the order of exposition, some consideration of definitions naturally finds an early place. But in the order of knowledge, finality of definition is attained only in a late stage of development. "The writers on logic in the middle ages," says Whewell, "made definition the last stage in the progress of knowledge; and in this arrangement at least, the history of science, and the philosophy derived from the history, confirm their speculative views."[1] From this standpoint, Adam Smith has been praised for the very sparing way in which he introduces definitions in the *Wealth of Nations*.

§ 2. *Conditions to be satisfied in framing economic definitions.*—It follows from what has been said in the preceding section that the main objects to be kept in view in discussing and framing definitions in political economy are—(1) to make as distinct and precise as possible the conceptions that are fundamental in the science, (2) to mark those distinctions between phenomena that are of chief economic importance. In other words, our aim should be to make our ideas at once *clear* and *appropriate*. It is hardly necessary to add that we should seek to express our definitions in a simple and intelligible form. There remain to be considered some special difficulties that present

[1] *Novum Organon Renovatum,* p. 40.

themselves in the attempt to frame satisfactory economic definitions.

Because economics is concerned with familiar phenomena of everyday life, and because of the precedent
set by the great economic writers of the past, economists have for the most part to content themselves
with terms that are already in current use in ordinary
discourse. There is some gain in this. Words borrowed
from common language are, as Whewell points out,
"understood after a very short explanation, and retained in the memory without effort." But, at the
same time, the problem of definition is made more
difficult. For if we use the terms of common language,
we must also endeavour to keep tolerably near to the
sense in which they are customarily employed. In so
far as this condition is not fulfilled, there is not only
danger of our being misunderstood by others, but, as
Dr Sidgwick remarks, we may also fall into inconsistency ourselves through the force of old associations and
the effect of habit on our own minds. Unfortunately,
the terms of ordinary language have not, as a rule,
any precisely determined connotation; they are used
vaguely and inconsistently. The distinctions indicated
by them, moreover, are by no means always those which
from the economic standpoint are of chief importance.
Hence arises a frequent conflict between the condition
that we are so to define our terms that the ideas

corresponding to them may be both clear and appropriate, and the further condition that we are to seek, as Malthus puts it, "to agree with the sense in which they are understood in the ordinary use of them in the common conversation of educated persons."[1] What then is the relative importance of these conditions? Some writers regard agreement with common usage as the ultimate and supreme test. So far, they consider, as we depart from the sense in which a term is used in common life, we necessarily fail in solving the problem of its best definition. In other words, the enquiry as to what a term ought to mean in political economy is practically identified with the enquiry as to its actual meaning in ordinary discourse.

In opposition to the above, the true solution seems to be as follows. In defining our terms, we should begin with a kind of Socratic induction, and enquire what is the main idea running through their ordinary use both in everyday discourse and in economic writings. Besides enabling us to minimise the divergence between our definitions and the current meaning of the terms defined, a study of the traditional use of language is likely to suggest both similarities and distinctions that might otherwise have escaped our notice. From this point of view, even the ambiguity of a term may not be without a certain compensating

[1] *Definitions in Political Economy*, p. 4.

advantage; for by enquiring into the source of the ambiguity we may gain light on the connexion between the phenomena denoted by the term in its two senses respectively[1]. Still, however important the enquiry into the current use of language may be, it ought not to be regarded as identical with the problem of determining what is the best definition to select for scientific purposes; and while agreement with ordinary usage is to be sought for, this aim must always be subordinated to the attainment of clear and appropriate conceptions. Hence, some deviation from the colloquial use of terms may ultimately be found inevitable. It need hardly be said that whenever we thus find ourselves compelled to employ an old term in a new and technical sense, we should spare no pains in emphasizing our divergence from previous usage.

A word or two may be added with regard to the frequent diversity in the use of terms amongst economists themselves. This diversity leads sometimes to misunderstanding, and probably tends to retard the progress of the science; it is, therefore, to be regretted; but we should not attach undue importance to it. Divergence in regard to questions of definition does

---

[1] Thus—to take a simple illustration—the ambiguity of the term *value* leads up to a discussion of the relation between exchange-value and utility. Again, the ambiguity of the expression *value of money* suggests the enquiry how changes in the general purchasing power of money are related to changes in the rate of discount.

not necessarily preclude substantial agreement either in the ultimate analysis of fundamental conceptions or in completed doctrine; and the conclusions of any given economist may have intrinsic value, although he is paradoxical in his phraseology. Moreover, where there is a want of agreement in definition, valuable lessons may sometimes be learnt from a study of its causes. Two different definitions of the same term may be complementary to one another, in the sense that each lays stress on some distinction that the other tends to slur over. And thus the criticism of definitions that are ultimately rejected may be by no means barren of result.

It will be gathered from what has been already said that in advocating one definition of a term rather than another, dogmatism is generally speaking out of place. Advocates of particular definitions are, however, far too apt to dismiss rival definitions as simply erroneous, not recognising that the question is usually one of degree of appropriateness, rather than of absolute right or wrong. It may for this reason be useful very briefly to consider the various grounds on which any proposed definition may be criticized and rejected. (1) *That it is based on an erroneous analysis of facts.* The real ground of a criticism of this kind is an underlying assumption, on the part of the framer of the definition, either that the denotation of the term is more or less fixed, or else that some given proposition in which the term occurs is true.   We have already pointed out that such assumptions as these do frequently underlie proposed definitions; and it is clear that any resulting controversy must turn on matters of fact, and not merely on questions of propriety of language or classification[1]. Whenever, therefore, such criticism can be shewn to be valid, the critic may rightly claim to be allowed to express dissent dogmatically.   (2) *Unintelligibility or obscurity.*   This again is a ground of criticism which, if it can be made good, justifies an unqualified rejection. (3) *Unsuitability.*   Here the basis of the criticism is that the classification implied by the definition is not one that is suitable or convenient for economic purposes. The unsuitability or inconvenience may of course be of an extreme and patent character; but frequently it is merely a question of degree, or of a balance of advantage and disadvantage, in regard to which a writer may have his own opinion, but should also be content to let others have theirs, without adopting a violently controversial tone.   For so long as economists agree in their fundamental analyses, a difference

---

[1] If, for instance, it is assumed that the normal value of freely produced commodities is determined by their cost of production, then the definition of cost of production involves questions of fact.   Similarly, if in defining wealth, it is assumed that whatever can be bought and sold is wealth; or if in defining a market, it is assumed that the Money Market is properly so called.

between them as to the precise point at which classes should be separated from one another may be a matter of comparative indifference. (4) *Departure from popular or previous economic usage.* There are here three cases which may be distinguished. (*a*) Where the writer intends to define the term in the popular or the usual economic sense, but fails to do so correctly. This is a valid ground for speaking of a definition as incorrect. (*b*) Where the writer is aware that he is departing from ordinary usage, but in his own subsequent use of the term unconsciously drops back into the old meaning. The charge here is one of internal inconsistency; and if it can really be shewn that the force of old associations is such that the very framer of the new definition is misled by them, it is a fair ground for rejecting the definition summarily. (*c*) Where the writer is aware that he is departing from ordinary usage, and is not open to the charge of inconsistency. Under these conditions, novelty of definition may be perfectly justifiable; and in no case does it afford ground for any accusation of positive error or incorrectness. The disadvantages of using terms in a novel sense are, however, obvious and indisputable; and the proposed innovation may be paradoxical in so high a degree that it stands for practical purposes self-condemned. Even short of this, a valid and sufficient ground for rejecting a proposed definition will be afforded if it can be shewn

that the definition involves a paradoxical use of language
that is unwarranted by the necessities of the case.

§ 3.   *Relativity of economic definitions.*—A serious
difficulty in the definition and use of economic terms
results from the fact that, in different departments of
economic enquiry, it may be convenient to vary the
point at which distinctions are drawn.   In other words,
a conception, which is appropriate from a given standpoint, may need to be modified, if it is to continue
appropriate as the standpoint is changed.   This has
been held to be the case in regard to such conceptions
as *wealth* and *capital*: from the point of view of
production, for example, it may be convenient to give
a definition of wealth, not in all respects identical with
the definition that is appropriate from the standpoint
of distribution; again, with special reference to its
measurement, there may be advantages in defining
wealth differently from the cosmopolitan, national,
and individual points of view respectively.   How then
are conflicting requirements to be satisfied?   One
possible solution would be the introduction of fresh
technical terms.   A great multiplication of technical
terms is, however, in itself an evil, since it tends to
restrict the study of the science.   Moreover, to have
entirely distinct names for conceptions that are closely
related to one another might lead to the disregard
of important relations and resemblances.   The original

terms might, again, be rigidly defined, careful qualifications being introduced to fit them for use in different connexions; but this would give rise to the necessity of very cumbrous and involved statements. A third alternative is frankly to allow the use of the same term in slightly different senses, according to the department of the science under discussion; and to vary the definition accordingly.

This last alternative has a great weight of authority in its favour; and, where the differences of meaning are really inconsiderable, it seems an admissible course to adopt, on the ground that the context will generally speaking suffice to mark the precise sense in which the term is being used in any given instance. It is an essential condition, however, that the fact of variation in the use of the term should be very carefully emphasized. In some cases, it may be possible to combine the first and third alternatives by forming a series of compound words, in which the term conveying the central conception remains unchanged. Thus, if it is thought desirable to define *capital* differently from the point of view of the individual and that of the community, the terms *revenue-capital* and *production-capital* may be used accordingly. By this plan all danger of ambiguity will be avoided, while at the same time the common element running through the different uses of the term will not be concealed from view. It will probably not be necessary to use the full compound word on all occasions.

It is to be added that definitions may be relative not only to different standpoints, or different departments of economic enquiry, but also to different periods of economic development; for at each new stage of economic progress, fresh characteristics of phenomena denoted by the same name may rise into prominence. In order, for example, to meet the circumstances of modern trade and financial organization, *money* requires a different definition from that which is appropriate to it in relation to earlier periods of industrial evolution. Again, a definition of the term *market*, that would be appropriate under the primitive conditions of the Middle Ages, would hardly be adequate under the more complex conditions of modern industry. As reflecting the characteristics of different periods, and as illustrating the different stages through which phenomena have passed, the actual history of the use of terms is worthy of special study[1].

[1] Compare Cunningham, *Growth of English Industry and Commerce during the Early and Middle Ages*, p. 17. "In the sixteenth century," says Dr Cunningham, "the change in the use of certain terms is very remarkable; and if we attend to it, we are enabled to realise the extraordinary transformation which was then taking place. A social change may be said to have been completed when it found expression in a new term, or fixed a new connotation on an old one." The use of an historical method of definition is advocated by Professor Nicholson in his address on *Political Economy as a Branch of Education*.

Whilst, however, many economic definitions may be allowed to possess a relative or progressive character, this relativity cannot be extended to the ultimate analysis of the fundamental conceptions of the science. If these conceptions assume a somewhat different character in different connexions, we shall still find something generic or universal in each one of them. Hence the admission of the relativity of economic definitions must not be absolute or unqualified.

Attention may further be called to a difficulty, which political economy—in common with many other sciences—frequently finds in applying its definitions. Limiting cases are met with, which it is far from easy to assign to their proper category. This remark applies pre-eminently to such distinctions as those between specialized and non-specialized capital, skilled and unskilled labour, productive and unproductive consumption, &c., where the two classes almost necessarily shade into one another by insensible degrees. But even in dealing with such conceptions as wealth, capital, money, direct and indirect taxation, protection to native industry, and so on, there is often the greatest difficulty in so formulating their definitions as to leave no doubt in any case as to whether given phenomena come under them or not. For instance—Is skill to be included under *wealth*, or is the goodwill of a business, or a merchant's

credit? Where precisely shall we draw the dividing
lines between *capital* and land on the one hand,
and labour on the other? Are bills of exchange
to be included under *money*? Is a tax on wages
indirect because by checking the supply of labour
it may lower profits? Is an import duty on tea
in England *protective* because it may cause some
persons to consume more beer or other home-made
drinks?

It is desirable that in the construction of definitions, difficulties of the above kind should not be
overlooked; but it is nevertheless no fundamental
objection to a definition that it does not enable them
to be solved offhand. If in the definition itself it is
sought to meet all limiting cases that may arise, the
resulting formula is likely to prove very cumbrous,
or more probably the attempt to obtain a definite
formula at all will finally be given up as hopeless.
But to conclude a discussion concerning the definition
of a term without providing a definition cannot be
regarded as satisfactory, however valuable in itself
the discussion may be. If, therefore, an economist
brings into prominence the many difficulties in the
way of an unexceptionable definition, it should also
be his aim to make it clear what formula affords
in his opinion the best available solution of the
difficulties.

The truth is that in drawing hard and fast lines—
as definitions compel us to do—there is necessarily
something artificial; for such lines are not drawn by
nature. Here, as elsewhere in economic matters, a
principle of continuity is in operation, and different
classes imperceptibly merge into one another. Hence
arises the necessity of being content, in some cases,
with definitions that are not absolutely unequivocal
and determinate. Where this is so, the characteristics
of the limiting cases that may arise will form a valuable
subject of consideration, and attention should be called
to them. But they may then be neglected, except
where, in special connexions, they rise into exceptional
importance.

CHAPTER VI.

ON THE METHOD OF SPECIFIC EXPERIENCE IN POLITICAL ECONOMY.

§ 1. *Preliminary functions of observation in economic enquiries.*—An endeavour will be made in the present chapter to shew that, except within a somewhat limited sphere, the method of specific experience cannot by itself afford a sure and adequate foundation for the attainment of general economic truths, and that political economy is accordingly not to be considered—as some maintain—a purely empirical or inductive science. At the same time, it may be well to say explicitly at the outset that herein one side only of the truth is presented. If pure induction is inadequate, pure deduction is equally inadequate. The mistake of setting up these methods in mutual opposition, as if the employment of either of them excluded the employment of the other, is unfortunately very common. As a matter of fact, it is only by the unprejudiced combination of the two methods that any complete development of economic science is possible.

At an early stage of economic enquiry, observation has functions to perform, which, though very important, are somewhat liable to be overlooked. In the first place, it is from observation that even deductive economics obtains its ultimate premisses. From this point of view, an introspective survey of the operation of those motives by which men are mainly influenced in their economic activities is of fundamental importance; and this introspective survey must be combined with observation of the conduct of other men in the economic sphere. Observation is also needed in order to determine how far and in what way economic motives may be compared and measured. The fact, learnt by observation, that as a rule they are measurable, is one of the principal reasons why political economy is able to resolve itself to a considerable extent into the form of a deductive science.

It is further necessary that there should be an investigation of the principal physical and other circumstances by which economic activities are conditioned. In particular, the legal structure of society in its general economic bearing must be examined. Of this kind of preliminary observation, and more generally of the part played by observation in connexion with the deductive method, a further consideration will follow in a later chapter. In the meantime, there is a certain distinction to which attention may be drawn. The observation that precedes deductive reasoning is in the main not observation of complex economic facts, but of elementary economic forces and the conditions under which they operate. It is by the agency of these forces that complex economic facts are built up[1].

In all economic investigations, however, it is also requisite that there should be some preliminary observation of the complex phenomena themselves, with a view to their description and provisional classification. The phenomena which really constitute the subject-matter of economic science are thus passed under review in their concrete manifestations; the problems to be solved are indicated; and means are afforded for guiding and controlling our subsequent reasonings.

The department of political economy which deals with economic phenomena from the descriptive standpoint may be spoken of as *descriptive economics*, as distinguished from *constructive economics*, which aims at establishing laws or uniformities. Descriptive economics has itself been further subdivided into a *formal* and a *narrative* branch[2]. The former of these analyses and classifies the conceptions, such as wealth, capital, value, money, &c., which are needed for understanding the nature of economic phenomena, and it involves the

[1] Compare Wagner, *Grundlegung der politischen Oekonomie*, 1892, § 92.

[2] See Mr W. E. Johnson's article on the *Method of Political Economy* in Mr Palgrave's *Dictionary of Political Economy*. Mr

logical processes of definition and division. The latter investigates historically and comparatively, and with the aid of statistics, the particular economic phenomena which are met with in different communities and at different epochs; it is essentially concrete and circumstantial.

Within the province of descriptive and classificatory economics, there is unlimited scope for valuable economic work. In a broad sense, descriptive economics includes the whole of economic history and economic statistics. But at the same time, the knowledge of particular facts, which is thus afforded, does not in itself constitute the end and aim of economic science, the central problems of which are constructive and not merely descriptive. It would not be necessary to dwell at all upon this, were not the view sometimes put

Johnson gives the following scheme of the chief departments of economic science from the methodological standpoint:

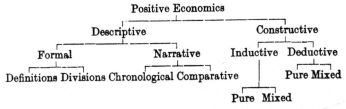

It will be observed that the divisions given under the head of constructive economics relate to the method of reasoning adopted, which may be predominantly inductive or predominantly deductive, whilst in each case a mixed method is recognised in which induction is modified by deduction, or deduction by induction.

forward that political economy is nothing more than an empirical science in its descriptive or classificatory stage. It is held by some writers that under existing conditions it is impossible for the economist to accomplish more than the provision of a nomenclature, and the description and classification of what is directly observed; and it is said accordingly that economics must "be content to observe and classify and describe and name."[1]

Political economy does not, however, deserve the name of a science at all, if the economist is not competent to reason about the phenomena of wealth, and discover laws of causal connexion. Mere description cannot constitute a science; and political economy has no purely classificatory stage, such as will enable it to be compared with sciences of the type of zoology and botany, which deal with material objects falling into a natural system of classification. The doctrine in question seems practically to overlook the fact that economics is of necessity a science of cause and effect. The economist cannot help endeavouring to trace effects to their causes, and to assign to causes their effects. But the detection of causal connexion needs the assistance of some apparatus of reasoning, inductive or deductive or a combination of these. Mere

[1] Compare Dr Cunningham's pamphlet on *Political Economy treated as an Empirical Science*. The somewhat similar doctrines held by the more extreme members of the German historical school will be discussed in greater detail subsequently.

reflective observation cannot possibly give the requisite insight[1].

It is to be added that while some preliminary description and classification of concrete economic phenomena rightly precedes the treatment of economic theory, still such description and classification must be regarded as in the first instance only provisional. Relations of cause and effect are often implied in what appears to be simple description. Hence without some examination of underlying principles, the description of economic facts, to say nothing of their classification, is apt to be unconsciously deceptive, an element depending upon the individual writer's personal bias being imported into what professes to be the mere holding up of a mirror to nature. The more complete our

[1] It has been already mentioned that Wagner recognises three theoretical problems in political economy, namely, the description of economic phenomena, their arrangement under types, and the explanation of the causes upon which they depend (see p. 37 and note 1 on p. 38). He adds, however, that the three problems really constitute three stages of a single problem, and that they must not only be all of them as far as possible solved, but also in the order in which they are given. Political economy, he goes on to say, would be, if still a science, at least no independent science, but only a part of historical science and descriptive statistics, if—in accordance with certain tendencies of the historical school—it were to limit itself to the first of the three problems. The second and third really constitute the special and chief problems of political economy, for the solution of which the first was merely preparatory; and it is only when the second and third problems are reached that political economy becomes a really independent and theoretical science (*Grundlegung der politischen Oekonomie*, 1892, § 58).

knowledge of the laws by which economic phenomena are regulated, the more accurate will our description and classification of them become.

Whatever importance then may be attached to purely descriptive economics, it is necessary to pass on from observation to processes of inference that will satisfy logical canons; and the first question to be considered is how far specific observation of industrial phenomena can lead directly to the establishment of economic laws. By the method of specific experience is here meant the method that passes slowly from particulars to *axiomata media*, and thence to the highest generalizations of the science, without ever reversing the order.

Two forms of the purely inductive method may be distinguished. In the first place, some single set of economic facts may be examined under special conditions, with a view to the application of the logical method of difference. In the second place, an elaborate collection of some particular class of economic facts may be made with a view to generalization from a large number of instances. In the former case, recourse is had to experiment or to some substitute for experiment. In the latter case, the sources from which our material is gathered are history and statistics.

§ 2. *Limited scope for experiment in political economy.*—Observation and experiment are sometimes

contrasted with each other as if they were distinct
methods of obtaining knowledge.   But this is of course
not the case.   Experiment is nothing more than the
process of deliberately producing phenomena for ourselves, so that we may be enabled to observe them
under the most advantageous circumstances[1].   In
experiment we have a control over the phenomena
under investigation, and generally a far more precise
knowledge of the conditions under which they occur,
than is possible in cases where they are brought about
independently of our own action.   Where there is
free scope for experiment, we can also multiply our
instances under varying conditions, and thus isolate
phenomena successively from those circumstances that
might obscure their true character.   It is accordingly
to experiment that recourse is usually had for the
application of the method of difference, which is the
only completely adequate method of reasoning from
specific experience.

The essence of the method of difference is the
comparison of two instances, which resemble one
another in all material respects, except that in one a

---

[1] We sometimes hear of "unintentional experiments," such as
a railway accident or a famine.   Experiment, however, in the logical
sense implies something that is brought about deliberately and of set
purpose: it is not merely any striking event from the investigation of
which special insight may be gained.   The conditions under which
such phenomena as the above may serve as *substitutes* for logical
experiment will be considered later on.

certain cause is present, while in the other it is absent. The effects of that cause are thus made manifest.

The requirements of the method can best be satisfied if the cause, whose effects are under investigation, comes singly into operation in a state of things with which we are so well acquainted that no material change can pass unobserved. It is also generally speaking essential that there should not be a long interval between the occurrence of the cause and the production of the effect; otherwise it is practically impossible to exclude the interference of extraneous and unknown causes. Under these conditions, the instances compared are the state of things before, and the state of things after, the given cause has come into operation; and this is the form of the method usually adopted when recourse is had to experiment.

We have a different form of the method, when one of the instances is the state of things brought about by the given cause operating in conjunction with other causes, while the second instance is the state of things brought about by causes similar to the latter operating alone. It is not essential here that the nature of the "other causes" should be completely known; the sole requirement is that they should occur equally in both instances. It is very difficult, however, to be sure that this requirement is really fulfilled; and hence the first way of applying the method is usually the more satisfactory[1].

It may now be asked how far effective experiment is possible in political economy, or how far without experiment the conditions requisite for the employment of the method of difference are capable of being satisfied.

It cannot be said that experiment is a resource from which we are absolutely debarred in economic enquiries. Experiment may assist in establishing the simpler laws of the production of wealth—as, for instance, those relating to the circumstances upon which the efficiency of labour depends, and the means whereby such efficiency may be increased. Thus, by the aid of experiment the economist may directly investigate the effect of the specialization of skill upon the dexterity of the workman, and hence be the better able to estimate the economic consequences of the division of labour. The law of diminishing returns can also be tested by experiment.

But these are problems that lie only on the threshold

---

[1] Illustrations of both the above varieties of the method of difference will be found later on. There is a third variety, in which the given cause operates in conjunction with other causes, whose nature and individual effects are accurately known both in kind and amount. In this case, the effect of the given cause may be determined by subtracting from the total effect the sum of the effects of the other causes. This form of the method of difference is technically known as the method of residues.

of economics. Indeed, some of the laws thus determined by experiment may be regarded as the contributions of other sciences to economics, rather than as conclusions obtained by it. In regard to problems of distribution and exchange, and the economic influence exerted by social institutions and governmental policy, the possibility of effective experiment is far more questionable. The phenomena are for the most part not such as can be manipulated at will; and even when some kind of experiment is possible, our power of controlling and varying the concomitant circumstances is very limited; nor can the experiment be freely repeated[1].

It is sometimes said that every new law is an experiment; and, in the popular sense in which the term experiment is used, this is true. In all legislation, new phenomena are produced by human agency;

[1] Cairnes, after stating that the economist is precluded from the use of experiment in the ordinary sense, suggests as an inferior substitute what he speaks of as "experiment conducted mentally." Hypothetical conditions are first formulated; then some new agency is supposed to come into operation under these conditions; and finally the effects of this new agency are deduced. In this way, Cairnes adds, "Ricardo employed, as far as the nature of his problem and the circumstances of the case permitted, that experimental method which those who would disparage his great achievements affect to extol. but the real nature of which, as their criticisms shew, they so little understand" (*Logical Method*, p. 81). The process referred to is a form of the deductive method, and is of the greatest utility. But to speak of it as in any sense "experimental" can hardly be considered a legitimate use of language.

the precise character of these phenomena either in kind or amount, it is generally impossible to foretell; and, although a return to the exact *status quo ante* may be out of the question, some further modification by subsequent legislation is always possible. But it is not the case that the primary object of every new law is to afford means of studying the effects which a change of conditions or the introduction of a new agency is capable of producing; nor is any effort made to arrange or modify the attendant circumstances so as to facilitate the attainment of this object. Legislation cannot, therefore, be generally speaking regarded as equivalent to experiment in physical science[1].

The statesman may, however, rightly be said to experiment when he adopts avowedly tentative measures, with the express object of gaining insight into their

[1] Bacon distinguishes between *experimenta lucifera* and *experimenta fructifera*. "Experiments, which are in themselves of no use, but avail only for the discovery of causes and axioms, we are wont to call *light-bringing* experiments, to distinguish them from *fruit-bearing* ones. They have in them a wonderful virtue and condition; namely, that they never deceive or disappoint. For since they are employed not to effect any result, but to reveal the natural cause in something, however they fall out, they equally satisfy our purpose, inasmuch as they settle the question" (*Novum Organon*, Book i, Aphorism 99). In modern works on logic, the term *experiment* is usually limited to *experimentum luciferum*; in other words, we mean by an experiment in the logical sense, some course of action whose immediate object is increase of knowledge, rather than material advantage. It is only in special cases that *experimenta fructifera* are also to any marked extent *lucifera*.

social and economic effects. Such a course may be adopted in a modification of tariffs, the duties on a few articles only being in the first instance altered; or in a reform of the Poor Laws, the change affecting in the first instance only one or two counties. Legislation of a permissive character may, again, be specially intended to resolve itself into local experimentation. Action of a novel kind may be taken by local authorities in certain parts of the country, and the results watched by those in other parts of the country. Thus the area of operation may gradually be extended, and perhaps with each extension fresh lessons may be learnt. It should be observed that in this case we are able to compare the condition of the locality where the experiment has been made, not only with the antecedent condition of the same locality, but also with the condition of other localities where there has been no such experiment. By the latter comparison we may be enabled to eliminate the effects of concurrent social and industrial changes that are affecting the country as a whole. There is here a combination of the two forms of the method of difference to which reference has been already made[1].

[1] Tentative legislation is strongly advocated by Jevons in one of his essays on *Methods of Social Reform* (pp. 253 ff.). He points out that by this means it is possible to make "direct experiments upon the living social organism," and to conduct social experimentation with a view to social progress. It may be observed that in the

It should be added that in special cases economic experiments may be made by private bodies of individuals; as, for instance, those of Robert Owen and his followers in communism. Another interesting example of a somewhat different kind is afforded by the year's trial of the "forty-eight hours' week" made in 1893 at the Salford Iron-works of Messrs Mather and Platt.

Still, at the best, experiments, such as the above, are made under very different conditions from those that are conducted in the laboratory of the chemist or the physicist. It by no means follows that whenever experiment of some sort is possible, the requirements of the method of difference can be adequately fulfilled. So far, for instance, as experiments involve tentative legislation, it is at any rate not possible to make them at will; and, therefore, the process of investigation for ordinary enquirers differs little from simple observation. Nor are the experiments actually made likely to be of

---

Middle Ages laws were frequently passed for a limited period of years. This remark applies, for example, to early legislation affording protection to native industries. Thus in 1455 the silk workers and spinners complained that their industry was being ruined by the Lombards and others, and a law was passed prohibiting for five years the importation of manufactured silk goods. In 1463—after an interval, during which the law was inoperative—a similar measure, but of a more general character, was passed; and again, after another interval, in 1482. There were several subsequent renewals, and it was not till the beginning of the following century that the prohibition was made perpetual. By experimental legislation of this kind, whatever its other drawbacks, fresh.experience was continually gained.

the kind that the theoretical economist would naturally select. It is to be added that even statesmen cannot indefinitely multiply the instances under varying circumstances; and thus one of the special advantages of experiment is lost.

It is further to be observed that in the economic world those effects, that are of the most consequence, are apt to be produced very gradually. There is, therefore, the greater opportunity for the independent occurrence of material changes over which we cannot possibly have control, and of whose occurrence we may even have no suspicion. It is, in other words, specially difficult to isolate any single cause from other causes whose effects may be mistaken for its own.

Experiments that involve the voluntary action of individuals are also under a peculiar disadvantage, inasmuch as the persons who are made the subjects of the experiment are likely to be themselves interested in the result. Thus, in experiments intended to throw light upon the economic effects of community of goods, it is impossible to exclude the interference caused by the fact that the majority of the members of the self-constituted societies, seeking to realise socialistic ideas, are probably—at any rate at the outset—specially selected persons, by no means typical or representative of mankind in general. They are likely to be persons, who are individually disinterested and unselfish, while they are at the same time peculiarly anxious that the results should be of a nature favourable to the scheme they have at heart. In some cases, the members of voluntary communistic societies have further been held together by special bonds of a religious nature. So far, then, as these considerations go, communistic experiments would appear to be unduly favourable to communism. It is true that such experiments as have actually been tried have more often met with failure than success. But in order to account for this, advocates of communism may call attention to another source of weakness in the experiments, that tells in the opposite direction. For it may be maintained that because of the small scale on which alone it is possible to experiment, and the uncongenial environment, and the fact that exceptional and sustained sacrifice of a purely voluntary kind is required on the part of the strongest and ablest of those concerned, the principle under trial is not allowed a fair chance. It cannot be said that no useful lessons are to be learnt from experiments of the kind referred to; but it seems clear that they cannot be regarded as by themselves providing conclusive evidence either one way or the other[1].

[1] Some of the above observations apply to the interesting experiment, already referred to, which was made by Messrs Mather and

§ 3.   *The employment of the method of difference*
independently of deliberate experiment.—On the whole—

Platt in 1893 in order to test the working of an eight hours' day; and
a very brief account of that experiment (taken from the *Economist* for
31 March 1894) may here be given.   The firm, who employed about
1200 men in the engineering and machinery trades, were anxious to
reduce the hours of labour, and they took their workmen into counsel
with them on the subject.   As a result, it was arranged that from
February 1893 to February 1894 the works should run 48 instead of
53 hours per week, the rate of wages remaining unaltered.   The
details of the scheme were discussed with the officials of the Amalga-
mated Society of Engineers, and the Society undertook that during
the year in which the experiment was to be tried no demand for
a reduction of hours should be made upon other employers.   It was
moreover pointed out to the workmen that if the new system was to be
a success, they must themselves contribute their share towards making
it so by greater punctuality and by increased energy and interest
during the shorter hours.   An earnest appeal was also made to the
foremen in the various departments to exercise foresight and vigilance
throughout the year in forwarding the work from process to process,
in furnishing materials well in advance, and in providing such simple
facilities and workshop conveniences, other than new tools, as might
from time to time be suggested by the men, especially the piece-work
men.   A special feature in the experiment was that no overtime
whatever was worked, except for breakdowns and repairs; extra men
being employed, on the double shift plan, to meet extra pressure of
work.   It was arranged with the men and with the trade-unions that
should the experiment prove a failure, the firm should be allowed to
modify the programme or revert to the old system.

The results of the experiment were worked out very fully by
Mr William Mather, the indirect, as well as the direct, advantages
and disadvantages of the new system being carefully calculated
and balanced one against another.   It is unnecessary to go into
details here; it will suffice to say that the results were found to be
very satisfactory from the point of view of the employers as well as
from that of the workmen.   The gross earnings of pieceworkers were
somewhat reduced, but this reduction was slight in comparison with
the reduction in their hours of labour; and the very slight increase in

leaving on one side the more elementary phenomena of the production of wealth—the help to be derived from deliberate experiment in political economy is but slight. It will for the most part be found that the exceptional cases, in which the method of difference can with some success be employed in complex economic enquiries, are not the result of experiment at all, but are due

the wages cost of production was counterbalanced by the saving in gas and electric lighting, and in wear and tear of machinery, &c.

It cannot be doubted that the experiment was a valuable contribution to the determination of the economic effects of a shortening of the hours of labour. At the same time it is possible to exaggerate its cogency, even if it be assumed that, in making his calculations, Mr Mather was able to eliminate interferences due to external changes in the state of the trade in which the firm was engaged.

As was pointed out by critics at the time, the conditions under which the reduction of hours of labour took place were in several respects exceptional in character, so that doubt may be felt as to whether the satisfactory results should not in large measure be credited to these collateral conditions rather than to the mere reduction of working hours. Thus some part of the gain might not unreasonably be attributed to the better organisation enjoined upon the foremen in the various departments, and to the additional facilities afforded to the pieceworkers to enable them to increase their output. It was moreover natural that throughout the trial year all concerned should do their utmost to make the trial a success. The men would naturally strain every nerve at the beginning in order to secure a permanent future advantage; and the employers would not be less anxious that the experiment which they had initiated should not result in failure.

Under a general eight hours' system these special incentives to increased production would be wanting. Hence any generalisation from a particular case of this kind must be made with caution; and the experiment ought to be considered along with much other evidence bearing on the point at issue rather than as by itself affording a decisive solution of the question.

either to the sudden but fortuitous introduction of influences, abnormal in their character or in the scale of their operation, or else to the rare chance of two communities existing side by side, in both of which all the agencies affecting their economic condition, save one, are similar in kind.

An example, to which the former of the above descriptions will apply, is afforded by the sudden diminution in the supply of labour on an altogether abnormal scale caused by the Black Death in the fourteenth century. By a comparison of the conditions of the labour market before and after this plague, some of the effects of a scarcity of labour on wages are distinctly indicated even by the aid of the imperfect data that alone are now obtainable[1]. Again, in the issue of assignats at the time of the French Revolution, in the suspension of the Bank Charter Act during a period of crisis, in a sudden burst of activity such as manifested itself in the American railroad construction of 1881, we have further examples of agencies coming suddenly into operation and producing effects that seem unmistakeable.

An example belonging to the second type is to be found in the first two chapters of the second

---

[1] An example of a somewhat similar character—the Irish potato-famine of the years 1845 to 1849—is adduced by Sir G. C. Lewis, *On the Methods of Observation and Reasoning in Politics*, Chapter 6, § 8.

book of Malthus's *Essay on Population.* Malthus
cites Norway and Sweden as two countries closely
resembling one another in their general economic
conditions, except that Sweden had some advantage
in a more favourable soil and climate. Nevertheless,
the average mortality in Sweden in proportion to its
population was considerably higher than in Norway,
the lower classes of the people were in a less flourishing
condition, and the increase of mortality in barren
seasons was peculiarly striking. Malthus accordingly
applies the method of difference in order to determine
the cause of this diversity; and he finds it to consist
in the superior force in Norway of preventive checks
to the increase of population. Thus, till within a few
years of the time when he wrote, every man in Norway
was subject to ten years' military service; and during
this period he "could not marry without producing a
certificate, signed by the minister of the parish, that
he had substance enough to support a wife and
family; and even then it was further necessary for
him to obtain the permission of the officer." The
general sentiment of the country was also opposed
to early marriages. Labour was little migratory, and
the division of labour was not carried far; every man
could, therefore, judge of the openings that existed
for his own employment and that of his children;
and thus the danger of a redundant population was

more clearly brought home to each individual. In Sweden, on the other hand, the variety of employment was greater; and the danger of redundancy, therefore, not so apparent. The average proportion of yearly marriages to the whole population was larger than in Norway, and this proportion increased at every temporary and occasional increase of food. At the same time, the continual cry of the government was for an increase of subjects, and practical evidence of this desire was given in the establishment of lying-in and foundling hospitals. The contrast was, therefore, very marked; and, taking it in connexion with the general similarity between the two countries in other respects, the conclusion drawn by Malthus seems difficult to gainsay[1].

Mill indicates in his *Logic* the conditions that he regards as alone adequate for the application of the method of difference in the protectionist controversy. "If two nations," he says, "can be found which are alike in all natural advantages and disadvantages; whose people resemble each other in every quality, physical and moral, spontaneous and acquired; whose habits, usages, opinions, laws, and institutions, are the same in all respects, except that one of them has a more protective tariff, or in other respects interferes more with the freedom of industry; if one of these

[1] Compare Bonar, *Malthus and his Work*, p. 132.

nations is found to be rich, and the other poor, or one richer than the other, this will be an *experimentum crucis*: a real proof by experience, which of the two systems is most favourable to national riches."[1]

The implication is that these conditions are necessarily incapable of being satisfied. It has been maintained, however, that a comparison of the economic progress of Victoria and New South Wales during the period succeeding the year 1870 actually provides an *instantia crucis* of the kind asked for. Both colonies gained ground after 1870, but the progress of New South Wales is said to have put that of Victoria into the shade, whether we take as our criterion population, or revenue, or exports and imports, or the value of rateable property. The method of difference has accordingly been applied to find the cause of this. The territories of the two colonies are contiguous; they closely resemble one another in natural advantages and disadvantages; their inhabitants belong to the same stock, and are similar in character and habits; they are governed on the same principles; their institutions have been for the most part the same. But in this respect there is one striking exception. In Victoria a policy of protection was in the ascendant, in New South Wales a policy of free trade. Here then, it is

[1] *Logic*, vol. ii., p. 472.

argued, is to be found the difference required to account for the diversity in the progress of the two colonies[1].

It cannot be denied that in such cases as the above some degree of cogency attaches to the employment of the method of difference even in complex economic enquiries; in other words, a connexion of cause and effect can be established by this method with a more or less high degree of probability. The cases of which this can be said are, however, exceptional; and even in the most favourable instances, confirmation by some independent line of reasoning is indispensable. For, in consequence of the complexity of the surrounding circumstances, and the length of time generally required for effects fully to manifest themselves, it is impossible that the conditions requisite for the valid employment of the method should be more than approximately fulfilled. Such conditions as are often satisfied in physical science are quite unattainable.

If we are sometimes inclined to accept without question economic arguments based on the method of difference, it is to a large extent because the way has been prepared by previous reasoning tending towards the same conclusion. 'How far we rely on

[1] Compare Lord Farrer, *Free Trade and Fair Trade*, Chapter 29; and Sir G. Baden-Powell on the *Results of Protection in Young Communities* in the *Fortnightly Review* for March 1882.

the previous reasoning, and how far on the *à posteriori* evidence pure and simple, it is often difficult to determine. The latter evidence may, as Cairnes points out, strongly arrest attention, because it deals with new and perhaps striking facts. But when the basis on which we really rest our conclusion is subjected to logical analysis, it will probably be found to combine induction and deduction, which mutually support and strengthen one another; and not to be—as at first it seemed—purely inductive.

It may be worth while to turn back to one or two of the instances given above, in order to examine their cogency in a little more detail. In the comparison drawn by Malthus between Norway and Sweden, it seems impossible to make quite sure that some vital difference between the two countries may not have been overlooked. Hence the argument has not the cogency that an ordinary argument based on the method of difference would have in physics or chemistry; nor does Malthus for a moment imagine that it has. He gives it as one item only in a mass of concurrent evidence; and as such its force is unquestionable. This exemplifies the true place of the method of difference in complex economic enquiries. Any given application of the method taken by itself has not the independent validity that belongs to the method under ideal conditions; for such conditions cannot be fulfilled. But it may usefully serve to strengthen or confirm evidence afforded by other methods.

Similar remarks apply to the free trade argument based on the comparison between New South Wales and Victoria. It is clear that in this comparison account ought to be taken of the circumstances of the two colonies before as well as after 1870. The gold discoveries dating from 1851 caused Victoria to develope with extreme rapidity, her gold fields being about six times as productive as those of New South Wales. Subsequently, however, there was a falling off in the Victorian production of gold from about ten millions annually to about three millions. May not the protectionist find here an obvious cause for the comparatively slow progress of Victoria after 1870? Again in 1870, in consequence of the previous rapid development of Victoria, the two colonies started from a different level. While Victoria is not much more than a quarter of the size of New South Wales, her population was in 1870 very considerably the larger, and so was her external trade. But it is a well recognised fact that *ceteris paribus* the higher the stage a country has reached, the more difficult is it likely to be for her to maintain a high rate of progress. It may further be argued, rightly or wrongly, that by her policy of protection Victoria laid the foundation of future greatness, whatever the immediate effects on her prosperity may have been. It is impossible, therefore, to base a perfectly conclusive argument upon a bare comparison of the circumstances of the two countries.

The truth is that between any two countries there are sure to exist to an almost indefinite extent differences that may conceivably affect their economic condition. These differences may be small in themselves and not apparent on the surface, and yet in the aggregate their economic influence may be considerable. "No two communities," says Sir Robert Giffen, "are sufficiently alike to be comparable in strict logic. The slightest differences in the race or moral condition of the two communities, who are to outward appearance much the same, might make a great deal of difference in their material progress. If the two are subjected to different economic *régimes*, how are we to tell whether the inferior progress of the one materially—even when we are sure about the inferiority—is due to the *régime*, and not to other differences in the character of the communities, which we cannot so well appreciate? External economic circumstances are, besides, incessantly changing, and may affect two communities apparently of much the same character and position quite differently. If it were possible to institute many pairs of comparisons and exhibit a uniform result in all, it might be safe to infer that it was the *régime* which did make the difference, no other uniform cause of difference being assignable; but this condition of course it is impossible to fulfil."[1]

So great is the danger of exaggerating the probative force of the method of difference in economic enquiries, that there is probably in popular economic reasoning

[1] *Essays in Finance*, Second Series, p. 200. Mill argues on *à priori* grounds that it is impossible for two countries to agree in everything affecting their economic condition with the one exception of their policy as regards free trade or protection. After the passage quoted on pages 192, 93, he continues: "But the supposition that two such instances can be met with is manifestly absurd. Nor is such a concurrence even abstractedly possible. Two nations which agreed in everything except their commercial policy would agree also in that. Differences of legislation are not inherent and ultimate diversities; are not properties of Kinds. They are effects of pre-existing causes. If the two nations differ in this portion of their institutions, it is from some difference in their position, and thence in their apparent interests, or in some portion or other of their opinions, habits, and tendencies; which opens a view of further differences without any assignable limit, capable of operating on their industrial prosperity, as well as on every other feature of their condition, in more ways than can be enumerated or imagined. There is thus a demonstrated impossibility of obtaining, in the investigations of the social science, the conditions required for the most conclusive form of inquiry by specific experience." This *à priori* argument has some degree of validity; but it is pushed a little too far. The adoption of a free trade policy instead of a protectionist or *vice versâ* might conceivably be due to fortuitous circumstances. It might be due, for instance, to the ascendancy of an individual statesman or statesmen, whose influence was exerted on the particular side in question. It might, therefore, possibly be unconnected with any other differences of economic importance. At the same time, while such an occurrence as this is "abstractedly possible," it is without doubt improbable in the highest degree.

no more common fallacy than a false argument from cause to effect based on an illegitimate application of this method[1].

Typical examples are to be found in the ordinary *à posteriori* arguments in favour either of protection or of free trade. The protectionist points to the prosperity of the United States, and the free trader to the prosperity of England. But economic prosperity or the reverse is of course the outcome of a variety of causes acting together, some of which tell in the same direction, while others more or less counteract one another. Granting that free trade tends towards prosperity, there may also be other powerful causes tending in the same direction; and these may operate with greater force in the countries that happen to be protectionist than in those that happen to levy no protective duties. Hence it is quite compatible with

---

[1] It may be observed in passing that we commit the fallacy of *post hoc ergo propter hoc* not only when we assign an effect to an antecedent that is really unconnected with it, but also when we assign it exclusively to an antecedent that only partially accounts for it. For example, Professor Marshall enters a caution "against treating the new forces of competition as exclusively responsible for those sufferings of the English working classes at the end of the last century and the beginning of this, which were partly due to war, bad harvests, and last, but not least, a bad Poor Law. That law was itself antagonistic to free competition, which it set aside in favour of a crude form of socialism, that exercised a degrading influence on character" (*Principles of Economics*, vol. i., 1st edition, p. 717, *note*).

the free trader's position that a given protectionist country should be more prosperous than a given free trade country. For it is not maintained that, however much other circumstances may vary, prosperity is always proportional to freedom of commerce; but simply that under given economic conditions the prosperity of a country is increased by free trade. On the other hand, if it be allowed that on the whole England very greatly prospered after the repeal of the Corn Laws, the beneficial effects of free trade are not by this single fact alone rendered unquestionable; for the conditions demanded by the method of difference fail altogether to be satisfied. Many other causes were in operation during the second half of the last century to which our prosperity might on similar grounds be rightly or wrongly attributed; for example, the progress of invention, the vast improvement in means of communication and the diminished cost of transport, the spread of education, the Australian and Californian gold discoveries, the extension of the field for emigration, and the further opening up of new countries. It must, moreover, be remembered that, even before the repeal of the Corn Laws, England occupied a unique position in the commercial world. Friedrich List, applying the *à posteriori* method, is led to attribute the commercial supremacy of Great Britain largely, if not mainly, to the restrictive policy pursued by her up to the early part of the nineteenth century[1].

All things considered, it must be said that the method of difference has no very important part to play in economics; and that even when it is employed under exceptionally favourable conditions, the argument is still not completely satisfactory, unless supported and strengthened by some independent line of reasoning. The function of the method of difference in political economy is to suggest or to confirm, rather than to afford complete and adequate proof. It should be added that the method needs to be employed with the greatest caution, even when it is used only for purposes of verification. So many counteracting causes may be in operation that the influence of a given cause, although undoubtedly exerted in a known direction, may be extremely difficult to detect in the complex facts, which alone are open to direct observation. More will be said upon this point in the following chapter.

[1] It would have seemed almost unnecessary to call attention to the above considerations were it not that the *à posteriori* argument in favour of free trade has recently been cited as a typical example of the value of the inductive method in economic enquiry. The inductive method, says Professor R. Mayo-Smith, is comparative,— "it compares economic institutions performing the same function among different nations of the same degree of civilisation, in order to discover which is the best" (*Science Economic Discussion*, p. 107); and he afterwards adds, as a special illustration of a general conclusion gained by induction, that we can reason "from the prosperity of England to the principle of free trade, at least for industrially developed nations" (*ib*. p. 114).

§ 4. *The method of inductive generalization from a multiplication of instances.*—It has been shewn in the preceding section that the economist cannot to any considerable extent rely upon inferences based on the examination and comparison of single pairs of instances. It remains to be considered how far he can substitute quantity for quality, and can generalize from the direct observation of a number of cases in which the same cause is in operation under varying conditions. Generalizations, thus based upon an accumulation of instances, will fall for the most part under Mill's method of agreement, or his method of concomitant variations, and will be in the strictest sense empirical.

The essence of the method of agreement consists in finding two phenomena constantly conjoined, while the remaining circumstances by which they are accompanied are none of them present in all the instances. Where this condition is fulfilled, it is inferred that there must be some causal connexion between the two phenomena in question.

The peculiarity of the method of concomitant variations is that it requires quantitative data. Causal connexion is inferred to exist between two phenomena, because variations in the one correspond in some manner with variations in the other.

In the endeavour to employ the above methods, the special sources from which material may be

gathered are the history of the past and the systematic observation of the present. The account of
existing economic phenomena need not necessarily
take a statistical or quantitative form. But since
economics is essentially concerned with quantities,
there is a tendency for contemporary economic records
to become more and more statistical in tone. The
same would be the case with the history of past times, if
statistical data relating to the past could be multiplied
at will. The further we go back, however, the fewer
and the more untrustworthy are the figures at our
disposal.

The functions of history and statistics in economic
enquiries are very important and very various. For the
present, however, their distinguishing characteristics
will not be dwelt upon; and they will be considered
in respect of one of their functions only, namely, as
constituting—along with the observation of everyday
economic facts—the basis of inductive generalization
from a multiplication of instances[1].

[1] It is to be observed that some writers who insist upon the
importance of the purely inductive method in economics use the term
inductive in a rather wider sense than is usual in works on logic.
"Finally, we may ask," says Professor R. Mayo-Smith, "what can
the inductive method do when it faces some great economic problem
which affects the whole community and civilisation itself? Such
a problem is the labour problem. What is the condition of the labouring class? Has that condition deteriorated or improved? The
inductive method has not shrunk from attempting to find an answer
to even such questions as these. Thorold Rogers has laboriously

The first and most obvious point to notice is that the importance of the place to be assigned to such generalization in economics varies according to the nature of the problems under discussion. As a rule, it is less and less to be trusted, as we work up from the more simple to the more complex phenomena with which the science is concerned. This is in accordance with the ordinary logical canon, that the greater the number of causes in operation, and the more compli-

traced the condition of the English labourer during the last six centuries, for the purpose of answering this question historically. Giffen has attempted, by statistics, to shew that the condition of the labouring class has materially improved during the last fifty years" (*Science Economic Discussion*, p. 111). What writers on logic, however, usually mean by induction and the inductive method is a process of reasoning, whereby on the strength of particular instances a general law is established In the above examples there is no establishment of any general law at all, and the enquiries are obviously of a kind that must proceed by a study of concrete facts. Not even the most extreme of anti-inductive economists has ever maintained that we can à *priori*, or by any other method than that of specific experience, determine the condition of the labouring classes at any given time, or compare their condition at different times. It should then be clearly understood that in expressing doubts as to the efficacy of pure induction in political economy, we are referring to the establishment of general laws on purely empirical data; we do not mean to deny—it would indeed be absurd to deny—the essential and paramount importance of direct appeals to experience in en quiries which are not concerned with the ascertainment of general laws at all, but merely with the investigation of economic phenomena at a particular time or place, or with their comparison at different times or places. In other words, we make no attempt to establish *descriptive* economics on any other basis than that of direct observation. The only question at issue is the place of induction in *constructive* economics.

cated the mode of their interaction, the less possible it becomes to fulfil the conditions required for valid inductive reasoning.

It is in regard to the circumstances affecting the production of wealth that the relative importance of direct generalization from specific experience is the greatest. It has, indeed, been already pointed out that, in this department of the science, all economists agree in adopting as their principal resource an inductive method. No doubt, even within this sphere, they seek deductively to connect their conclusions with general principles of human nature. In other words, deduction and induction, here as elsewhere, supplement one another. Still, the inductive element is more prominent than the deductive. This is the case, for instance, in the investigation of the circumstances upon which the degree of productiveness of productive agents depends, and in the comparison of production on a large and on a small scale.

Again, in investigating the laws of the increase of capital, while the deductive argument from a psychological analysis of motives is important, the effects of external circumstances upon the operation of such motives can be ascertained only by fresh observation and direct generalization. It is experience that teaches what states of society most encourage saving, though no doubt the facts that experience brings to light can afterwards be psychologically accounted for.

Similar remarks apply to theories of population. In the suggestion and development of such theories, the history of population, and statistical records of the manner in which the rate of increase of human beings has in fact varied with varying conditions, are of the first importance. This is exemplified in the second and later editions of Malthus's *Essay on Population*. Malthus pursues an inductive method of enquiry. His reasoning is directly based on historical and statistical data. He collects and compares recorded facts which throw light on the forces controlling the growth of population in a number of different countries, civilised and uncivilised, in past times and in modern Europe.

As further examples of a valid treatment of economic problems, in which induction is placed in the foreground, reference may again be made to Cairnes's analysis of the economic characteristics of slave labour, and to Mill's discussion of peasant proprietorship in its economic aspects. It is worth specially pointing out that Mill's argument is based on the method of agreement, not on the method of difference. He is not able, satisfactorily or on any considerable scale, to compare different systems of land tenure under conditions identical in all other material respects—identical, that is to say, in climate, fertility of soil, national character, methods of cultivation, and so forth.

Some additional illustrations of the appropriate use of the empirical method in political economy will be found in the chapters that follow on economic history and statistics. To give here one more example of a typical character, it may be pointed out that in regard to the possibilities of co-operative production in its various forms we are in a marked degree dependent upon direct generalization from experience.

When recourse is had to the empirical method it must always be remembered that the mere number of the instances is not so important, as that they should be diverse in character, and collected over a wide and varied range. The object is to eliminate the effects of adventitious circumstances; and it is, therefore, important that the instances, upon which the argument is based, should have as little as possible in common, except those circumstances which constitute the special subject of investigation. A dozen well-selected instances fulfilling this condition are worth more than a hundred all of a similar character.

It should be added that, taking empirical generalizations at their best, great caution is necessary in extending them beyond the limits of actual experience. For, however wide and varied the range of economic conditions that has been examined, there may still be other conditions, in relation to which the inferred law needs considerable modification. Jevons truly remarks,—"However useful may be empirical knowledge, it is yet of slight importance compared with the well-connected and perfectly explained body of knowledge, which constitutes an advanced and deductive science. It is, in fact, in proportion as a science becomes deductive, and enables us to grasp more and more apparently unconnected facts under the same law, that it becomes perfect. He who knows why a thing happens, will also know exactly in what cases it will happen, and what difference in the circumstances will prevent the event from happening. Though observation and induction must ever be the ground of all certain knowledge of nature, their unaided employment could never have led to the results of modern science."

It follows that even when we rely primarily on induction, it is of great importance that our conclusions should be confirmed and interpreted by deductive reasoning. Hence, in saying that in certain departments of economic enquiry induction is fundamentally important, it is not meant that the need of deduction from more general principles is superseded; but merely that the induction may usefully precede the deduction.

§ 5. *Limitations of the empirical method.*—There
remain to be briefly considered those very important
departments of economic enquiry, in which direct
generalization from complex economic facts, without
a prior appeal to underlying principles, is generally
speaking in a high degree untrustworthy, and in
which, if we depend upon inductive reasoning alone,
our conclusions are more likely than not to be erroneous.
In this category are included the central problems
of the exchange and distribution of wealth. It is of
these problems that Cairnes is thinking when he
speaks of the "utter inadequacy" of the inductive
method in political economy. Bagehot is also referring
to them, when he remarks: "The facts of commerce,
especially of the great commerce, are very complex.
Some of the most important are not on the surface;
some of those most likely to confuse *are* on the
surface. If you attempt to solve such problems
without some apparatus of method, you are as sure
to fail as if you try to take a modern military fortress
—a Metz or a Belfort—by common assault: you must
have guns to attack the one, and method to attack
the other." By this reference to an "apparatus of
method," Bagehot means that we are to proceed, not
by the unaided analysis of complex economic facts,
but by a synthesis, based on a previous examination
of the nature and action of the elementary forces,

through whose operation the complex facts are produced. The need of an *à posteriori* investigation of the concrete phenomena themselves, at a certain stage of the reasoning, remains; but no trust is to be put in an *à posteriori* method pure and simple.

The argument, on which the above view is based, turns on the enormous complexity of the phenomena of the distribution and exchange of wealth. In the technical language of logic, the method of direct generalization is inapplicable, because of plurality of causes and intermixture of effects. There is plurality of causes, *i.e.*, the same phenomenon may on different occasions be traced to wholly different agencies; and there is intermixture of effects, *i.e.*, the same cause is continually operating in conjunction with other causes, whose effects coalesce and combine with its own. In consequence of the latter circumstance, the effect proper to a given cause is, in one place, counteracted by some other influence operating simultaneously; in another place, it is intensified; in another, it is modified and led to change its character. Mill shews clearly in the third book of his *Logic* (without any special reference to political economy) that where effects result from the union of many causes, the method of simple observation is in general inappropriate. The difficulty is increased by the length of time that is in the majority of cases required if the full effects of economic causes are to be allowed to manifest themselves. In these cases, even if the purely *à posteriori* method enables us to detect the immediate but transient effects of given economic changes, the ultimate and more permanent effects are likely to elude our grasp unless we are assisted by some "apparatus of method." Many of the problems of political economy are further complicated by the relation of mutuality that so often exists between the phenomena with which the science is concerned. Instead of one phenomenon determining a second, and the second determining a third, without any influence being in either case exerted in the opposite direction, the three phenomena may mutually determine one another. This is the case, for example, with supply, demand, exchange-value, and with other economic phenomena that are of equally fundamental importance. To deal with relations of this kind by the method of direct generalization is out of the question. We must, as Professor Marshall puts it, "work with the aid of a special organon."[1]

For these reasons, it is impossible to frame any general theories of value, interest, wages, rent, &c. by purely *à posteriori* methods of reasoning. Recourse must needs be had to a method, in which deduction from elementary principles of human nature occupies a position of central, though not exclusive, importance.

[1] *Present Position of Economics*, p. 31.

Upon this point there is practical unanimity amongst economists, with the exception of the extreme wing of the historical school; and they do not so much affirm that general theories can be obtained by the method of specific experience, as that it is useless attempting to obtain general theories at all. They turn aside, therefore, upon the track of a quite different class of problems.

Leaving general theories, a typical instance may be added of an economic problem of a more special character, towards whose solution the purely *à posteriori* method avails little or nothing. Suppose that it is desired to determine the relation, if any, between the general commodity-purchasing power of money and the price of securities yielding a fixed rate of interest. Can the method of concomitant variations suffice for a solution? Statistics are available in abundance. The average price of Consols—which may be taken as representative of securities yielding a fixed rate of interest—is known for every year in the century; and numerous tables have been compiled, shewing how, during a number of years, the average aggregate price of certain selected wholesale commodities has varied. In the construction of these tables certain difficulties present themselves, but however perfect they might be made, we could never, by simply comparing them with the price of Consols or any other kind of security, obtain even approximately a solution of the given problem. For whatever may þe the effect of the general purchasing power of money on the price of securities, it is at any rate likely to be insignificant by the side of other influences, such as the condition ot the money market or the political outlook. It is true that the investigation, if it is to be complete, requires knowledge of the general characteristics of periods of rising and falling prices, such as can be gained only by experience. But it also of necessity involves deductive reasoning of some degree of complexity.

In some cases it is possible approximately to satisfy the conditions of valid induction; and yet the conclusion so obtained cannot be regarded as more than suggestive and provisional, until deductive explanation and verification are forthcoming. Theories of periodic movements in the money market may be cited as an instance in point.

It is remarkable that some writers on economic method should imply that while the deductive method might be applicable to a simple and stationary condition of industry, it becomes valueless in face of the increasing complexity of the modern economic world; and that under such conditions, at any rate, it must give way to the method of specific experience[1]. We

---

[1] Compare Cliffe Leslie's essay on *The Known and the Unknown in the Economic World.*

have already indicated reasons why the reverse is nearer the truth. It is needless to say that as the forces in operation become more numerous and their modes of interaction more intricate, and as changes in the general conditions of industry succeed one another more rapidly, the problems of economics become more difficult whatever method may be employed for their solution. The deductive method needs to be applied with the greater caution, and the apparatus of facts with which it has to be supplemented increases in importance. But, on the other hand, facts by themselves leave us the more helpless, and mere empiricism is the more misleading. Compare, for example, the investigation of the connexion between changes in gold supply and prices, or between changes in gold supply and the rate of discount, under simple and comparatively stationary industrial conditions, with the same investigation under complex industrial conditions, where credit and banking are fully developed, and where prices, and the condition of the loan market, are liable to alterations from an indefinite number of causes. If a mere *à posteriori* examination of statistics, without any appeal to deductive argument, might in the former case be of some value, it would certainly in the latter case be almost worse than useless[1].

---

[1] Compare Sir Robert Giffen's admirable investigations on the above-mentioned subjects in the Second Series of his *Essays in*

There is a special reason why no attempt should be made to ignore or disguise the weakness of pure induction in complex economic enquiries. The prevalence of a low type of inductive reasoning in the treatment of economic questions is one of the most fertile sources of economic fallacy; and, however legitimate the employment of the inductive method may be under certain conditions, there can be no doubt that this method is liable to serious abuse.

Finance. In these essays the necessity of having recourse to a deductive method of investigation is clearly shewn, whilst it is at the same time pointed out that the deductive argument must not ignore the actual working of modern commerce and modern banking. The use of the deductive method has been so constantly misrepresented, that it is well to lose no opportunity of repeating that to fall back upon a deductive line of reasoning by no means involves our going on our way regardless of actual facts.

CHAPTER VII.

ON THE DEDUCTIVE METHOD IN POLITICAL ECONOMY.

§ 1. *Nature of the deductive method.*—In so far as the method of specific experience fails to afford reliable knowledge of economic laws, recourse must be had to a method, whose essence consists in the preliminary determination of the principal forces in operation, and the deduction of their consequences under various conditions. For an *à posteriori* argument depending entirely upon the examination of concrete facts in all the complexity of their actual presentation, is substituted an *à priori* argument depending upon knowledge of the general characteristics displayed by men in their economic dealings one with another. "The problem of the deductive method," says Mill, "is to find the law of an effect from the laws of the different tendencies of which it is the joint result." The method in its complete form consists of three steps. It is necessary, first, to determine what are the principal forces in operation, and the laws in accordance with which they operate. Next comes the purely deductive stage, in which are inferred the consequences that will ensue from the operation of these forces under given conditions. Lastly, by a comparison of what has been inferred with what can be directly observed to occur, an opportunity is afforded for testing the correctness and practical adequacy of the two preceding steps, and for the suggestion of necessary qualifications. It will be observed that only one of these three steps—namely, the middle one—is strictly speaking deductive. The so-called deductive method in its complete form is thus seen to be not an exclusively deductive method. It may more accurately be described as a method which, whilst predominantly deductive, is still aided and controlled by induction. This point will be further brought out in what follows, but it seems desirable to call attention to it at the outset.

§ 2. *The application of the term "hypothetical" to economic science.*—Political economy, in having recourse to the deductive method, is usually described as essentially hypothetical in character. This description of the science needs, however, to be carefully explained and guarded, as there is some danger of confusion of thought in regard to the implications contained in it.

All laws of causation may be said to be hypothetical, in so far as they merely assert that given causes will *in the absence of counteracting causes* produce certain effects. As a matter of fact, in the instances that actually occur of the operation of a given cause, counteracting causes sometimes will and sometimes will not be present; and, therefore, laws of causation are to be regarded as statements of tendencies only. It follows that all sciences of causation, and pre-eminently sciences employing the deductive method—including political economy and astronomy—contain a hypothetical element.

The above may be expressed somewhat differently by saying that the use of the deductive method in economics involves, at a certain stage, a process of abstraction, necessitating a frequent recurrence of the qualification *ceteris paribus*. The abstraction is carried furthest in reasonings where the motive of self-interest is supposed to operate unchecked in a state of economic freedom; that is, in reasonings which involve the conception of the "economic man." But in all cases where the deductive method is used, it is present more or less. For in the deductive investigation of the economic consequences of any particular circumstance or any particular change, the absence of interfering agencies and of concurrent but independent changes is of necessity assumed. So far as other changes themselves result from the one change or the one circumstance specially under consideration, account must of course be taken of them; but the distinguishing characteristic

of the deductive method consists in seeking, in the first
instance, to effect a mental isolation from the operation
of all modifying forces that are not in some way connected causally with the particular subject of enquiry.
The distinction between *dependent* and *independent*
changes, here indicated, is of fundamental importance,
and is in itself simple enough. At the same time, a
difficulty is often found in keeping it clearly in view
throughout the course of a complicated argument; the
faculty of succeeding in this is essential to sound
economic reasoning, and needs special cultivation.

It does not, however, follow that because a law
is hypothetical in the above sense, it is therefore
unreal or out of relation to the actual course of
events. Although laws of causation may from a
certain point of view be regarded as hypothetical,
they are from another point of view categorical.
For they affirm categorically the mode in which
given causes operate. Moreover, even though a cause
may be in a manner counteracted in consequence of
the operation of more powerful causes acting in the
opposite direction, it will still continue to exert its
own characteristic influence, and will modify the
ultimate result accordingly. No one supposes that
the law of gravitation ceases to operate when a
balloon rises in the air or water rises in a pump; and
this may serve as a simple illustration of what is of

constant recurrence in regard to economic phenomena. An intensification, for instance, in the demand for a commodity may take place concurrently with an increase in supply; and hence the absolute effect of the change in demand may not be apparent in any actual change of price. It may even be that the price falls, whereas the change in demand operating alone would have caused it to rise. Were it not for the latter change, however, the price would, in the supposed circumstances, have fallen still more. It remains true, absolutely and without qualification, that every change in demand tends to cause price to be different from what it would otherwise have been.

Take, again, the theory that an increase (or diminution) in the quantity of money in circulation tends *ceteris paribus* to be followed by a general rise (or fall) in prices. This is, in a sense, a hypothetical law: it does not enable us to say that whenever there is an actual increase in the quantity of money in circulation there will actually be a rise in prices; nor does it even enable us to say that if we find an increase in the amount of money in circulation taking place concurrently with a general rise in prices, the latter phenomenon must of necessity be wholly due to the former. For the cause in question is not the only one capable of affecting general prices. Its effects may, therefore, be counteracted by the concurrent operation of more powerful causes acting in the opposite direction, or exaggerated by the concurrent operation of causes acting in the same direction. But while this is true, it is also true that wherever the cause in question is present, it does exert its due influence in accordance with the law laid down, and plays its part in helping to determine (positively or negatively) the actual effect produced. The given law, therefore, notwithstanding the hypothetical element that it contains, still has reference to the actual course of events; it is an assertion respecting the actual relations of economic phenomena one to another.

But the question may be raised whether deductive political economy is not hypothetical in a more fundamental sense than has yet been indicated. It is clear that whenever conclusions are reached by deductive reasoning, their applicability to actual phenomena must remain hypothetical, until it has been determined how far the premises which form the basis of the reasoning are realised in fact. May it not accordingly be said that some at least of the conclusions of deductive political economy are hypothetical in the sense that they require, not merely the absence of counteracting causes, but the realisation of certain *positive* conditions, which are not as a matter of fact always realised? If this question is answered in the affirmative, it must not be understood to carry with it the implication that political economy employs arbitrary or fictitious premisses, or premisses whose relation to the actual phenomena of economic life is doubtful. This, however, appears to be what is meant by those who speak of the deductive method disparagingly, on the ground that it yields only hypothetical conclusions —conclusions which are affirmed to be useless for all practical purposes, however much their hypothetical validity may be beyond question.

It is certain that in their use of the deductive method, economists do very frequently work from positive assumptions not universally realised. Indeed their premisses need to be varied in order to meet different cases; and this being so, it is clear that the applicability of their conclusions must depend upon circumstances. For instance, in dealing with problems that relate to rent, certain conditions of land tenure are assumed; and in treating monetary questions, certain regulations as to coinage, legal tender, instruments of credit, and so on, are supposed to be in force. Again, in working out theories of wages, it is a not unusual assumption that each grade of labour, or even the working class as a whole, has its own definite standard of comfort. Even those assumptions that may be summed up under the general head of absence of disturbing causes have a positive side. For the relevancy of the argument, so far as the explanation of actual phenomena is concerned, requires that, as a matter of fact, the causes, whose influence is neglected, shall be strictly "disturbing" causes, and shall not exert an influence so powerful as to reduce that of other agencies to insignificance.

It must, however, always be borne in mind that the deductive method does not consist of the deductive step alone. This appears to be forgotten by those who speak scornfully of the hypothetical character of deductive political economy. Mere deductive reasoning may indeed be symbolized by a hypothetical statement of the form, If P and Q are true, R is true. But the deductive method is not concerned merely with establishing the connexion between the truth of P and Q and the truth of R. In its complete form, it includes a preliminary investigation of the forces actually in operation, and the various conditions under which they operate; and it also tests the applicability of its results to actual phenomena by appeals to the concrete realities that are open to direct observation. There is sometimes a convenience in taking the deductive stage of economic work more or less by itself; and in the pure theory of economics special prominence is given to it. But still the premises are not chosen arbitrarily. For while the pure theory assumes the operation of forces under artificially simplified conditions, it still claims that the forces whose effects it investigates are *verae causae* in the sense that they do operate, and indeed operate in a predominating way, in the actual economic world[1].

A brief reference may here be made to laws of normal value, normal wages, &c. In the process of arriving at these laws, account is professedly taken only of the comparatively universal and permanent forces in operation, leaving on one side the varying influence exerted by the local and temporary causes that may happen also to act at any given moment. The laws are, therefore, arrived at by a very deliberate process of abstraction, and they may appear to have an exceptionally hypothetical character. If, however, the forces whose influence is calculated can be shewn to be really the predominant and more permanent ones operating in any given economic society, then it may be a legitimate postulate that the modifying forces act in different directions on different occasions, so that in the long run they tend to balance and neutralise one another. In these circumstances, although the conclusions of the deductive reasoning may fail to correspond with the observed facts in any individual instance, they will nevertheless be realised, if instances are taken in the mass and if the general conditions of economic life

[1] It is this point that Senior is anxious to insist upon, when, although holding that political economy "depends more on reasoning than on observation," he yet refuses to speak of it as a hypothetical science.

remain unchanged for a sufficiently long period of time[1]. Laws of normal value &c. are, therefore, not necessarily hypothetical in any sense that implies unreality. They are nearly always not merely of greater scientific importance, but also of greater practical importance, than the ever-varying phenomena observable in individual instances. It is indeed essential that the operation of local and transient influences should not be ultimately overlooked or disregarded. But until knowledge has been gained of general and permanent tendencies, that which is local or transient will in all probability be itself misinterpreted.

The conclusions reached in this section may be briefly summed up by saying that deductive political economy is rightly described as hypothetical, if by this nothing more is meant than that, in the first place, its laws are statements of *tendencies* only, and are therefore

[1] It has to be recognised that the predominant and more permanent forces in operation are themselves liable to variation over long periods, and this undoubtedly, as Professor Marshall points out (*Principles of Economics*, vol. i. 1895, p. 426), increases the difficulties that are met with in applying economic doctrines to practical problems. The question at issue may be made more clear if we explicitly distinguish two points that are involved in the determination of laws of normal value, normal wages, &c. In the first place, we abstract from the operation of local and transient causes; in the second place, we assume that the general conditions of economic life are stationary, so that the predominant forces in operation are themselves constant. It is only within the limits up to which this second assumption is, as a matter of fact, realised that *normal* value can be identified with *average* value, *normal* wages with *average* wages, &c.

usually subject to the qualifying condition that *other things are equal*; and that, in the second place, many of its conclusions depend upon the realisation of certain *positive* conditions, which are not as a matter of fact always realised. Given the conditions, however, the laws may be stated categorically. The conditions are, moreover, not arbitrarily assumed, but are chosen so as to correspond broadly with the actual facts in the different forms in which economic phenomena manifest themselves. In saying, therefore, that political economy, in so far as it has recourse to the deductive method, is a hypothetical science, it is necessary to guard against the idea that this implies unreality or want of correspondence with the actual order of economic phenomena[1].

[1] Much of what Cairnes says in his *Logical Method of Political Economy* about the hypothetical character of the science is perfectly sound, and expressed with his usual lucidity and effectiveness. But a few of his statements—as, for instance, when he remarks that an economic law is not an assertion respecting the actual order of economic phenomena (p. 99), and again that an economic law can be established or refuted only by an appeal to some mental or physical principle (p. 107)—are likely to give rise to misunderstanding, even if they admit of justification when carefully explained. Consider, for example, in reference to the above statements, the attempt to refute the doctrine of cost of production as the regulator of value by an appeal to certain social facts, summed up in the phrase—"immobility of labour and capital." If the doctrine is considered purely hypothetical, this objection might be dismissed as simply irrelevant. But we cannot think that Cairnes would have been content so to dismiss it. In his hands, and in those of his school generally, the doctrine means that under existing economic conditions cost of production does actually

§ 3. *Functions of observation in the employment of the deductive method.*—The part played by specific experience in guiding and giving reality to deductive economic reasoning is of the utmost importance. It may be said without qualification that political economy, whether having recourse to the deductive method or not, must both begin with observation and end with observation. As already pointed out, there is a tendency to forget that the deductive method in its complete form consists of three stages, only one of which is actually deductive, the two others being the inductive determination of premises, and the inductive verification of conclusions. The true character of the deductive method is in particular misapprehended by those of its critics, who reject its aid in political economy on the ground that its employment means closing one's eyes to facts, and trying to think out the laws of the economic world in entire neglect of what is actually taking place[1].

exert a very material influence upon the price of the great majority of commodities. Consider further the doctrine of the existence of grades of labour between which competition is sluggish and ineffective. This doctrine is indicated by Mill, but is given greater prominence by Cairnes, who bases upon it a modification of the received theory of value. By appeal to what mental or physical principle, however, can it be said to be established? It is rather to be regarded as a modification of premises, suggested by observation and having for its object to bring economic theories into closer relation with actual facts.

[1] Speaking of induction as supplementary to deduction, Wagner observes that "according to our past experience and probably also in

It is true that in working out the pure theory of economics, the part played by specific observation may be subordinated and kept temporarily in the background. It is true also that the intellectual bias of some investigators naturally inclines them to cultivate specially this side of the subject. Again, for purposes of illustration, and with the object of familiarising ourselves with the kind of reasoning requisite in dealing with economic problems, it may sometimes be useful to frame hypotheses that have little relation to actual facts[1]. Still it is only partially and temporarily that the economist can thus remain independent of specific experience. The special functions of observation as supplementary to deductive reasoning are at once suggested by the analysis of the deductive method already given.

In the first place, observation guides the economist in his original choice of premises. Even in the most abstract treatment of political economy, it is necessary to begin by considering what are the general characteristics actually displayed by men in their economic dealings with one another, and by investigating the

the future, we must expect more from induction as a means of control than as an independent method. We shall probably owe to induction not so much new results as corrections, refinements, and enlargements of propositions obtained in the first instance deductively" (*Grundlegung der politischen Oekonomie*, 1892, § 95).

[1] On the subject of illustrative hypothesis, compare Venn, *Empirical Logic*, pp. 288, ff.

physical and social environment in which their economic activities are exercised. As already implied, however, it is not necessary that the propositions assumed in regard to men's motives or their material and social surroundings should be true universally or without qualification. To attempt any exact correspondence with what has been called the "full empirical actuality" would be to sacrifice generality, and to involve ourselves afresh in those complexities of actual economic life from which it is the special object of the deductive method temporarily to escape. The requirements are, first, that the motives taken into account shall be exceptionally powerful in the economic sphere, and so far uniform in their operation that the kind of conduct deduced from them shall correspond broadly with what actually happens; and, secondly, that the circumstances in which the motives are supposed to operate shall be of a representative character, either as regards economic life in general, or, at any rate, as regards a special aspect of it over a given range.

The observation requisite for the selection of premisses may sometimes involve little more than the reflective contemplation of certain of the most familiar of every-day facts. But it is to be remembered that the economist does not always work from one and the same set of assumptions; and in some cases knowledge of a much more extended character is required in order to determine what the premisses shall be. This remark applies to the working out of the theory of the foreign exchanges, of movements in general prices, of the effects of trade-unions or of machinery on wages, and the like. In dealing with problems of this kind the necessity for a somewhat intimate acquaintance with concrete economic phenomena arises at the very commencement of our enquiries. The general principles that should guide the economist in his selection of premisses will be indicated in rather more detail subsequently[1].

In the second place, observation enables the economist to determine how nearly his assumptions approximate to the actual facts under given economic conditions. He thus learns how far his premisses require to be modified; or to what extent, where no actual modification of premisses is necessary or feasible, allowance must be made for the effects of so-called disturbing causes. The use of observation for the above

---

[1] Cairnes observes that "the economist starts with a knowledge of ultimate causes" (*Logical Method*, p. 75); but this statement should at any rate be limited to the pure theory of economics. As remarked by Professor Dunbar in his essay on *The Reaction in Political Economy*, the method to be employed in carrying economic science into regions never penetrated by Ricardo is simple; it is only necessary to draw from the actual observation of affairs fresh premisses relating to forces of the secondary order (*Quarterly Journal of Economics*, October, 1886, p. 10). Professor Marshall's *Principles of Economics* affords numerous striking examples of the fresh developments of which deductive political economy guided by observation is capable.

purpose is one of the principal respects in which the more concrete is distinguished from the more abstract treatment of political economy. Its importance for the adequate understanding of the economic phenomena of any given period is very great. "Nothing but unreality," as Bagehot puts it, "can come of political economy till we know when and how far its first assertions are true in matter of fact and when and how far they are not."[1]

Considering this function of observation from a somewhat different standpoint, it will be seen that observation determines the limits of the positive validity of laws deductively obtained. The economic world is subject to continual changes. Certain assumptions may be realised at one stage of economic progress, and nevertheless be in violent opposition to facts at another stage. Hence without the aid of an extensive knowledge of facts, there is danger of ascribing to economic doctrines a much wider range of application than really belongs to them. This point will be further considered in treating of the relation between economic theory and economic history.

---

[1] *Economic Studies*, p. 71. Bagehot himself illustrates this statement by an inductive investigation of the effect of differences in the real wages of labour upon movements of population. An important postulate in regard to the nature of this effect is involved in the ordinary deductive determination of laws of normal wages. See also Mr L. L. Price's *Industrial Peace*, pp. 108, ff.

In the third place, the economist has recourse to observation in order to illustrate, test, and confirm his deductive inferences.   It is important here to observe that the verification may, and in fact will generally, consist in the satisfactory explanation of actual phenomena, not necessarily in the discovery of phenomena that would justify as direct generalizations the conclusions that have been deductively obtained[1].

Of course in some cases, instead of any confirmation of theory, there will be revealed a clear discrepancy between the actual course of events and the results of the deductive reasoning, shewing that the latter, if not positively erroneous, are at any rate insufficient to account for the facts.   The problem then is to determine the source of the error or incompleteness.   It is possible that empirical enquiry may indicate the operation of agencies, exerting an important influence upon the phenomena in question, but of which no

---

[1] Amongst recent economic treatises, Professor Nicholson's *Money* may be mentioned as affording numerous effective examples of the way in which actual occurrences may serve to illustrate and confirm deductive arguments.   If we want examples, however, we cannot do better than go back to the *Wealth of Nations*.   As Professor Marshall observes,—"Adam Smith seldom attempted to prove anything by detailed induction or history.   The data of his proofs were chiefly facts that were within everyone's knowledge, facts physical, mental, and moral.   But he illustrated his proofs by curious and instructive facts; he thus gave them life and force, and made his readers feel that they were dealing with problems of the real world, and not with abstractions."

account has been taken[1]; or it may be that whilst the right forces have been taken into account, their relative strength has been wrongly estimated, or the mode of their individual operation miscalculated; or there may have been error in the deductive reasoning itself.

The serious difficulties which sometimes attend the process of verification must not be overlooked. Mill goes so far as to say that "the ground of confidence in any concrete deductive science is not the à priori reasoning itself, but the accordance between its results and those of observation à posteriori."[2] This statement needs to be slightly qualified. For we may have independent grounds for believing that our premisses correspond with the facts, and that the process of deduction is correct; and we may accordingly have confidence in our conclusions, in spite of the fact that there is difficulty in obtaining explicit verification.

There must not of course be a manifest discrepancy between our theoretical conclusions and the actual facts. But we should not hastily draw negative conclusions, or suppose theories overthrown, because instances of their operation are not patent to observation. For the complexity of the actual economic world, which in the first place makes it necessary to have recourse to

---

[1] The operation of these agencies having once been suggested by observation, it is not improbable that we may be again aided by deduction in determining the precise nature of their influence.

[2] *Logic*, vi. 9, § 1.

the deductive method, may also render it difficult to determine whether or not the actual effects of any given agency really correspond with the results of our deductive calculations[1].

Again, laws of normal value, wages, &c. are, as we have already pointed out, verifiable only by instances taken in the mass and not by instances taken individually. It follows that, as in framing empirical generalizations, so in verifying from observation the results of deductive reasoning, it is in general necessary to extend our investigations over a wide range of facts, and especially to allow sufficient time for effects fairly to manifest themselves. If these precautions are not taken, misunderstanding may easily ensue and economic theory be unjustly discredited.

The doctrine that taxes on commodities are, under ordinary conditions, paid by consumers may serve as a simple example; for this doctrine is in no way inconsistent with the fact that a new tax may in the

---

[1] The problem of the effect exerted on general prices by the quantity of money in circulation is first worked out deductively, and then illustrated and tested by the examination of instances in which changes in the amount in circulation have occurred on a considerable scale. In some cases the confirmation may be very clear and decisive; but sometimes there may be the greatest difficulty in allowing properly for the effects of an increase or diminution in the general volume of trade, for the effects of an expansion or contraction of credit, and so forth, the tendency of which is to counteract or exaggerate the effects proper to the cause specially under investigation.

first instance bear very heavily upon the industry that
is taxed.   The whole reasoning by which the doctrine
is established shews that it relates solely to what will
happen in the long run.   In other words, it relates only
to taxes of old standing or to such as have been long
anticipated[1].

As another simple instance, it may be pointed out
that in accordance with the principles of deductive
political economy, the repeal of the Corn Laws must
have tended to bring about a permanent fall in the
price of wheat in England.   Yet no such fall occurred
immediately.   The explanation of the apparent discrepancy is to be found in the interference of such
circumstances as the failure of the potato crop, the
Crimean War, and especially the depreciation of gold,

---

[1] The deductive theory of the incidence of taxes on commodities
has been a frequent source of perverse misunderstanding.   "The
deductive economist's theory of profits and prices," writes Cliffe
Leslie, "will be found to claim to be true, under all circumstances,
in the case of every individual in trade and of every particular
article, and to foretell the exact rates at which goods will be sold.
His theory of taxation is an application of his theory of profits and
prices; and it proceeds on the assumption that prices will actually
conform to the cost of production, so nicely in every particular case,
that every special tax on any commodity will be recovered by the
producer from the consumer, with a profit on the advance" (*Essays*,
1888, p. 229; compare also p. 64).   In so far as isolated passages
from the writings of deductive economists may appear to justify such
statements as the above, it is only because they have not always been
sufficiently careful to emphasize the distinction between the immediate and the ultimate incidence of taxation.

which contributed to maintain the price up to 1862, notwithstanding free trade. Time, moreover, was required in order to allow the area of cultivation in new countries to be increased, and means of communication to be developed, so as to meet the new demand[1].

§ 4. *Ricardo's use of the deductive method.*—The above considerations indicate certain requirements that need to be satisfied in the right use of the deductive method, and also certain limitations to which the method is subject. One essential point is that there shall be a clear and definite enunciation of the assumptions upon which any given piece of reasoning is based. Sometimes, in addition to giving a careful explanation of the conditions under which the inferred results hold good, it will be advantageous to indicate the directions in which these results are likely to be modified by alterations in the conditions. In discussing the effects of economic changes it is further requisite to specify in general terms the period of time taken into consideration, distinguishing clearly between immediate and ultimate effects. It must always be remembered that assumptions need to be varied in order to meet varying economic circumstances; and *à priori* dogmatism must be avoided in regard to the application of conclusions to any given state of society. Before such applications

---

[1] Further illustrations of the part played by observation in connexion with the deductive method will be found in chapters 9 and 10.

can be justified, empirical tests must be applied—
tests, which in some cases lie ready enough to hand,
but which not infrequently involve systematic observation and statistical research of greater difficulty than
the deductive reasoning itself.

Ricardo's writings, and in particular his *Principles
of Political Economy and Taxation*, are frequently
quoted as affording typical and representative examples
of the use of the deductive method in economics; and
any objections, to which either his methods or his results
are open, are accordingly regarded as in all respects
equivalent to objections to the deductive method as
such.   It must be said, however, that while Ricardo's
writings contain some of the most brilliant and instructive examples of close deductive reasoning to be
found in economic literature, and while a thorough
study and mastery of his works may rightly be regarded as a part of the necessary equipment of the
economic student, still his manner of employing the
deductive method is not free from grave faults.   For
instance, the explanations and qualifications, which are
continually necessary in the interpretation of his results,
have usually to be supplied by the reader himself.
Neither the subsidiary postulates, nor those that underlie the greater part of the reasoning, are explicitly
indicated; and there is sometimes an unexplained
change from one hypothesis to another that is specially

perplexing. Again, the necessity of attending to the element of time is insufficiently emphasized, and far too little importance seems to be attached to the characteristics of the periods of transition, during which the ultimate effects of economic causes are working themselves out. The tone adopted by Ricardo suggests further an undue confidence in the absolute and universal validity of the conclusions reached; and in his illustrations there is a remoteness from the facts of actual life that is not really essential to the employment of the deductive method.

There is still another respect in which Ricardo's chief work fails to satisfy the requirements of a perfect deductive system. As a science grows more deductive, the logical arrangement of its different parts, and the due subordination of some parts to others, become considerations of increasing importance. Ricardo, however, never makes sufficiently clear the exact relation between his different theorems, and the manner of their dependence one upon another. In some respects, the different chapters of the *Principles of Political Economy and Taxation* read more like independent essays than consecutive chapters of a connected and logically complete system.

An explanation of much of the above is to be found in the special circumstances and conditions under which Ricardo wrote. While his premisses were suggested by the actual economic world in which he lived, his observation was partial, and confined to a narrow range. He was consequently led to interpret his results without adequate limitation. It is, moreover, very doubtful whether it was his deliberate intention to produce a complete systematic exposition of economic science. It has been suggested on very plausible grounds that his chief work was originally written not for publication, but with the object of formulating his own ideas on various economic questions, and for private circulation amongst an inner circle of acquaintances. If this view is correct, the not unfrequent incompleteness of the argument from the strictly logical standpoint is to a considerable extent accounted for. Nothing can be more natural than that anyone writing for those whom he knows to be already familiar with his general attitude should omit an explicit statement of postulates and qualifications, that are certain in any case to be present to the minds of his readers[1].

[1] Compare a very suggestive note on *Ricardo's Use of Facts* in the *Quarterly Journal of Economics*, July, 1887, p. 474. Compare, also, *Letters of Ricardo to Malthus*, edited by Dr Bonar. "It is not difficult," says the editor, "for men living two generations after Ricardo, and having (as he himself expressed it) 'all the wisdom of their ancestors and a little more into the bargain,' to point out many unjustified assumptions, many ambiguous terms, and even many wavering utterances in Ricardo's *Principles*, in spite of their appearance of severe logic. The author's detached practical pamphlets were in those respects far more powerful than this volume of imperfectly connected essays on general theory. The flattering importunities of

Whatever may be the explanation, however, of Ricardo's shortcomings, it is certain that the deductive method is not exemplified in anything approaching an ideal form in his pages.

§ 5. *The premisses of deductive political economy.*— In those abstract reasonings, which constitute the most prominent part of economic theory, the principles by which the economist is guided in his choice of premisses are generality and simplicity: the former, in order to widen as far as possible the range over which the theory may be applicable as an instrument for the solution of concrete problems; the latter, in order that the process of deductive reasoning may not be too difficult[1]. The principle that men desire to increase their sum of satisfactions with the smallest possible sacrifice to themselves, the law of decreasing final utility as amount of commodity increases, the law of diminishing return from land, and the like, are premisses which possess the requisite degree of universality. The hypothesis of free competition, again, affords a fairly simple basis

friends had induced an unsystematic writer to attempt a systematic treatise" (p. xvii).

[1] "The function of a pure theory," says Professor Marshall, "is to deduce definite conclusions from definite hypothetical premisses. The premisses should approximate as closely as possible to the facts with which the corresponding applied theory has to deal. But the terms used in the pure theory must be capable of exact interpretation, and the hypotheses on which it is based must be simple and easily handled."

for deductive reasoning, and, so far at any rate as modern trade is concerned, is approximately valid in relation to a large number of economic phenomena. The alternative hypothesis of pure monopoly is in certain respects even simpler, but the cases in which it is approximately realised cover a much narrower area[1].

Passing to the consideration of more concrete problems, the above statement requires to be slightly modified. The first requirement now is that the premisses shall ultimately include all the circumstances which exert any very important influence upon the phenomena in question at the period and place to which the investigation has primary reference. The second requirement is again one of simplicity. The hypotheses adopted should be capable of being made the basis of deductive inference; they should therefore take a definite and precise form, and should be as few and as simple as is consistent with keeping fairly close to the facts[2].

---

[1] Cournot in his *Recherches sur les Principes Mathématiques de la Théorie des Richesses* takes the hypothesis of pure monopoly on the part of sellers as his starting-point.

[2] Wagner, without attempting a complete enumeration of postulates, gives as the first important hypothesis of deductive economics (*a*) the assumption that everyone acts from economic self-interest (*Grundlegung der politischen Oekonomie*, § 67). To this he adds two other fundamental hypotheses, namely, (*b*) that all concerned know and understand their own interests, and (*c*) that they are not

Bagehot in his unfinished *Postulates of Political Economy* proposed to enumerate the principal assumptions of economic science, and to examine the validity or the limits of the validity of each in turn. Such an enumeration and examination may under certain conditions be highly instructive; but unless the object in view is carefully explained, it may also prove misleading. In the use of the deductive method in political economy, and especially in the pure theory,

hindered by law from pursuing their interests. We thus postulate as the general basis of our argument (*a*) the desire, (*b*) the ability, (*c*) the permission, to act in accordance with the dictates of self-interest. Wagner goes on, however, to point out (§ 70) that each of these three assumptions is capable of being modified as circumstances may require. Such modifications will of course not be introduced arbitrarily, but with the object of making our hypotheses correspond more and more nearly with the facts; and the facts will themselves vary according to the particular nation, period, place, or class of economic phenomena, under investigation. Thus, the first assumption may be varied by taking into consideration the operation of other motives as co-operating factors along with self-interest; the second assumption may be varied by the recognition of inequalities in the knowledge and ability required in order to pursue one's own interests to the best advantage, the extent of the modification depending upon the particular class of persons under consideration; the third assumption may be varied by considering various ways in which individual freedom in economic affairs may be interfered with. In these ways Wagner thinks that we may approach more and more nearly to complete coincidence between our assumptions and the full reality, although it is allowed that the altered hypotheses may not always be easy to work with, and that the ideal of mathematical procedure may not be attainable. It might be added that as our general command over the processes of deductive reasoning in economics increases, the greater will be our success in working from these modified assumptions.

there are some half dozen premisses that are more fundamental and of more constant recurrence than others. But unless great care is taken to emphasize the distinction between abstract and concrete economics, the recognition of a limited number of definite assumptions as fundamental and sufficient tends to give to the science a formal and unreal aspect that is not properly characteristic of it considered in its totality[1].

The validity, moreover, of economic postulates varies not only from time to time, and place to place, but also in different connexions at the same time and place. Hence even if a preliminary enumeration of premisses, supposed to underlie the whole science of economics, were really feasible, it would not be possible to examine once for all the validity of such premisses; and on the whole it seems best to regard any preliminary enumeration and examination of economic postulates, not as definitive or exhaustive, but simply as illustrative of the general character of economic theory[2].

[1] The notion that the whole of the science is built up from just one or two premisses has always been seized upon for comment by adverse critics. Compare, for instance, Mr Frederic Harrison's criticism that "political economy has two postulates—production as the sole end, competition as the sole motive—postulates of which the human race and its history can shew no actual example."

[2] The enumeration of postulates proposed by Bagehot was unfortunately never completed. Enumerations of the kind referred to will, however, be found in Senior, *Political Economy*, p. 26; Cairnes,

§ 6. *Special modifications of the deductive method.*—
There are certain modifications of the deductive method

Logical Method, Lecture 2, § 2, and Lecture 3, § 1; Cossa, *Introduction to the Study of Political Economy*, Theoretical Part, Chapter 6, § 2; Sidgwick, *Principles of Political Economy*, 3rd edition, Introduction, Chapter 3, § 4. Compare also the postulates formulated by Wagner, as given in the note on page 241. It may be useful to quote from Senior and Cairnes. Senior says, "We have already stated that the general facts on which the science of political economy rests are comprised in a few general propositions, the result of observation or consciousness. The propositions to which we then alluded are these:— 1. That every man desires to obtain additional wealth with as little sacrifice as possible. 2. That the population of the world, or, in other words, the number of persons inhabiting it, is limited only by moral or physical evil, or by fear of a deficiency of those articles of wealth which the habits of the individuals of each class of its inhabitants lead them to require. 3. That the powers of labour, and of the other instruments which produce wealth, may be indefinitely increased by using their products as the means of further production. 4. That, agricultural skill remaining the same, additional labour employed on the land within a given district produces in general a less proportionate return, or, in other words, that though, with every increase of the labour bestowed, the aggregate return is increased, the increase of the return is not in proportion to the increase of the labour." Cairnes indicates the following as the ultimate premisses of economic science, —first, "the general desire for physical well-being, and for wealth as the means of obtaining it"; next, "the intellectual power of judging of the efficacy of means to an end, along with the inclination to reach our ends by the easiest and shortest means"; thirdly, "those propensities which, in conjunction with the physiological conditions of the human frame, determine the laws of population"; and lastly, "the physical qualities of the soil and of those other natural agents on which the labour and ingenuity of man are employed." It is clear that such enumerations as these cannot lay claim to completeness. Some postulate is, for example, essential in regard to the nature of the social customs and legal institutions relating to property. Some postulate is also requisite in regard to the variation of utility with amount of commodity; for it would not be possible from Senior's or which render it comparatively easy to deal effectively with problems of considerable intricacy. It is Cairnes's premisses alone to deduce laws of demand. Even the principle of free competition is not clearly enunciated. This principle is indeed so complex, and involves so many different subsidiary assumptions in different connexions, that it would be difficult to analyse once for all its full content in the various economic reasonings in which it plays a part.

A well-arranged enumeration of postulates is given by Mr W. E. Johnson in his article on the *Method of Political Economy* in Mr Palgrave's *Dictionary of Political Economy*. Mr Johnson does not profess that any complete enumeration of premisses is possible. Agreeing, however, with the view taken in the text, he considers that there are some half dozen premisses which may be regarded as typical and which are almost universally applied. "Of these six data, two belong to each of the divisions, physical, psychological, and social. (1) The two physical or natural laws presupposed are the law of Diminishing Returns, which arises from the necessity of having recourse to inferior agents of production, or to their use under less advantageous circumstances; and the law of Increasing Returns, which results from the increased possibilities of industrial organisation under extension of supply. But these laws represent *tendencies* ascertained by ordinary observation, which work in opposite directions. Hence more exact knowledge as to the magnitude of the forces in particular circumstances has to be supplied by further detailed observation. (2) The two psychological data are general expressions of the nature of Demand and of Supply, so far as these depend on the characters of individuals. The law of demand is to the effect that the utility afforded by any increment of any kind of desired object diminishes with increase of the amount possessed: the law of supply is to the effect that every one tries to procure material well-being with the least possible sacrifice. These assumptions are common to almost all economic reasonings of a deductive type, though they are not always explicitly formulated. Here, as in the case of the physical presuppositions, further detailed observation is required to determine the precise degree in which these psychological forces act under any circumstances. In particular, the law of supply requires to be made more definite by an estimate of the influences of habit, particularly helpful to work up gradually from simple to more and more complex hypotheses. The conditions assumed at the outset may fail to represent even approximately the actual facts. But the problem having first been treated in the simplest conceivable form, it may be possible to grapple with it under somewhat less simple conditions. And so we may go on, until at last the assumptions do fairly correspond with the facts. As remarked by Bagehot, "the maxim of science is simply that of common sense—simple cases first; begin with seeing how the main force acts when there is as little as possible to impede it, and when you thoroughly comprehend that, add to it in succession the separate effects of each of the encumbering and interfering agencies."[1]

Mill's working out of the theory of international values affords a familiar example of the above method of procedure. He begins by supposing that international dealings are carried on between two countries

inertia, ignorance, or custom, which materially affect its application. (3) The two sociological data relate to the conditions of freedom and restraint under which the economic activities of a community take place. Speaking generally, it is assumed on the one hand that individual action is controlled by certain legalised institutions with regard to property, and, on the other hand, that individuals are free to act according to their own will within certain limits. A similar remark applies here, as before, namely, that the precise degree of freedom or of restraint, operative under any circumstances, has to be determined by specific observation."

[1] *Economic Studies*, p. 74.

only, and in two commodities only, which commodities
are directly exchanged the one for the other, without
the intervention of money in any form. The countries
are supposed contiguous, so that cost of carriage may
be left out of account; neither country has any international liabilities except in payment for imports; and
complete free trade exists, neither export nor import
duties being imposed on either side. The problem
having in this simplified form been solved, the various
limitations are one by one removed until an hypothesis
is at last reached that includes all the essential conditions of actual trade between different communities.
Similarly, in seeking to determine the circumstances
that regulate the range of general prices, the most
serviceable method is to begin with a very simple
artificial hypothesis, and thence pass gradually to the
complex realities of modern trade[1].

---

[1] Compare Professor Nicholson's treatment of this problem in his
book on *Money and Mone'ary Problems*. He begins as follows,—
"Now, under the present conditions of industry and exchange, the
causes which lead to general movements of prices are exceedingly
complex and various, and in order to understand them it is necessary to begin with the simplest case, and then gradually to introduce
the less obvious, though equally effective, causes of movement.
I would then beg the reader to get rid, as far as possible, of all the
notions he may have formed of the causes of the actual movements
in prices in recent years in the complex industrial world of to-day,
and, in order to isolate and examine the most important cause of
all, to take up an attitude of observation in what, for fault of a
better term, may be called a 'hypothetical market.' The phrase is

Another interesting and useful variety of the deductive method is where a number of alternative conditions are taken, which between them cover all cases that are practically possible, and an enquiry is instituted as to what will happen under each in turn. In this way the limits within which the truth will lie may be determined; and in so far as it is possible in any concrete instance to discover the relation of the actual to the hypothetical conditions, the deductive solution may be turned to practical account. Unless the different alternatives are formal contradictories, a preliminary investigation of facts will of course be

suggestive of unreality, but no more so than the suppositions or hypotheses constantly made in physics and mathematics, of bodies perfectly rigid, smooth, or without weight, or of lines without breadth, or of points without parts or magnitude. Let the following, then, be assumed as the laws and conditions of our market: (1) No exchanges are to be made unless money (which, to be quite unreal and simple, we may suppose to consist of counters of a certain size made of the bones of the dodo) actually passes from hand to hand at every transaction. If, for example, one merchant has two pipes but no tobacco, and another two ounces of tobacco but no pipe, we cannot allow an exchange of a pipe for an ounce of tobacco unless money is used. Credit and barter are alike unknown. (2) The money is to be regarded as of no use whatever except to effect exchanges, so that it will not be withheld for hoarding; in other words, it will be actually in circulation. (3) Let it be assumed that there are ten traders, each with one commodity and no money, and one trader with all the money (100 pieces) and no commodities. Further, let this moneyed man place an equal estimation on all the commodities" (p. 56). All this sounds artificial enough; but it is only the starting point. Before the discussion is finished, the reader finds himself dealing with actual concrete problems of to-day.

necessary in order to determine what alternatives should be chosen.

Let the problem be to determine the ultimate consequences of a strike of workmen, its immediate success being assumed. Enquiry may be made as to what will happen under three different suppositions: first, in so far as the rise in wages leads to an increase of efficiency on the part of the workmen, and is therefore not at the expense of other members of the community; secondly, in so far as it raises prices, and is therefore at the expense of consumers; thirdly, in so far as it lowers profits, and is therefore at the expense either of earnings of management or of interest. In the first of these cases, there is, *ceteris paribus*, no reason why the success of the strike should not be permanent. In the second case, it is necessary to consider the possibility of a reaction in so far as higher prices lead ultimately to the use of substitutes or stimulate foreign competition[1]. Besides this, there is a further subdivision of alternatives according as, before the strike, wages in the given trade were or were not below the general level of wages (of course taking into account the net advantages of different occupations). If they were, then, except for the reasons suggested above, there need be no reaction, and the strike may merely

---

[1] And in these circumstances the effects on wages in allied trades have also to be considered.

have expedited a rise that would inevitably have occurred sooner or later. If, however, wages were already at the normal level, then after the rise there is likely to be a reaction in consequence of an influx of labour from other trades, the extent to which this happens and its rapidity depending on the effectiveness of competition. Under the third original hypothesis, there is again a subdivision of alternatives according as before the strike profits were or were not abnormally high in the trade in question. If they were, the rise in wages is likely to be maintained, although if competition is effective it may have to be shared with other trades. If profits were not abnormally high, then capital and business power may move to other trades; and ultimately the question arises how far either earnings of management or interest generally will bear reduction without reacting seriously on the demand for labour.

The above is of course not intended as an actual solution of the given problem, but only as an illustration in bare outline of the manner in which it may be dealt with by the deductive method. We see how by the aid of the deductive method an analysis can be given which will enable us to understand our whereabouts, so that if we wish to investigate any actual case we may know what are the special facts for which it is most important to look.

There are other modifications of the deductive method in which use is made of mathematical symbols and diagrams.   The nature of the aid that can thus be afforded is discussed in the following chapter.

CHAPTER VIII.

ON SYMBOLICAL AND DIAGRAMMATIC METHODS IN POLITICAL ECONOMY.

§ 1. *Mathematical character of political economy.*— Political economy is declared by Jevons to be essentially mathematical in character; and if the term *mathematical* is used in a broad sense so as to include all enquiries that deal with quantitative relations, the propriety of thus describing the science admits of easy demonstration. For political economy is not concerned simply with questions as to whether events will or will not happen. It deals with phenomena whose quantitative aspect is of fundamental importance, and one of its main objects is to determine the laws regulating the rise and fall of these phenomena. Its principal theorems relate accordingly to the manner in which variations of one quantity depend on variations of another quantity.

The quantitative, and therefore in a broad sense mathematical, character of economic reasonings might be illustrated by opening almost at random any economic work that fairly covers the ground of the science.

Thus Mill in his treatment of supply and demand as regulators of value introduces conceptions that are strictly mathematical. He insists, for example, that the idea of a *ratio* between supply and demand is out of place, what is really involved being an *equation*. Other instances are afforded by his general treatment of the value of money, and his theory of international values. In the latter case he employs undisguised mathematical formulae[1]. If further illustrations are wanted, it· may be pointed out that all discussions concerning a measure of value, involving as they do the conception of a *unit*, are intrinsically mathematical in character. Methods of measuring changes in the purchasing power of money must also of necessity be based upon mathematical considerations.

The fact that political economy is essentially concerned with quantitative relations, and therefore involves mathematical notions, needs to be insisted upon, because to some economists the very idea of a mathematical treatment of economic problems is not only repugnant, but seems even absurd; and further because the importance of seeking to make our economic conceptions quantitatively precise has not always received due recognition. Something more than the above, however, is needed in order to establish the position that economic knowledge can be advanced

[1] *Principles of Political Economy*, Book III, Chapter 18, § 7.

by the explicit use of geometrical diagrams or mathematical formulae. Simple quantitative relations can after all be clearly expressed in the forms of ordinary speech; and the need of careful quantitative analysis may accordingly be admitted, whilst there remains an unwillingness to have recourse to mathematical symbolism. We are thus still left with a question of method demanding discussion; and the object of the present chapter is briefly to enquire what is the nature of the advantage, if any, to be derived from the use of mathematical formulae and diagrams in economic reasonings[1].

§ 2. *The employment of arithmetical examples.*— Up to comparatively recent years, the mathematics introduced into ordinary economic treatises has for the most part taken the form of arithmetical examples; and a word or two may be said at this point in regard

[1] It may here be pointed out that mathematical methods in economics fall into two subdivisions, the algebraic and the diagrammatic. The application of the former requires knowledge of various technical processes, and as employed by Cournot and Jevons involves the infinitesimal calculus. The diagrammatic or graphic method, on the other hand, requires no more than an elementary knowledge of the first principles of geometry. The two methods are frequently combined. It is to be observed that diagrams lend themselves naturally to the registering of statistics, while to express statistics equationally is not possible until their laws have been determined. The employment of diagrammatic methods by the theorist is accordingly more likely than that of algebraic methods to be indirectly of assistance to the statistician.

to the part capable of being played by such examples in political economy. By taking particular numerical premisses and working out results, we may illustrate conclusions that have been obtained by means of ordinary reasoning processes; and hypothetical illustrations of this kind are certainly not without value. By their help students are likely to be materially assisted towards understanding the operation of such laws as that of supply and demand. Numerical examples have, moreover, a probative force in certain cases where it is not desired to do more than disprove a universal proposition, or—what comes to the same thing—establish a particular one; as, for instance, if we merely wish to shew that it *may be* profitable for a country to import commodities that it could itself have produced with a less expenditure of effort than is required in the country from which it obtains them.

The citation of examples is not, however, a method whereby general conclusions can be obtained; and the use of arithmetical illustrations may involve the danger of our forgetting that after all they are nothing more than illustrations. It is difficult or even impossible to guarantee the typical or representative character of the particular numerical data that have been selected, or to be certain that if they were varied the same general conclusion would always result. The consequence may be a failure to discriminate between that which is essential and that which is merely accidental[1].

§ 3. *Exact numerical premisses not essential to the employment of mathematical methods.*—If the use of mathematical symbols and diagrams is rightly to be called a *method*, it must do more than yield merely isolated examples, and must be free from imperfections such as those just pointed out. The economist must by the aid of his symbols and diagrams be enabled to deduce conclusions having general validity under conditions that can be precisely determined. It is, however, necessary here to guard against a misapprehension that has led some economists to reject mathematical methods far too summarily. Professor Cairnes, for instance, seems to imply that the employment of such methods is necessarily barren unless we can obtain premisses capable of being stated with numerical accuracy[2]. He is here indeed only following in the footsteps of Mill, who remarks that mathematical principles are "manifestly inapplicable, where the causes on which any class of phenomena depend are so imperfectly accessible to our observation, that we

---

[1] A noteworthy instance in which the employment of a numerical example leads to error of the above-mentioned kind is to be found in Mill's *Political Economy*, Book IV, Chapter 3, § 4. This is pointed out by Professor and Mrs Marshall in their *Economics of Industry*, p. 85, *note*.

[2] *Logical Method*, 1875, p. vii.

cannot ascertain, by a proper induction, their numerical laws."[1] Professor Cliffe Leslie argues similarly against the application of mathematics to political economy on the ground that economic premisses are not capable of exact quantitative determination[2]. And Dr Ingram says bluntly,—"The great objection to the use of mathematics in economic reasoning is that it is necessarily sterile. If we examine the attempts which have been made to employ it, we shall find that the fundamental conceptions on which the deductions are made to rest are vague, indeed metaphysical, in their character. Quantitative conclusions imply quantitative premisses, and these are wanting. There is then no future for this kind of study, and it is only waste of intellectual power to pursue it."[3]

The impossibility of obtaining exact numerical premisses in political economy is fully recognised by Cournot and other mathematical economists. But at the same time they shew clearly that such premisses are not always essential to the employment of mathematical methods. Cournot, for instance, remarks that while the law of demand for any commodity might conceivably be expressed by an empirical formula or curve, we cannot as a matter of fact hope to obtain

---

[1] *Logic*, Book III, Chapter 24, § 9.
[2] *Essays in Political and Moral Philosophy*, 1888, pp. 69, 70.
[3] *History of Political Economy*, pp. 181, 2.

observations sufficiently numerous or exact for this purpose. But he adds that it by no means follows that the unknown law of demand cannot by means of symbols be usefully introduced into analytic combinations. For one of the most important functions of mathematical analysis is to discover determinate relations between quantities whose numerical values are unassignable. Functions, while remaining numerically unknown, may possess known properties; and on the assumption that certain general relations between quantities hold good, it may be possible mathematically to deduce further relations that could otherwise hardly have been determined[1].

---

[1] *Principes Mathématiques de la Théorie des Richesses*, § 21. Again, in his preface, Cournot remarks that some economists seem to have a false notion of the nature of the applications of mathematical analysis to political economy. "On s'est figuré que l'emploi des signes et des formules ne pouvait avoir d'autre but que celui de conduire à des calculs numériques; et comme on sentait bien que le sujet répugne à cette détermination numérique des valeurs d'après la seule théorie, on en a conclu que l'appareil des formules était, sinon susceptible d'induire en erreur, au moins oiseux et pédantesque. Mais les personnes versées dans l'analyse mathématique savent qu'elle n'a pas seulement pour objet de calculer des nombres; qu'elle est aussi employée à trouver des relations entre des grandeurs que l'on ne peut évaluer numériquement. entre des fonctions dont la loi n'est pas susceptible de s'exprimer par des symboles algébriques" (pp. vii, viii). The possibility of mathematical reasoning without numerical data is discussed and illustrated in considerable detail by Professor Edgeworth in his *Mathematical Psychics*, pp. 1—9, and 83—93. "It is necessary," he says, "to realise that mathematical reasoning is not, as commonly supposed, limited to subjects where numerical data are attainable. Where there are data which though not *numerical* are

Cournot himself exemplifies the process which he thus describes. He starts with simple formulae to express relations between demand and price, cost of production and price, and the like, and assuming that these relations will conform to certain specified conditions, deduces by mathematical manipulation some of the consequences resulting therefrom. He deduces, for example, with the greatest clearness and precision the general laws determining what price will yield to a monopolist a maximum profit; and he then proceeds to deal with the difficult problem of the incidence, under different suppositions, of taxes on monopolies. Other problems are treated in a similar manner with more or less success; and at no point in the reasoning is it essential that numerical values should be assigned to the symbols.

What is true of algebraical formulae is true of diagrams also. Representing, for example, by a curve the manner in which the demand for a commodity varies with its price, general laws to which this curve will conform may be determined, and results deduced.

quantitative—for example, that a quantity is _greater_ or _less_ than another, _increases_ or _decreases_, is _positive_ or _negative_, a _maximum_ or _minimum_—there mathematical reasoning is possible and may be indispensable. To take a trivial instance: _a_ is greater than _b_, and _b_ is greater than _c_, therefore, _a_ is greater than _c_. Here is mathematical reasoning applicable to quantities which may not be susceptible of numerical evaluation."

But this does not necessitate that curves of demand for different commodities should be capable of being drawn with numerical accuracy.

§ 4. *Advantages resulting from the use of symbolical and diagrammatic methods in political economy.*—The employment of symbolical and graphic methods independently of specific numerical data is of course confined mainly, if not wholly, to the pure or abstract theory. Those, therefore, who deny the utility of abstract political economy in any form, and maintain that the only fruitful method of economic enquiry is inductive and empirical, will naturally reject mathematics as an instrument. This general question has, however, been sufficiently discussed already; and, therefore, in briefly enquiring what kind of advantages may result from the employment of mathematical methods, it will be taken for granted that the economist ought sometimes to have recourse to abstract and deductive reasoning. The advantages are partly direct, and partly indirect; and a brief reference may in the first place be made to the latter.

When mathematical processes are employed in the solution of a problem, attention can hardly fail to be called to the conditions assumed as the basis of the argument, and due importance is likely to be attached to the exact enunciation of these conditions; a more thoroughgoing quantitative analysis of fundamental conceptions is also necessary; it becomes less easy to slur over steps in the reasoning; and difficulties are brought to light that might otherwise have remained hidden. Hence there arises a higher standard of precision in abstract economic reasonings, even in cases where non-mathematical methods are still employed. As a further consequence, a check is put upon the tendency to overlook the limitations to which purely abstract and deductive methods of reasoning are subject. Professor Foxwell has well remarked that "there is no greater safeguard against the misapplication of theory than the precise expression of it"; and he rightly indicates that precise expression is necessitated when use is made of mathematical analysis[1]. It is now generally recognised that the introduction of mathematical methods and habits of thought into economics has exerted a wide-reaching and important educational influence in stimulating precision both of thought and of expression, and hence eliminating errors due to slovenly and inaccurate reasoning[2].

[1] *Quarterly Journal of Economics*, October, 1887, p. 90.

[2] Mr L. L. Price points out in an effective passage that the mathematical and historical methods have, in spite of their apparent antagonism, co-operated with one another in helping to make economic theory more accurate and more comprehensive. "By emphasising its limiting conditions, the historical treatment has checked the misapplication of theory; and the mathematical treatment, proceeding from a different starting-point by a different road, has reached the same goal, and tended to induce greater precision of statement" (*Economic Science and Practice*, p. 309).

Amongst the characteristic direct advantages of mathematical analysis and diagrammatic representation is the fact that the significance of *continuity* in the variations of phenomena is brought into prominence. This remark applies pre-eminently to the diagrammatic treatment of the law of supply and demand. Such a treatment affords, for example, the simplest means of dealing with the ingenious criticisms to which Mr Thornton has subjected this law. He adduces cases which at first sight look like exceptions overturning the law altogether; but the method of diagrams at once shews them to be extreme or limiting cases due to a break in the continuity either of demand or of supply. They are thus accounted for, and their true signification easily apprehended[1].

Another characteristic advantage of mathematical methods is increased power of treating variables (*e.g.*, demand, cost of production) in their true character, and not as constants. Professor Edgeworth observes that "to treat *variables* as *constants* is the characteristic vice of the unmathematical economist."[2] So to treat them may indeed be necessary for purposes of simplification, if we are limited to the comparatively clumsy instrument afforded by ordinary language and ordinary

---

[1] Compare Thornton, *On Labour*, Book II, Chapter 1; and Professor Fleeming Jenkin's essay on "the Graphic Representation of the Laws of Supply and Demand, and their Application to Labour."

[2] *Mathematical Psychics*, p. 127, *note*.

propositional forms. It is, however, clear that under such conditions the solution obtained cannot be regarded as more than a first approximation. Many of Ricardo's and Mill's reasonings are in this way rendered incomplete; for example, in discussing the incidence of tithes, and the effects of agricultural improvements, they assume that demand is unaffected by a rise or fall in price. A more striking and important instance is to be found in the treatment of cost of production as a constant, and the consequent failure to recognise the part played by demand in the determination of normal, as well as market, value. It is true that in the earlier editions of his *Economics of Industry* Professor Marshall expounded the correct theory without any explicit reference to symbols or diagrams. But it is no secret that his important contributions to the theory of value are mainly to be attributed to insight gained through working at economics mathematically on the lines first indicated by Cournot. It may be added that the full force and signification of Professor Marshall's theories are best apprehended by the aid of diagrams, even where their use is not absolutely necessary; and that in certain of the more complex developments of the theories, some assistance of a symbolical kind remains essential.

A point closely connected with the one just considered is the assistance which mathematical methods afford towards understanding the relation of *mutual* dependence which may subsist between different phenomena, *e.g.*, supply, demand, and price. This conception is of central importance in economics. For, as Professor Marshall has observed, "just as the motion of every body in the solar system affects and is affected by the motion of every other, so it is with the elements of the problem of political economy." The conception is, however, one that is found to be specially difficult of realisation by those who are without mathematical training. Arguments involving this conception are, moreover, apt to be lengthy, as well as difficult to follow, if expressed wholly in ordinary language[1].

It may, indeed, be added as amongst the special advantages of mathematical methods that they lead not only to accuracy and precision, but also to conciseness and the avoidance of circumlocution. In some cases it is possible by means of a single diagram to make intelligible at a glance what would otherwise require a more or less elaborate explanation. This remark applies to the ambiguity of the phrase *increase of demand*, pointed out by Professor Sidgwick[2]. The real import of the distinction between a mere *extension*

---

[1] Compare Professor Edgeworth's British Association Address on the Application of Mathematics to Political Economy, *Statistical Journal*, December, 1889, p. 541.

[2] *Principles of Political Economy*, 1901, p. 186.

of demand due to a fall in price, and an *intensification* of demand at a given price, can be made more clear by the aid of a diagram than by a long verbal explanation. The effects of an intensification of demand can also be more quickly and easily realised by diagrammatic aid than in any other way[1].

Much of the above is well expressed by Cournot in his remark that "even when the employment of mathematical signs is not absolutely necessary, it can facilitate the exposition, make it more concise, put it on the way towards more extended developments, and prevent digressions of vague argumentation."[2]

It can, however, hardly be affirmed that there are economic truths of fundamental importance which are incapable of being expounded except in a mathematical form. Jevons's theory of utility and its applications are in many respects the most striking outcome of

---

[1] Other illustrations are given by Professor Edgeworth in his British Association Address. "In the case of international trade," he remarks, "the various effects of a tax or other impediment, which most students find it so difficult to trace in Mill's laborious chapters, are visible almost at a glance by the aid of the mathematical instrument. It takes Professor Sidgwick a good many words to convey by way of a particular instance that it is possible for a nation by a judiciously regulated tariff to benefit itself at the expense of the foreigner. The truth in its generality is more clearly contemplated by the aid of diagrams such as those employed by the eminent mathematical economists Messrs Auspitz and Lieben" (*Statistical Journal*, December, 1889, p. 540).

[2] *Principes Mathématiques*, p. viii.

mathematical economics; and it is difficult to do full justice to this theory unassisted by mathematical methods. Nevertheless, without the explicit use of diagrams or algebraical formulae, what is essentially the same theory has been independently worked out by Menger and the Austrian school[1].

[1] Menger's *Grundsätze der Volkswirthschaftslehre* was published in 1871, the same year as that in which Jevons's *Theory of Political Economy* appeared. It may be said that the work of Menger and his followers is mathematical in tone, though not in language. Professor Walras of Lausanne, another independent worker in the same field, is like Jevons an ardent champion of mathematical methods. So is Mr Wicksteed, who in his *Alphabet of Economic Science* retains the mathematical form, and expounds Jevons's doctrines with admirable clearness. Professor Marshall is a mathematical economist of a different type inasmuch as—unlike Jevons and Walras, and also unlike Cournot, with whom he has in many respects more affinity—he subordinates his mathematics. He employs diagrams for the illustration and further development of his theories, but shews that his main doctrines are capable of being expressed without mathematical aids. He here proceeds on the principle that even in cases where mathematical symbolism is specially appropriate, and even where truths have actually been reached wholly or partially through the instrumentality of mathematical analysis, still some effort may rightly be made to avoid the use of mathematics in writing for the general economic public. The reason for this, like most other points connected with the subject under discussion, is very happily expressed by Professor Edgeworth. "Mathematics," he says, "is as it were the universal language of the physical sciences. It is for physicists what Latin used to be for scholars; but it is unfortunately Greek to many economists. Hence the writer who wishes to be widely read—who does not say, with the French author, *J'imprime pour moi*—will do well not to multiply mathematical technicalities beyond the indispensable minimum, which we have seen reason to suppose is not very large. The parsimony of symbols, which is often an elegance in the physicist, is a necessity for the economist."

On the whole, we arrive at the conclusions, first, that political economy involves conceptions of a mathematical nature requiring to be analysed in a mathematical spirit; and secondly, that there are certain departments of the science in which valuable aid may be derived from the actual employment of symbolical or diagrammatic methods. Mathematics may not up to the present time have proved an absolutely indispensable instrument of economic investigation and exposition; but it would be difficult to exaggerate the gain that has resulted from the application of mathematical ideas to the central problems of economic theory.

CHAPTER IX.

ON POLITICAL ECONOMY AND ECONOMIC HISTORY.

§ 1. *Functions of economic history in theoretical investigations.*—The nature of the distinction between economic history and economic theory, though sometimes apparently overlooked, needs no detailed discussion. The former describes the economic phenomena existing at any given period in the past, and traces the actual progress of such phenomena over successive periods; the latter seeks to determine the *uniformities* of coexistence and sequence to which economic phenomena are subject. The propositions of economic history are accordingly statements of particular concrete facts; economic theory, on the other hand, is concerned with the establishment of general laws.

Neither of the two can take the place of the other. For, on the one hand, mere historical research cannot by itself suffice for the solution of theoretical problems; and, on the other hand, the actual evolution of economic habits and conditions cannot be constructed *à priori*.

At the same time, economic history and economic theory in different ways assist and control one another; and their mutual relations become specially important as the history approaches the period with which the theory is more particularly concerned.

Reference may first of all be made to the desirability of a general historical study of the gradual development of those phenomena which are made the subject of theoretical enquiry. This applies to any treatment of economics that is not of the most abstract character. Thus, independently of any assistance that may be derived from actual historical generalizations, we shall gain a clearer insight into the general principles now regulating the distribution of wealth in England, if we can follow the process of development through which our system of distribution has passed. The really characteristic and significant features of the existing system will in this way be more distinctly perceived, and their economic consequences more exactly traced.

As an instance of a more special character, it may be observed that certain of the problems to which trade-unionism gives rise are more likely to be effectively dealt with, if attention is paid to the circumstances in which trade-unions originated. Another simple instance is to be found in the theory of the London Money Market, and the influence exerted therein by the Bank of England. The present position and functions of the Bank in the Money Market cannot be properly understood, as Mr Bagehot shews in *Lombard Street*, unless account is taken of its origin and history. It may be added that in the treatment of the general theory of modern banking, it is helpful to study the different ways in which modern banks had their beginning, and the various purposes which it was their original object to fulfil.

In a similar way, most theoretical enquiries, unless they are of a particularly abstract and general character, may with advantage commence with a brief historical introduction, tracing the mode of development of the phenomena under discussion.

The kind of aid, however, which the theorist thus gains from studying the evolution of economic phenomena, though very real, is indirect and perhaps somewhat indefinite. The more specific functions of economic history in connexion with the theoretical problems of political economy may be roughly classified as follows: first, to illustrate and test conclusions not themselves resting on historical evidence; secondly, to teach the limits of the actual applicability of economic doctrines; thirdly, to afford a basis for the direct attainment of economic truths of a theoretical character. It is to the last named function that reference is more particularly made when the application of the *historical method* to political economy is spoken of.

§ 2. *Economic theories illustrated by history.*—
Even when the general line of argument adopted
by the economist is of a deductive character, it is
desirable that concrete historical illustrations should if
possible be found. The kind of qualifications requisite
in applying theoretical conclusions to problems of real
life will thus be made prominent; and the student will
at the same time be reminded that hypothesis and
abstraction are employed but as means to an end, the
ultimate aim of the science being the explanation
and interpretation of the phenomena of the actual
industrial world. Historical digressions may also assist
the student in grasping the true import of a piece of
reasoning that is in itself severely abstract. For example, the effect exerted on the general level of prices
in a country by the quantity of money in circulation
may be illustrated from the debasement of the currency
under Henry VIII. and Edward VI. and the great discoveries of the precious metals in America during the
Tudor period, from the history of the *assignats* of
the French Revolution, from the period of the Bank
Restriction in England, and from the gold discoveries
in Australia and California in the nineteenth century[1].

[1] Compare Nicholson, *Money and Monetary Problems*, pp. 58 ff.
Cairnes shews in his *Leading Principles of Political Economy*,
pp. 377 ff., how the occurrences following the gold discoveries in
Australia also serve to illustrate in a striking way the abstract theory
of foreign trade.

It is to the economic history of the last hundred years that we most naturally turn for illustrations of current economic theories. Earlier economic history is, however, for some purposes available. Thus records of prices in the Middle Ages afford opportunities for illustrating the economist's general theory of values. For example, the movements in the price of grain resulting from the dearth of the years 1315, 1316, illustrate very forcibly the effect exerted on price by changes in supply. The price of wheat rose to more than three times what it was in ordinary years; and the fact that the rise was proportionately greater than any that has been experienced in recent times verifies the theoretical conclusion that the more limited the range from which supplies are drawn, the greater will be the influence exerted on the market by variations in the seasons. A comparison between medieval and modern prices illustrates, further, the influence of extended markets, and increased facilities of communication, in diminishing fluctuations and unifying prices throughout the country in ordinary years.

An objection may perhaps be raised to drawing illustrations of modern economic theories from prices in the Middle Ages, on the ground that the influence of custom, and the operation of legal restrictions, must necessarily have obscured or even nullified the effects of supply and demand. It is true that very great caution is requisite in applying to earlier times theories that presuppose thoroughgoing competition; but even in the medieval industrial world competition was always at work in some form or other. Each case requires special investigation, and it is at any rate clear that law and custom did not exert an absolute and decisive influence on the price of grain at the period above referred to[1]. In so far as they were in some degree operative, the figures become in one respect still more striking, since they shew how changes in supply are capable of overriding both custom and legal enactments.

As regards wages, one of the most obvious of early historical illustrations is afforded by the revolution in the history of labour in this country caused by the ravages of the Black Death in 1348, 1361, and 1369. Notwithstanding the differences of opinion as to the probable population of England at the beginning of the fourteenth century, it is generally agreed that not much less than half the people must have been swept off by the plague. An opportunity is thus afforded of studying on a large scale the effect on wages of a sudden diminution in the supply of labour, and also the conditions under which a rise in wages, once

---

[1] Compare Rogers, *History of Agriculture and Prices in England,* vol. i. Preface; and vol. iv. p. 427.

obtained, is likely to be permanent. At first the whole industrial machine was thrown out of gear; wages were doubled and, in some cases, even trebled. Even when things had somewhat settled down, nominal wages[1] appear to have risen on the average about fifty per cent. The whole of this rise was not maintained; but still wages during the next hundred years remained from twenty-five to forty per cent. higher than they were before the plague.

All this is in accordance with the general economic theory of wages. Especially it should be noticed that theory leads to the conclusion that if a general rise in wages is to be rendered permanent, it must be able to exert an influence upon the labourer's standard of comfort before an increase in the population has had time to bring about a reaction. This conclusion is borne out by the permanent improvement in the position of the labouring classes that was effected in the case before us. It is true that after the plague had spent

---

[1] The plague was accompanied by a dearth, and this, together with the general dislocation of industry and the check given to the proper cultivation of the land, resulted in a considerable rise in the price of corn. Moreover a general slight rise in prices was in operation, in consequence of successive depreciations of the coinage in 1346 and 1351. The rise in real wages was, therefore, not quite so great as the rise in nominal wages would seem to indicate; but no very great deduction need be made on this score, since the general increase in the money value of commodities was slight as compared with the increase in wages.

its force, population increased rapidly—a fact which may be noted as illustrating the Malthusian doctrine of population—but the diminution in the supply of labour was so great that the filling in of the gaps could not take place fast enough to prevent the rise in wages from permanently establishing itself.

Continual efforts were made by the legislature to restore wages to their old level; but though the statutes passed with this object may have been partially successful in certain localities, they were in the main inoperative[1]. This failure of legislative enactments to override the ordinary action of supply and demand is very significant. It has been suggested that where economic conditions are changing very

[1] Professor Rogers suggests that even in those cases where the Statute of Labourers was nominally operative, it was in reality evaded. "The Statute of Labourers may indeed have produced some effect on farm labour. I seem to detect its operation from a fact which I have frequently noticed in the accounts after the Black Death. Entries of payments on certain rates are cancelled, and lower sums are substituted for them. Of course in the tables which I have constructed I have not taken the figures which have been cancelled, but those which are substituted. But I cannot help thinking that these changes point to evasions of the statute, and that perhaps the labourer was compensated to the full extent of the previous entry, but in some covert way, or by some means which would not come within the penalties of the statute. Thus there might be larger allowances at harvest-time, or the permission to make fuller use of common rights, or, as I have seen in the case of a shepherd, a licence to turn his sheep into his lord's pasture, or some analogous equivalent to a necessary but illegal money payment" (*History of Agriculture and Prices in England*, vol. i. p. 300).

slowly, wages and prices may appear to be regulated by laws or customs entirely irrespective of competition, whereas in fact the laws or customs are being themselves gradually modified from generation to generation, so that at any given time the rates which they sanction are not materially different from the normal rates that the free operation of supply and demand would itself have brought about[1]. If there is any truth in this theory, it will explain how it was that although law and custom sometimes exerted considerable influence in medieval industrial economy, they failed to do so in the particular period succeeding the ravages of the Black Death. Here was a crisis in which economic conditions changed not gradually, but suddenly; customary and legal rates of wages were unable to adapt themselves quietly and by degrees, but became strikingly divergent from competition wages; and they had to give way accordingly.

Whilst attention is called to the value of historical illustrations such as the above, attention may also be called to the weakness of historical records as compared with contemporary observations. It is almost impossible to be equally sure of the accuracy and adequacy of the available data; and it is very easy to misinterpret them, particularly if they are of a statistical character. Many unrecorded and unsus-

Compare Marshall, *Present Position of Economics*, pp. 48 to 50.

pected influences may also have been in operation, and undue importance may consequently be attached to those of which a record remains. This danger becomes the greater, if we set out with the object of illustrating a foregone conclusion.

There is a further difficulty sometimes involved in the use of historical illustrations. In order that they may not be cumbrous, there is danger of their becoming either inadequate as illustrations, or else inaccurate from the historical standpoint. Separated from their context, they are apt to lose a good deal of their force, while there is at the same time a certain liability to exaggeration. A theory may be satisfactorily tested and confirmed by an historical record taken in its entirety, and yet it may be difficult to point to any separate portion of the record as constituting by itself an adequate illustration or exemplification. Illustrations avowedly fictitious are preferable to historical illustrations that require to be doctored in order to serve their purpose; and on the whole, while it is desirable to have recourse to historical illustrations wherever suitable ones present themselves, it is chimerical to expect that such illustrations can wholly supersede and replace illustrations of a hypothetical character.

§ 3. *Economic theories criticized by history.*—It has been said that the true function of economic history in relation to theoretical investigations is criticism; and this is undoubtedly one of its most important functions. For history does not merely illustrate and confirm; it also brings mistakes to light, and shews where doctrines have been laid down without due qualification or limitation. The history of wages, for example, shews the error of the assumption that the standard of comfort of the labouring classes automatically determines the rate of wages, whilst it is itself unaffected by changes in that rate.

In particular, economic history teaches the limits of the actual applicability of economic doctrines. It calls attention to the shifting character of economic conditions, and shews how, as these conditions vary, some at least of the principles by which economic phenomena are regulated vary also. The relativity of economic doctrines is discussed in some detail in a note at the conclusion of the present chapter; and hence no more than a passing reference to the subject need be made at this stage. It will suffice to remark that the almost universal recognition of such relativity by recent economists, so far at any rate as concrete economic doctrines are concerned, may be regarded as one of the most striking and legitimate triumphs of the historical school. The question how far there remain economic principles for which universality may still be claimed will be considered later on.

§ 4. *Economic theories established by history.*—The question next arises how far historical material may be of service for the discovery of economic uniformities, and not merely for the confirmation or criticism of theories arrived at in some other way. There are, without doubt, many problems which require for their solution a combination of deductive reasoning and historical investigation so to speak on equal terms; and there are other cases in which our main reliance has to be placed upon historical generalizations.

The effects of machinery on wages, the occurrence of credit cycles, the extent of the evils resulting from bad currency regulations, the effects of gold discoveries or of a scarcity of gold on trade and industry, the working of a system of progressive taxation, the economic consequences of different systems of poor relief, and of State interference of various kinds, may be given as instances where the economist is more or less directly dependent upon historical material. It is true that deduction from elementary principles of human nature also finds some place in the argument. Deduction at some stage or other of the reasoning is, indeed, in most cases essential to its cogency, for the fallibility of purely empirical laws must constantly be borne in mind. Still instances of the above kind serve at once to invalidate the view that economic history never provides premises for the economist or forms the basis of his doctrines.

For purposes of illustration the problem of the effects of machinery on wages may be considered in rather fuller detail. This problem really involves two questions, as is pointed out by Professor Nicholson in his essay on the *Effects of Machinery on Wages*: first, the immediate or closely proximate effects of the extended use of machinery—the characteristics, that is to say, of the state of transition; and secondly, the general characteristics—as affecting wage-receivers— of a system of industry in which much machinery is used, compared with one in which little machinery is used.

In dealing with the first of these questions we may to a considerable extent employ deductive reasoning based on the general theory of distribution. We have to consider the increased efficiency of production due to the use of machinery, yielding a larger dividend for distribution; the greater aid which capital is able to afford to labour, tending to raise the capitalist's share at the expense of the wage-receiver's[1]; the impetus

---

[1] This is a more satisfactory method of treatment than to argue from the increase of fixed at the expense of circulating capital. Considering that the amount of capital at the disposal of an employer is not a definite sum, but may within certain limits be increased by the aid of credit, without diminishing the resources of other employers, it does not follow that an extended employment of machinery will necessarily diminish circulating capital. Assuming that the substitution of machine for hand labour lowers prices, demand will be stimulated; and it is possible that this may be the case to such an extent that in

given to the accumulation of capital; the change in the kind of labour required, skilled labour of a given kind being superseded by unskilled labour or by skilled labour of another kind. These are the main factors to be taken into account, and we can argue from them deductively to the kind of effects that will be produced. Of course the actual effects will vary with varying conditions; but still arguing for the most part deductively, we can determine what are the most influential of these conditions: *e.g.*, the continuity or want of continuity in the changes, and the time over which a given alteration is spread[1]; also, the adaptability of the labourers, depending mainly on their general intelligence and technical education.

the production of the given commodity all the labour that was formerly employed may still be employed in addition to the machinery —the employers by means of credit discounting the future, so that although they have to purchase the machinery they can still advance as much in wages as before. This is the more likely to hold good if the machinery is introduced gradually, so as to allow demand to increase *pari passu*. So far as a different kind of labour is required, the old skilled workmen suffer because their particular skill is superseded, and not because there is less circulating capital with which to maintain them. It is always true, however, that, *ceteris paribus*, the extended use of machinery increases the relative importance of capital in the work of production.

[1] Professor Nicholson, in the essay to which reference has been made above, formulates the following *Law of Continuity*: "A radical change made in the methods of invention will be gradually and continuously adopted; and these radical changes, these discontinuous leaps, tend to give place to advances by small *increments of invention*." A proposition of this kind can of course be established only by direct historical evidence.

In all the above we may, in the manner indicated
in the two preceding sections, appeal to the experience
of the last hundred years to illustrate, confirm, or
correct our conclusions; still, so far, the use of history
is mainly supplementary. We need more definitely to
look to the past, when we turn to the second of the
questions involved in the given problem, and seek to
determine how wage-receivers are affected by the
general characteristics of an age of machinery as
compared with one of hand labour. In order to solve
this problem, it is necessary, not only to consider the
effects of cheapened production, but also to ask such
questions as the following,—how far, and under what
conditions, the use of machinery leads to the increased
employment of women and children, to the concentra-
tion of industry in large towns, to a widening of the
gulf between employers and employed, and to longer
hours of labour; how far it increases the monotony of
work and dispenses with technical skill or the reverse[1];
how far it increases or diminishes the specialization of
skill; how far it increases or diminishes fluctuations
in wages. Only to a limited extent do these questions
admit of abstract treatment. At any rate so far as
deductive reasoning is employed, it does but follow
the suggestions of history, and starts from premisses

[1] Experience seems to shew that on the whole the use of machinery
increases rather than diminishes the demand for skilled labour.

that are established historically. It is clear that the problem as a whole cannot be adequately dealt with except on an historical basis.

At the same time, and in consequence of the method employed, great care is necessary if we are to avoid attributing in too high a degree to the use of machinery effects that are partly or wholly due to some other cause. There is need also to guard against the danger of unduly extending the range of our generalizations, in consequence of overlooking the way in which the problem is affected by the special conditions of particular trades. Inductions that may seem to be justified by the facts should as far as possible be deductively checked; and it should in particular be remembered that the characteristics of machine-using epochs may vary at different stages, and that the use of very much machinery may not be related to that of much, as the use of much is to that of little, or the use of little to that of none.

In more general problems relating to economic growth and progress the part played by abstract reasoning is reduced to a minimum, and the economist's dependence upon historical generalizations is at a maximum. Theories of economic growth and progress may, indeed, be said to constitute the philosophy of economic history. For only by the direct comparison of successive stages of society can we reasonably hope to discover the laws, in accordance with which economic states tend to succeed one another or to become changed in character[1].

There are in fact few departments of political or social science in which the *à priori* method avails less than in the study of economic development. J. S. Mill in his *Political Economy*, Book IV., discusses the influence of the progress of society on production and distribution; and his method is to begin by assuming certain factors unchanged, and then to deduce the consequences of changes in others. Some additional light is thrown on the general laws of rent, profit, and wages, under the hypothesis of effective competition; but the discussion yields very little in the way of a true theory of economic progress. It has been already pointed out that in studying the mode of development of economic conditions, the economist is more than ordinarily dependent upon general sociological knowledge; and it may almost be regarded as a corollary that he is also more than ordinarily dependent upon historical investigation. The realistic and historical conceptions of political economy go hand in hand, and the spheres

---

[1] The historical comparison may, however, in some cases be usefully supplemented by a contemporary study of oriental and savage countries, in the manner exemplified by the investigations of Sir Henry Maine. The study, for example, of village life in India and Ceylon gives insight into the nature and development of the agricultural communities of earlier times in Europe.

within which they are specially appropriate may for the most part be identified.

§ 5. *Functions of economic theory in historical investigations.*—Turning to the other aspect of the relation between economic history and economic theory, we may pass on to enquire how far theoretical knowledge is of service in historical investigations. The first point to notice is that a knowledge of theory, *i.e.*, of previously established general propositions relating to economic phenomena, teaches the historian what kinds of facts are likely to have an important economic bearing. Even when we are engaged in the mere collection and registration of events, it is often advantageous, as Jevons has pointed out in the case of the physical observer, that our attention should be guided by theoretical anticipations. Industrial phenomena are exceedingly complex, and unless we know what special facts to look for, it is quite possible that some of the most vital circumstances may fail to attract our notice. Knowledge of cause and effect in the economic world is, accordingly, of assistance for discriminating between the facts to be specially noted and those that may without risk of error be disregarded.

But while theoretical anticipations may serve a very useful purpose, they may also be a serious source of danger. It has often been pointed out how the mere narration of events is influenced by the narrator's theoretical views. He is apt so to arrange and co-ordinate his facts—emphasizing some and slurring over others—that they cannot but suggest the conclusions he himself is inclined to draw from them. The history, for example, with which List commences his *National System of Political Economy*, though in many respects both sound and interesting, is more or less open to this criticism; that is to say, it is history read in the light of a particular theory, which theory is afterwards to a considerable extent based on the history.

If then a writer's theoretical views are likely to exert an influence upon his narration of facts, it is clearly of material importance that his preliminary study of theory should be careful and exact. It is also of importance that the theoretical position taken by the historian should not be disguised. As remarked by Professor Marshall, "the most reckless and treacherous of all theorists is he who professes to let facts and figures speak for themselves, who keeps in the background the part he has played, perhaps unconsciously, in selecting and grouping them, and in suggesting the argument *post hoc ergo propter hoc*."[1]

If the historian is properly to fulfil his function, he must avowedly attempt to establish relations between phenomena, and trace causes and effects. But it is an error to suppose that this is possible without the appli-

[1] *Present Position of Economics*, § 16.

cation of general propositions previously established. Causes in history are not, as has been affirmed, "given to us in each case by direct evidence," if by this is meant that each set of events can be studied separately, and causal connexions assigned without the assistance either of deductive reasoning or comparison with other instances. All that is really given to us in each case by direct evidence is a complex sequence of events, in which the true bonds of causal connexion may be disguised in a thousand different ways, so that, far from being patent to every observer, they can be detected only by the trained student thoroughly equipped with scientific knowledge. It follows that some familiarity with economic theory is needed for the interpretation of industrial phenomena, such as it falls within the province of the historian to give.

The above remarks apply with special force to the economic history of the last hundred years, both because the interactions between economic phenomena become more and more complicated as we approach recent times, and the interpretations of economic science are therefore the more indispensable; and also because modern economic analysis has a more direct and immediate bearing on this period than on earlier periods. Still the application of what has just been said need not be limited to recent economic history, although it is true that as regards earlier times no elaborate apparatus of theory is required. It may be added that the economic historian will be benefited by having received a scientific training in economic reasoning, even where there is little scope for the application of particular economic dogmas. Just as it is a function of history to criticize theory, so it may be regarded as a function of theory to criticize history. Theory often cannot tell definitely what actual results will follow from any given change; but it can determine the kind of effects that are probable or possible, and it can often particularise the conditions under which each will occur. It can, therefore, usefully criticize and test any given account of what actually took place. It is often competent to declare that a given effect cannot have been due to the assigned cause, or at least that this cannot have been the case under the stated conditions.

There has been some dispute as to whether the study of economic history should precede that of economic theory, or *vice versa*; it may also be argued, as a third alternative, that since their dependence upon one another is mutual, the study of the one and the other should be carried on more or less *pari passu*. It is difficult to lay down a general rule applicable to all circumstances. But, on the whole, so far as elementary study is concerned, it seems best that some treatment of general economic science in its simplest and broadest outlines should come first.   For unless the history is limited to an early period—say to that preceding the seventeenth century—the history essential to the illustration and due limitation of the general principles of economic reasoning can more easily and more safely be supplied incidentally, than can the theory essential to the right understanding of the history.

§ 6. *Economic history and the history of economic theories.*—Distinct from the history of economic facts, but closely related thereto, is the history of ideas and theories concerning the facts.   In the industrial sphere, as in other departments of human action, facts and ideas act and react upon one another, so that there results a complex bond of connexion between the historical succession of phenomena and the historical succession of theories.   Economic theories may accordingly be considered, not merely in relation to their absolute truth or falsity, but also in relation to the economic facts that helped to produce them, and those that they themselves helped to produce.

The theories of industry and commerce current at any period often throw light on the actual industrial facts of that period.   From the study of the theories new points of view from which to regard the facts may be obtained, and fresh clues may be suggested leading to a more thorough knowledge of the actual course of events. For this reason alone the economic historian would be led to examine the drift of economic opinion over the period of his investigations[1].

Another reason why the historian of economic facts concerns himself with the history of economic theories is to be found in the direct influence which the opinions current at any period exert on subsequent events. The course of economic development is controlled and modified not only by actual legislation, but also by social institutions and current habits of thought; and it is clear that all these are under the influence of theories and ideas. In early times, indeed, it is principally by their influence on actual phenomena that it becomes possible to trace the progress of ideas; and up to a certain stage, the history of thought on economic

---

[1] "Among the facts with which we are concerned," says Dr Cunningham in his *Growth of English Industry and Commerce during the Early and Middle Ages*, "none are of greater importance than those which shew that certain ideas were prevalent at a certain time, or were beginning to spread at a particular date. It is only as we understand the way in which men viewed the dealing and enterprise of their own time, and can thus enter into their schemes of advancement or their aims at progress, that the whole story may come to possess a living interest for us" (p. 17). Dr Cunningham adds that from the preambles of statutes and other documents and the economic literature of each century, "we can generally learn what men thought and what they wished, so that we can better apprehend the meaning of what they did" (p. 21). It ought no doubt to be borne in mind that the preambles of statutes taken by themselves may sometimes be misleading. Their primary object being to provide justification for the statutes that follow, they cannot in all cases be regarded as unbiassed expressions of opinion.

questions is almost necessarily merged in the history of the facts themselves. As we approach modern times, the theories begin to find more articulate and definite expression in literature, and we are able more and more clearly to distinguish between economic history and the history of political economy[1]. But it remains none the less true that the development of economic institutions and the course of economic legislation are always the outcome of the progress of thought concerning the phenomena of wealth. Even individual theorists may exert a striking influence on subsequent economic legislation. Adam Smith prepared the way for the triumphs of *laisser faire* which culminated in the repeal of the Corn Laws; and the reform of the English Poor Law in 1834 was largely due to the direct and indirect influence exerted by the writings of Malthus.

The reciprocal influence exerted by facts upon theories constitutes a further fundamental reason why the history of economic doctrines cannot be divorced from that of actual economic phenomena. The theories of any period are almost always based at least partly

[1] Blanqui fails to make the distinction sufficiently clear when he describes the history of political economy as "a summary of the experiments which have been made amongst civilised nations to improve the lot of mankind." Political economy, even if regarded as fundamentally an art, is not properly to be identified with economic legislation.

upon assumptions that have a special application to the actual circumstances of that period. With every change in economic conditions fresh problems arise for solution, and the solutions offered cannot but be to some extent affected by the contemporary current of events. No writer can altogether free himself from the characteristic influences of his age and country; nor is it desirable that he should do so. It follows that the theories of the past cannot be properly understood, or their validity fairly estimated, unless they are taken in connexion with the actual phenomena that were at the time attracting attention, and helping to mould and colour men's views.

As a simple example of the interaction of facts and ideas, the contempt expressed by Xenophon and other ancient writers towards the manual arts, with the one exception of agriculture, may be connected with the circumstance that in ancient communities manual labour was to a very great extent performed by slaves. At the same time, this contempt would naturally tend to perpetuate the state of things which up to a certain point accounted for it.

Another example is to be found in the strong moral feeling that existed in the Middle Ages against the taking of interest. Under modern economic conditions individuals, as distinguished from nations, borrow mainly in order that they may make a profit. But in the eleventh and twelfth centuries the field for the investment of capital was limited, and for the most part recourse was had to the money lender only in circumstances of misfortune or special need. Hence the taking of interest naturally presented itself in a different aspect from that in which we are now wont to regard it. It should, however, be added that while the theory of the immorality of interest was relatively justified, many of the arguments adduced in support of the theory were as fallacious in reference to the economic conditions of the Middle Ages or any other period, as they would be in reference to existing economic conditions. The actual prohibitions of the Church against usurious practices were also in some cases apparently pushed beyond the point which the circumstances of the time are likely to have rendered expedient; as, for instance, when wholesale merchants were forbidden to make a difference between cash prices and credit prices in their dealings with retail traders; for it seems clear that in this case credit would usually be taken with the object of making a trade profit. As a matter of fact, however, the prohibitions were constantly evaded by means of ingenious legal fictions; and it is probable that they were seldom really operative except in cases where they had some practical utility.

The Mercantile System and the doctrines of the

Physiocrats have been clearly shewn by recent historians to have been the natural products of the times and circumstances in which they respectively arose. The need of reading particular economic works in the light of contemporary phenomena has also been copiously illustrated by reference to our three great English economists, Adam Smith, Malthus, and Ricardo. A word or two may be said here in regard to the last of the three only, whose doctrines, sometimes spoken of as pure abstractions, had in reality a special relation to the facts that came under his observation.

As observed in a previous chapter, the main condition essential to the correct understanding of Ricardo is the precise determination of the assumptions upon which his reasoning proceeds. What these assumptions are, however, the reader is usually left to his own ingenuity to discover. Ricardo himself never explicitly formulated them—probably because they seemed to him in no sense arbitrary abstractions, but patent facts to which it was unnecessary specially to call attention. The reason of this is to be found in his personal circumstances, and in the general economic conditions of his time. His fundamental assumption is the operation of thoroughgoing uncontrolled competition; and this may, in the first place, be connected with his position in the City, and on the Stock Exchange,—a market that may be taken as a type of the theoretically

perfect market, where competition is unceasing, and
supply and demand all powerful. Ricardo's personal
surroundings are, however, comparatively unimportant
from our present point of view. What is really of
importance is that he wrote at a moment when in
the industrial world itself, so far as internal trade was
concerned, the principle of competition was very active
and self-assertive. Old statutes that sought to regulate
industry were giving way before it. No Factory Acts
had yet been passed. Trade combinations of workmen
were still illegal. The industrial revolution of which
Adam Smith hardly saw the commencement was in
progress; and in the general movement caused by it,
the subtle hindrances to competition which were still
in operation were the more easily overlooked.

Ricardo has frequently been represented as laying
down the "iron law" that wages cannot permanently
rise above what is sufficient to provide the bare necessaries of life. He explicitly recognises, however, that
the "natural price of labour," even when estimated
in food and necessaries, is not absolutely fixed and
constant. "It varies," he says, "at different times in
the same country, and very materially differs in different
countries. It essentially depends on the habits and
customs of the people."[1] At the same time, in the
course of his reasonings, e.g., in his treatment of taxes

---

[1] *Principles of Political Economy and Taxation* (McCulloch's
edition), p. 52.

on raw produce, he constantly assumes that the working classes have so low a standard of comfort, that an alteration in the price of necessaries must very quickly react upon the nominal rate of wages. This assumption may be taken in connexion with the deterioration in the state of the working classes at the beginning of the nineteenth century,—a deterioration due mainly to the industrial revolution and the demoralizing conditions under which poor relief was administered, supplemented by the Napoleonic wars and an extraordinary series of bad harvests.

A minor assumption involved in many of Ricardo's reasonings is that all the agricultural produce consumed in a country is grown in the country itself. This again was a natural assumption to make at a time when, except in years of scarcity, the importation of wheat was virtually prohibited. Even had free trade seemed within the range of practical politics, Ricardo could not have anticipated that the development of the wheat-producing capacities of North America and India, combined with the discovery of cheap and rapid means of transit, would ever bring about a condition of affairs in which England would import nearly twice the quantity of wheat and flour that she produced for herself. Such a state of things, even if its possibility were contemplated, would seem so remote from facts as to make its economic consequences not worth discussing.

NOTES TO CHAPTER IX.

A. ON THE LIMITS OF THE VALIDITY OF ECONOMIC DOCTRINES.

§ 1. *The relativity of concrete economic doctrines.*—By some of the older economists, for example, Senior, political economy was regarded as a system of doctrines possessing universal validity. The science was declared to belong to no one nation and to no one country; wages, profits, and other economic phenomena were held to be governed by immutable laws comparable to the law of gravitation. De Quincey's eulogy of Ricardo may serve as an illustration. "Previous writers," he says, "had been crushed and overlaid by the enormous weights of facts, details, and exceptions; Mr Ricardo had deduced, *à priori*, from the understanding itself, laws which first shot arrowy light into the dark chaos of materials, and had thus constructed what hitherto was but a collection of tentative discussions into a science of regular proportions, now first standing upon an eternal basis."[1]

This claim to offer something unconditional and true in the same way for all times, lands, and nationalities,

[1] *Confessions of an English Opium-Eater* (edition of 1856), p. 255.

is termed by Knies the *absolutism of theory*[1]. He considers that it is countenanced as a tacit assumption by some writers who would not perháps defend it on principle; and in opposition to it, he and other economists of the historical school affirm the *relativity* of economic doctrines. On the ground that the economic phenomena of each age and each community are subject to special laws, an absolute system possessing universal validity is regarded as necessarily an impossibility; every people and every epoch are considered to have a political economy of their own more or less peculiar to themselves. The idea of the relativity of economic doctrines follows indeed immediately from the conception of economic life as exhibiting continuous organic growth, and this conception is itself the natural outcome of historical study[2].

---

[1] While sometimes using the phrase *cosmopolitanism* of theory in much the same sense as absolutism, Knies points out that it is not strictly speaking sufficiently broad in its signification. This phrase indicates the disregard of the special conditions given by territorial differences and differences of nationality, but it fails to indicate the disregard of distinctions brought about by differences of time— whether in the case of one and the same people or of all peoples. To express this second element in absolutism of theory, the term *perpetualism* is suggested. *Die politische Oekonomie vom geschichtlichen Standpunkte*, 1883, p. 24.

[2] Richard Jones and Frederick List are to be regarded as important forerunners of the historical movement rather than as themselves typical representatives of the movement itself. What is most characteristic, however, in their teaching is the insistance upon relativity in two particular spheres. Jones specially insisted on the limited applicability of the Ricardian theory of rent as regards both place and time. A theory based on the assumptions of individual ownership and freedom of competition could not, he pointed out, apply to oriental states of society in which joint ownership is the

It is to be added that the affirmation of the relativity of economic doctrines is not confined to the historical school. Mr Bagehot, who was an economist of an essentially conservative type, expressly limits the science to a single kind of society, "a society of grown-up competitive commerce," such as existed in England in the nineteenth century. His object is, however, just the reverse of that of the historical school. The aim of the historical school is to concentrate attention on economic history and on the study of economic development as opposed to the study of economic relations in a given society. Bagehot, on the other hand, seeks to concentrate attention on current economic phenomena, and to avoid the distraction that must result from turning aside to the superficially corresponding but yet essentially different phenomena of earlier epochs.

In the discussion of the question here raised, the distinction between abstract and concrete economics rises into

rule and rents are regulated by custom, nor even to those instances nearer home in which land is held on a customary tenure, as in the métayer system. Similarly, as regards limitation in time, he shewed that the Ricardian law could not hold good in a condition of affairs such as existed in medieval economy, where land was to a great extent held in common, and the relations between the owners and the tillers of the soil were not controlled by free competition. List based his defence of protective duties on the recognition of relativity in another sphere. He held that all civilised communities of the temperate zone pass through successive economic stages, and that for any given community at a given time the solution of the problem of protection *versus* free trade depends upon the stage of development that has been reached. The principle of relativity in the sphere of economics was expressed in a more general form by Roscher, and still more definitely by Knies, as indicated above (see also note B to this chapter, pages 317, 319).

importance. The former may at any rate be regarded as an *instrument* of universal application. It discusses principles that are universal in the sense of pervading all economic reasoning. To this point we shall return presently. Confining our attention in the meantime to concrete economic doctrines, it may be said that their relativity follows immediately from the realistic conception of this portion of the science adopted in an earlier chapter. It is as true of economic conditions, as of social conditions in general, that they are ever subject to modification. They vary with the legal form of society, and with national character and institutions.

Even where the forces in operation are the same, the relative strength that should be assigned to each may vary indefinitely. Law, custom, competition, combination, are agents in determining the distribution and exchange of wealth, no one of which is probably at any time altogether inoperative[1]. But the extent of their influence, and the

---

[1] Just as in modern industrial societies, where competition is the dominant force, some values are nevertheless regulated by law or custom (*e.g.*, parliamentary railway fares, lawyers' fees), so in more primitive societies, where custom is the most powerful influence, competitive prices are not altogether unknown. Sir Henry Maine in his *Village Communities*, Lecture vi, gives several instances of competitive prices existing side by side with customary prices. There are cases, for example, where members of the same group never think of trading together upon commercial principles, but where dealings between members of different groups are entirely unshackled by customary rule. There are also cases where "natives of India will pay willingly a competition price for one article, when they would think it unjust to be asked more than a customary price for another. A man who will pay the price of the day for corn collected from all parts of India, or for cotton-cloth from England, will complain if he is asked an unaccustomed price for a shoe."

manner is which it is exerted, are constantly varying; and such variations are always of importance as affecting the relevancy of economic doctrines in relation to actual economic phenomena.

Not much needs to be said in illustration of the above statements. It has become a commonplace that many modern economic theories have little or no direct application to medieval Europe. The contrasts presented by medieval and modern societies, and by contemporary Oriental and European societies, considered in their economic aspects, are indeed such as can hardly be overlooked[1]. As regards the former of these contrasts, Cliffe Leslie puts the case very forcibly in brief compass,—"The structure and phenomena of medieval society in Germany, as elsewhere, were far from suggesting an economic theory based on individual interest and exchange. Common property in land, common rights over land held in severalty; scanty wealth of any kind, and no inconsiderable part of it in mortmain, or otherwise intransferable; labour almost as immovable as the soil; production mainly for home consumption, not for the market; the division of labour in its infancy, and little circulation of money; the family, the commune, the corporation, the class, not individuals, the component units of society: such are some of the leading features of medieval economy."[2] The Ricardian law of rent, in

---

[1] Less striking contrasts, but contrasts that ought not to be neglected, are observable when we consider different modern communities of the European type in respect of particular economic phenomena, such as the tenure of land, the mobility of labour, and so forth. On this point see also pp. 309, 10.

[2] *Essays in Political and Moral Philosophy*, 1888, p. 84.

the ordinary form in which it is stated, may be taken as a special example. Every economist recognises that this law does not apply universally, although the physical fact of different returns to different doses of capital may remain[1].

It must not, indeed, be supposed that current economic theories are wholly inapplicable to earlier periods of history. Instances of their applicability have been given in the preceding chapter. Dr Cunningham draws a clear distinction in this respect between market prices and rents. "Many of the phenomena of medieval industrial life," he remarks, "were governed by conditions precisely similar to those which operate now; competition was quite as real, though there was more 'friction, and its action was less obvious. Market prices of all kinds, such as the price of wool or of herrings, were determined by supply and demand as truly as now, and none of the frequent efforts to interpose barriers could alter the forces at work, though they might affect the rate of their operation. But with rents it was different; free competition and market rates did not control agricultural operations as they do now, and the theory which rightly assumes them for the present day does not serve to explain the variations of medieval rents."

The following statement may be quoted as an example of the tendency to over-estimate rather than to under-estimate the relativity of economic doctrines. "The middle ages," says Dr Seligman, "were a period of customary, not of competitive prices; and the idea of permitting agreements to be decided by the individual preferences of vendor or

---

[1] Compare pp. 312, 13.

purchaser was absolutely foreign to the jurisprudence of the times. The 'higgling of the market' was an impossibility simply because the laws of the market were not left to the free arbitrament of the contracting parties. It would have seemed preposterous for the producer to ask as much as he could get, or, on the contrary, to demand less than his neighbour, and thus undersell him."[1] Professor Rogers has, however, shewn that "producers were very acute during the middle ages, and for the matter of that, buyers, too, in doling out their supplies to the market, or in making purchases, according to their interpretation of the amount in hand or available for sale. The most critical sales of the year were those effected in early summer, when the amount of the last year's produce was known pretty correctly, and the prospects of the ensuing harvest could be fairly guessed."[2] This brings out a point that is of considerable importance in the operation of the law of supply and demand, namely, the manner in which estimates of future supply influence the amounts immediately demanded by purchasers and those immediately offered for sale by vendors. Take, again, the following reference to the price of iron in the fourteenth century, as a simple instance of the effect of demand on price. "A very dry summer caused much wear and tear of implements, and consequently an increased demand and a higher price; so that the bailiff's accounts frequently mention the 'dearness of iron on account of drought.'"[3]

[1] *Science Economic Discussion*, p. 6.
[2] *Six Centuries of Work and Wages*, p. 144.
[3] Ashley, *Economic History*, vol. i., p. 36. Professor Ashley in a lecture on the study of Economic History (*Surveys Historic and*

Again in regard to contemporary economic phenomena of a different type from our own, although prices may appear to be wholly under the influence of custom, competition may still operate in a disguised form—a change in the quality of the goods sold taking the place of a change in price. Sir Henry Maine indicates that in the more retired villages in the East, where the artificer who plies an ancient trade still sells his wares for the customary prices, he is prepared to change their quality under conditions which in the West would lead to a change in price[1].

Still, whilst it is an exaggeration to regard doctrines based on the hypothesis of competition as wholly inapplicable to the past or to oriental societies at the present time, it is strictly true that such doctrines can never be safely applied without special enquiry and the most careful investigation of economic conditions.

And the progress of society does not merely affect the solution of old economic problems; it also gives rise to new ones. There are many doctrines relating to complex problems of money, credit, international trade, and the like, that can apply only to advanced economic societies. In relation to earlier states of society these doctrines are not so much false as irrelevant.

Economic, p. 12) observes in criticism of the use here made of this quotation, "Surely the power of tracing so obvious a connexion between phenomena demands nothing more than plain common sense." Granted that this is so, however, it seems in no way to affect the appropriateness of the instance in relation to the particular point at issue. The question raised in the text does not turn on the nature of the proof of the law connecting changes in price with changes in demand, but simply on the range of the application of the law.

[1] *Village Communities*, pp. 190, 1.

The above remarks relate to economic theorems. The recognition of the relativity of economic maxims is even more imperative; and, as suggested in an earlier chapter, unless we carefully distinguish the theorems from the maxims, we shall naturally be led to exaggerate the relativity of the former. In theoretical investigations hypothesis and abstraction are often indispensable; but when we apply our theory with the object of laying down rules of practice, it is desirable to have recourse to hypothesis and abstraction but sparingly. It is indeed doubtful whether, in the examination and criticism of particular economic institutions and policies, we can advantageously carry our abstraction even to the stage of neglecting social and political considerations of an altogether non-economic character. But the bearing of such considerations, even more than of purely economic considerations, will vary with the circumstances of different nations and different ages. Hence a given economic policy can in general be recommended only for nations having particular social and economic surroundings, and having reached a certain stage of economic development. It may be possible to formulate as having universal validity certain negative precepts, namely, that certain lines of action cannot in any circumstances be advisable; but on the whole the principle of relativity may be accepted with little qualification so far as economic precepts are concerned.

Legislation directed against speculative dealings in any commodity may be mentioned as a simple instance of the relativity of economic politics. The expediency of such legislation depends largely on the extent to which the economic conditions of place or time render it possible for

individuals or combinations to succeed by speculative purchases in gaining an effective control over the whole supply
of the commodity[1]. Speaking more generally, we may say
that the less favourable the conditions to the maintenance
of thoroughly effective competition, the more expedient
become legal interferences with competition. Thus the
justification of the Assize of Bread and Ale, and other
similar medieval laws regulating prices, is to be found in
the probable failure of competition in the case of retail
exchanges. The aim was merely to ensure—what really
effective competition would of itself have brought about—a
correspondence between retail prices and variations in the
price of the raw material.

§ 2. *Undesirability of limiting political economy to the
theory of modern commerce.*—The recognition of the relativity of economic doctrines led Mr Bagehot, not to the
adoption of the historical method in any form, but to the
limitation of political economy to "the theory of commerce,
as commerce tends more and more to be when capital
increases and competition grows." Mill is criticized for
"having widened the old political economy either too much
or not enough." "If it be," says Bagehot, "as I hold, a
theory proved of, and applicable to, particular societies
only, much of what is contained in Mr Mill's work should
not be there; if it is, on the contrary, a theory holding
good for all societies, so far as they are concerned with
wealth, much more ought to be there, and much which is
there should be guarded and limited."[2]

A good many reasons may be urged against adopting

[1] Compare Ashley, *Economic History*, vol. i., p. 187.
[2] *Economic Studies*, pp. 19, 20.

a definite limitation of political economy such as is here indicated. It is true that the modern economist will formulate principally a doctrine that applies to the economic world in which he finds himself; he will frequently select assumptions that hold good only in such a world; and wherever this is the case, it is essential that it should be carefully borne in mind. But we need not work with one and the same set of assumptions throughout. We may investigate the economic phenomena of more societies than one; and we shall find that the application of our doctrines has to be narrowed or may be widened according to circumstances. While some of our conclusions may be true only of the more advanced countries of the world, and that only in the present stage of their development, others may have a far more extensive application, or may at any rate require to be only slightly modified in order that this may be the case. It is probably true that the law of supply and demand directly applies to some classes of exchanges in almost every state of society; and there are many other laws to which a very wide range of application may be given, e.g., Gresham's law—that bad money drives out good money. Moreover, the wider the range of our investigations the more complete and serviceable is likely to be our knowledge of the present[1].

Mr Bagehot speaks of the periods preceding the modern commercial era as *pre-economic*[2]; but this conception is

---

[1] It has been shewn in the preceding chapter that certain theories of prices and wages may be very well exemplified by statistics of the fourteenth and fifteenth centuries. But the England of that period was certainly not an example of a modern industrial society.

[2] *Economic Studies*, p. 65.

open to criticism. Granted that in ancient Greece and Egypt, in feudal Europe, in the village communities of India and Ceylon which still survive, the phenomena of wealth are found to be in many vital respects different from those of modern Europe, and to be partially at least governed by different laws; still they remain economic phenomena, and—except in so far as adequate data are unattainable—it is not beyond our power to investigate them. We are compelled to recognise eras of varying economic types, and the existence of primitive societies in which industrial organization is but rudimentary; but until we find an age or a society in which exchanges— even in a disguised form—are unknown, and appropriated wealth does not exist, we have not in a strict sense reached the pre-economic.

We are told, for instance, how in the village community of Ceylon the craftsman "exchanges the results of his handiwork and specially acquired skill against a share of the produce on the threshing-floor of his neighbours."[1] The exchange takes place without the intervention of any medium of exchange, and is regulated by custom, not by competition. Nevertheless it is an economic phenomenon of a kind that the economist ought not to neglect. Sir Henry Maine has pointed out, further, how the importance of studying the economic phenomena of the East is increased by the fact that in the midst of striking diversity, they nevertheless do resemble in many respects the economic phenomena of the West. "If Englishmen settled in India," he remarks, "had found there kinds of property

---

[1] Sir J. B. Phear, *The Aryan Village in India and Ceylon*, p. xvi.

such as might be attributed to Utopia or Atlantis, if they had come upon actual community of goods, or an exact equality of all fortunes, or, on an exclusive ownership of all things by the State, their descriptions would at most deserve a languid curiosity. But what they found was very like, and yet appreciably unlike, what they had left at home. The general aspect of this part of social mechanism was the same. There was property, great and small, in land and moveables; there were rent, profits, exchange, competition; all the familiar economical conceptions. Yet scarcely one of them exactly corresponded to its nearest Western counterpart. There was ownership, but joint ownership by bodies of men was the rule, several owner-ships by individuals was the exception. There was the rent of lands, but it had to be reconciled with the nearly universal prevalence of fixity of tenure and the consequent absence of any market standard. There was a rate of profit, but it was most curiously under the influence of custom. There was competition, but trade was conducted by large bodies of kinsmen who did not compete together; it was one large aggregate association which competed with another."[1]

A further reason for not accepting Bagehot's conception of political economy is that it is impossible so to limit the science that all its concrete doctrines shall be relative to precisely the same condition of society. It cannot be said of the modern commercial world itself that it is a fixed and stationary state of society, subject no longer to variation or modification. The economic condition of the United

[1] *The Effects of Observation of India on Modern European Thought,* Rede Lecture, 1875.

States to-day is not the same as that of England—the
postulate, for instance, of the free mobility of labour from
place to place and from occupation to occupation is probably more fully realised in the former country than in the
latter; nor is the economic condition of England—in
regard, for instance, to the tenure of land—the same as
that of France. Still more striking is the contrast between the economic England of the twentieth century
and the economic England of Adam Smith's time. Even
in the commercial era, therefore, it is necessary carefully
to examine the applicability of our premisses, and to
recognise still a relativity. As a matter of fact, there
is comparatively little risk of our misapplying modern
economic theories to savage or oriental states of society.
It is when we come nearer home that the danger of the
undue extension of economic doctrines is the greater; and
that danger is at least not diminished by Bagehot's conception of a transcendently economic era, in regard to
which it may be supposed that the application of economic
theories is absolute, needing no qualification.

§ 3. *In what sense universality may be claimed for the
principles of abstract economics.*—The relativity of concrete
economic doctrines does not establish the impossibility of
an abstract theory having a certain character of universality; and it remains to be indicated in what sense
universality may still be claimed for the principles of
abstract economics.

In the first place, abstract economics analyses the
fundamental conceptions of the science, such as utility,
wealth, value, measure of value, capital, and the like. It
has been pointed out in an earlier chapter that even the

definitions of political economy may sometimes be relative or progressive. But in the analysis of such conceptions as the above it is not too much to look forward ultimately to a certain finality. It has been already observed that if the conceptions take on a somewhat different character in different connexions, we shall at least find something that is generic and universal in each one of them; and a consideration of them in their general character will be a valuable preliminary to more concrete economic enquiries.

Abstract economics next proceeds to discuss certain fundamental principles that are universal in the sense of pervading all economic reasonings. One of these principles is the law of the variation of utility, which is the key-note of Jevons's principal additions to the science. This principle applies not only to material commodities determining the law of demand for them, but also to services; and hence it is of the greatest importance in the whole theory of distribution. Thus, other things being equal, the aid which a dose of capital of a given description can render to the labour with which it is co-operating diminishes as the number of doses is increased; similarly, other things being equal, the aid which a unit of labour of a given kind can afford to capital, and to the other kinds of labour which it is assisting, diminishes as the number of units is increased. The truth of this elementary principle is quite independent of social institutions and economic habits, though the results which it actually brings about may vary considerably. Another principle of a similar character is that, other things being equal, a greater gain is preferred to a smaller; or, as we may put it, every man so far as he is free to choose will choose the greater apparent good[1].

On the basis of its analysis of fundamental conceptions, assisted by principles such as the above, abstract economics is enabled to draw certain negative or formal inferences which possess the character of universality. As, for instance, that a general rise in values is impossible; that if two kinds of commodities have the same law of utility, that which is the rarer will be the more valuable; that of different methods of production which can be used for obtaining a given result, the one that can do the work the most cheaply will in time supersede the others[2]; that facilities of transport tend to level values in different places, while facilities of preservation tend to level values at different times. In the same category may be placed such propositions as that no commodity or service can serve as a universal measure of value between different times and places, and that general over-production in a literal sense is impossible.

We have already spoken of the relativity of the Ricardian law of rent as ordinarily stated. But compare with this the principle of economic rent in its most abstract and generalised form. The Ricardian law, so far

[1] It is of principles such as these that Jevons is probably thinking when he remarks that "the first principles of political economy are so widely true and applicable, that they may be considered universally true as regards human nature" (*The Future of Political Economy, Fortnightly Review*, vol. xxvi., p. 624); and again, "the theory of the science consists of those general laws which are so simple in nature, and so deeply grounded in the constitution of man and the outer world, that they remain the same throughout all those ages which are within our consideration" (p. 625).

[2] This is one form of the important Law of Substitution.

as it claims to determine the actual payments made by
the cultivators of the soil, is a relative doctrine, that is
to say, it is based on assumptions, which, as regards both
time and place, hold good over a limited range only. The
theory of economic rent in its most generalised form,
however, merely affirms that where different portions of
the total amount of any commodity of uniform quality
supplied to the same market are produced at different
costs, those portions which are raised at the smaller costs
will yield a differential profit; and there is now no similar
limitation to its applicability. This principle may even
be said to hold good in a socialistic community, for the
differential profit does not cease to exist by being ignored
or by being municipalised or nationalised.

In this way may be built up a system of general
theorems relating to economic phenomena which, with
due modifications, are applicable under widely different
conditions. It has to be admitted that the body of doctrine thus built up is mainly hypothetical in character;
that is, it will not by itself enable us to lay down definitely
the laws according to which wealth is distributed and
exchanged in any given society. In order to determine
the latter, we have further to take into account the special
conditions under which the general principles operate; and
such conditions are indefinitely variable. But what is
here maintained is that the abstract theory is invaluable
as a preliminary study. The principles involved and the
modes of investigation employed have a significance and
importance which it would be misleading to call merely
relative; and the economist who would deal with the more
concrete problems of any particular age or state of society

cannot afford to neglect them. Thus, as we have already seen, there is a good deal of abstract reasoning in regard to the laws of supply and demand that has a very wide application indeed. These laws work themselves out differently under different conditions, and in particular there are differences in the rapidity with which they operate. Their operation may, however, be detected beneath the surface even in states of society where custom exerts the most powerful sway. And this would in all probability be overlooked were not our attention turned in the right direction by the method of analysis afforded by abstract economics.

B. On the Conception of Political Economy as a distinctively Historical Science.

It has been shewn in the preceding chapter that the study of economic history plays a distinct and characteristic part in the building up and perfecting of political economy There are many problems belonging to economic science whose solution must necessarily remain incomplete, apart from the aid afforded by historical research; and the historical method is, therefore, rightly included amongst the methods to which the economist ought to have recourse. Nevertheless economics is not to be considered, as some maintain, an essentially historical science.

This view is opposed to the doctrines of those more advanced members of the historical school who maintain that their method should supersede, and not merely supplement, other methods, and who seek to bring about thereby a complete transformation of political economy. A claim of this kind is sometimes put forth explicitly. Thus Cliffe Leslie treats the deductive and historical methods as necessarily antagonistic, and rejects the former on the ground that its professed solutions of economic problems are illusory and false. It yields, he says, "no explanation of the laws determining either the nature, the amount, or the distribution of wealth"; the philosophical method of political economy must, on the other hand, "be historical, and must trace the connexion between the economical and the other phases of national history."[1] From a similar point of view, Dr Ingram blames Jevons for seeking to "preserve the *à priori* mode of proceeding alongside of, and concurrently with, the historical." He adds that "the two methods will doubtless for a time coexist, but the historical will inevitably supplant its rival."[2]

Other writers, while professing that they do not entirely reject the deductive method, still set it contemptuously on one side as having already done all it can do, and played to the full its unimportant part in economic investigations. The necessity for a completely new departure is no less strenuously insisted upon. Even if the doctrines reached by the methods of the older economists possess a relative truth, they are, it is said, of little importance; and political economy can do fruitful work in the future only by taking on a new form and becoming a distinctively historical science. The abstract method, says Professor Schmoller, has degenerated into intellectual consumption;

---

[1] *Essays in Political and Moral Philosophy*, 1888, p. 189.
[2] *History of Political Economy*, pp. 232, 3.

the spring of its vitality is dried up.   A necessary revolution is in progress, whereby things are viewed from a totally different side—the historical.   "In the future a new epoch will come for political economy, but only by giving value to the whole historical and statistical material which now exists, not by the further distillation of the already-a-hundred-times-distilled abstractions of the old dogmatism."[1]

The extreme "historismus" of which we are now speaking is characteristic only of the more advanced wing of the historical school, and not of Roscher, who is usually regarded as its chief founder, or of its more moderate representatives such as **Wagner**, whose treatment of the whole subject of economic method is admirable[2].

Roscher, for instance, insists on the necessity of taking

---

[1] *Zur Litteraturgeschichte der Staats- und Sozialwissenschaften*, p. 279.

[2] See previous references to Wagner on pp. 27, 8, and elsewhere. Wagner is spoken of by a writer in the *Revue de Belgique* (15 April 1889) as *un déductif modéré*, and as such is contrasted with Schmoller, who is *un historique avancé*, with Menger, who is *un déductif intransigeant*, and with Brentano, who is *un historique modéré*.   He explicitly includes himself, however, amongst the representatives of the historical school of national economy in Germany; and the fact that he is nevertheless described as *un déductif modéré* may be considered a tribute to the judiciousness with which he combines rival methods, and holds the balance between them.   A moderate writer whose attitude is one of compromise is likely to be regarded as belonging to the one hostile camp or the other according to our own point of view.   There are in fact all shades of opinion among recent German economists who more or less sympathise with the historical reaction, and this makes it very difficult broadly to describe their position without doing injustice to some.   Even individual writers take up sometimes a more and sometimes a less extreme position.   In the present note we are purposely dealing only with the more extreme views of the more extreme writers.

into consideration the varying character of economic habits
and conditions, and attacks especially the fallacy of
criticizing economic institutions, regardless of a people's
history and the stage of social and industrial development
to which they have attained. But he neither effects nor
seeks to effect a complete transformation of political
economy. Whilst his chief treatise on the subject abounds
in historical and statistical illustrations, and is full of
information about the history of economic principles, the
doctrines taught in it follow in the main the orthodox
lines both in substance and in manner of exposition. He
even "has no doubt that the future will accord both to
Ricardo and Malthus their full meed of honour as political
economists and discoverers of the first rank."[1] This very
moderation of Roscher is, however, by some of his more
advanced followers made a subject of reproach. The
dogmatic and the historical matter in his *Principles* are
said to be juxtaposed rather than vitally combined; and
he is charged with not having been sufficiently under the
influence of the method which he himself was one of the
first to characterize[2].

In criticizing the conception of political economy as a
distinctively historical science the main difficulty consists
in understanding what the conception really amounts to.

---

[1] *Principles of Political Economy*, Preface.

[2] Knies deplores the fact that Roscher did not make stronger
steps forward after having taken up a position that promised so much.
He considers that the historical method, as exemplified by Roscher's
actual treatment, becomes historical description enlarged rather than
political economy set right. *Die politische Oekonomie vom geschicht
lichen Standpunkte*, 1883, p. 35.

It is far from being easy to gain a clear idea of the form to be assumed by economics when its "transformation" has been effected. Much that is said by the historical school consists of mere negative criticism; and on the positive side, there is often wanting an adequate discrimination between what really belongs to economic science, and what is no more than economic history pure and simple[1].

---

[1] Cliffe Leslie enumerates a number of problems which he asserts are left entirely unsolved by the deductive method; but most of these problems will be found to be of a purely historical character. On the other hand, when he comes to deal with theoretical questions, he himself constantly implies or presupposes the use of a deductive and *à priori* method of reasoning on fundamental points. For instance, "Only high profit can permanently support high interest, and low profit can afford only a low recompense to the lender of capital. The rate of profit determines in general both the maximum and the minimum of interest; the maximum must be below it, or the borrower would make nothing, and the minimum must not be so low as to drive the owners of capital to employ it themselves, instead of lending it, or to spend it" (*Essays*, p. 255). Again, "A falling-off in the foreign demand for British produce, such as is sometimes argued from the small proportion of exports, would have the opposite effect of diminishing the proportion of imports, by altering the equation of international demand to the disadvantage of Great Britain. A diminution of exports might result from hostile tariffs, but imports would fall off more. A good market abroad for our exports raises their value measured in foreign commodities, and swells the amount of goods given for them; while a declining demand in foreign countries would compel us to give more for our imports; the ratio of exports would increase, exporters would sell at ever-increasing disadvantage and diminishing profits" (p. 257). The doctrine here laid down appears to be based on Mill's theory of international values, which represents the deductive method in a somewhat high stage of development. Other typical instances, in which Cliffe Leslie employs the deductive method after the fashion of ordinary deductive economists, are cited by Professor Sidgwick in an article on *Economic Method* in the *Fortnightly Review* for February, 1879, pp. 304, 5. Compare also

According to Knies, the historical conception of political economy is based on the ideas of economic evolution and the relativity of economic doctrines. Economic institutions and economic theories are products of historical development. No given economic system can be final. It is itself the result of special conditions of time, place, and nationality; and as these vary, it will be subjected to progressive modifications. Every nation, therefore, and every age has a political economy of its own. Hence follows the denial that there are any absolute or universal economic laws. Every economic principle is relative to the particular phase of development to which a nation has at any given time attained. And so political economy resolves itself into a description of the various stages of industrial evolution, and the principles appropriate to each in turn[1].

The relativity of economic doctrines has been discussed in the preceding note; and only two remarks need be

—with reference to other economists of the historical school— Sidgwick, *Scope and Method of Political Economy*, pp. 35, 6.

[1] "In opposition to the absolutism of theory, the historical conception of political economy rests upon the fundamental principle that the theory of political economy, in whatever form we find it, is—like economic life itself—a product of historical development; that it grows and develops—in living connexion with the whole social organism—out of conditions of time, space, and nationality; that it has the source of its arguments in historical life, and ought to give to its results the character of historical solutions; that the laws of political economy should not be set forth otherwise than as historical explanations and progressive manifestations of the truth; that they represent at each stage the generalizations of truths known up to a certain point of development, and neither in substance nor in form can be declared unconditionally complete; and that the absolutism of theory—even when it gains recognition at a certain period of historical

made at this point in regard to the bearing of such relativity upon the question whether economics must be regarded as a distinctively historical science[1].

In the first place, the mere fact of a progressive evolution of industrial conditions by no means establishes the impossibility of general economic laws. There may be much that is common to the different stages of development; the same tendencies may be in operation in varying circumstances. Nothing more, therefore, than special modifications of the general laws may be requisite in order to suit special cases as they arise. It has been shewn that, notwithstanding the relativity of concrete economic doctrines, a certain character of universality belongs to the abstract theory of political economy.

In the second place, in so far as each epoch has a political economy peculiar to itself, the question still remains how that political economy is to be established. Hence, regarded as a system dealing primarily with the economic problems of our own age, no need is shewn for a transformation of the existing science. At most all that is necessary is the recognition that in regard to many of

development—itself exists only as the offspring of the time, and marks but a stage in the historical development of political economy" (*Die politische Oekonomie vom geschichtlichen Standpunkte*, 1883, pp. 24, 5). Knies allows abstraction and the deductive method a place in political economy, provided that they are employed with due precautions, and that the results obtained by their aid are empirically tested before being regarded as conclusively established (p. 499). The position granted to other methods than the historical remains, nevertheless, a very subordinate one.

[1] But see, further, the concluding paragraph of this note (p. 327), where the argument is turned the other way.

its doctrines, as ordinarily laid down, some limitation of their sphere of application is essential.

Professor Schmoller of Berlin goes further in the direction indicated by Knies, and in some of his utterances seems practically to identify economic science with the philosophy of economic history, or even with economic history itself in its broadest outlines. He holds that at the stage we have now reached we had better not attempt to formulate economic laws. We must rest content to work on at specific historical investigations, observing and recording actual economic phenomena, classifying them, and searching into their causes. There is an underlying implication that this search is likely to be successful, notwithstanding the alleged impossibility of formulating economic laws.

The denial that it is possible to arrive at economic laws seems, however, not intended to apply to laws of economic development. At any rate an express exception in regard to the latter is made by some extreme advocates of the historical method. While the changing nature of industrial conditions is insisted upon, it is held that the laws of these changes may be discovered, and that such laws will be universal in their character. Political economy is accordingly to be transformed into "a doctrine of the laws of the economic development of nations."[1]

Somewhat similarly, Professor Ashley—after remarking that among economists who employ the historical method there is 'considerable divergence of opinion as to the kind of results to be aimed at, and the shape political economy

[1] This was Hildebrand's ultimate object. Compare also Ingram, *History of Political Economy*, pp. 201 to 206; and Cliffe Leslie, *Essays in Political and Moral Philosophy*, pp. 83, 190.

should assume—expresses what may be taken for his own view as follows: "An increasing number—'the historical school' in the strict sense of the word—hold that it is no longer worth while framing general formulas as to the relations between *individuals* in a given society, like the old 'laws' of rent, wages, profits; and that what they must attempt to discover are the laws of social development —that is to say, generalizations as to the stages through which the economic life of society has actually moved. They believe that knowledge like this will not only give them an insight into the past, but will enable them the better to understand the difficulties of the present."[1]

Political economy is here resolved into a philosophy of economic history. It is held to be possible to determine economic laws; but such laws belong to a different sphere from that of the laws ordinarily formulated by economists. Two propositions have to be established in order to make good this position: first, that any theory of economic development must rest on an historical basis; secondly, that an economic science worthy of the name is an impossibility except in so far as it consists of a theory of economic development.

The first of these propositions would now meet with almost universal acceptance. It has been laid down in the preceding chapter that so far as any satisfactory theory of economic development can be formulated, its foundation must be sought principally in a direct appeal to history. Assistance may be derived from a comparison of European, oriental, and savage states of society at the present time;

[1] *English Economic History and Theory*, Preface.

but the main resource must be a comparison of successive states of society in the past. Whilst, however, the theory of economic development affords the most appropriate sphere for the employment of the historical and comparative method, it should be added that the function of establishing general laws of economic evolution is to be regarded as one which the method may fulfil in the future, rather than one which it has up to the present time gone very far towards fulfilling.

Passing to political economy, regarded as a statical science, the ultra-historical doctrine under discussion involves not so much its regeneration as its simple negation. We must not ask what new theories of value, rent, money, international trade, &c., are to replace those that it is sought to destroy. Such theories, we are told, it is "not worth while" to formulate; or rather, with the materials at present available, they cannot be formulated so as to be of any real utility or importance.

Positively to meet this attack would require a careful statement and detailed defence of particular economic laws, shewing not merely their hypothetical truth, but also their effective bearing on concrete economic phenomena. Such a defence of political economy cannot be attempted here. It must suffice to refer to the best contemporary treatises on the science. In examining, however, the claims put forward on behalf of the purely historical method, it is important to observe that if the impossibility of establishing economic laws throws us back upon specific historical investigations, still such investigations cannot in themselves constitute a science of political economy. Instead of economics being converted into a distinctively historical science, it is made to stand aside in order that economic history may take its place. The claim that the historical method shall dominate political economy resolves itself from this point of view into the assertion of the supreme and paramount importance of the work of the historian as compared with that of the theorist[1].

But we are told that the establishment of economic laws is only postponed. "It is by no means a neglect of theory," says Professor Schmoller, "but the necessary basis for it, if at times we proceed mainly in a descriptive manner. Only in so far as the descriptive material is defective are reproaches against this method justifiable."[2] Theoretical economists, however, have never denied that there is an ample field of work for economic historians, and they welcome any assistance in their own sphere of enquiry that historians may be able to afford. What they protest against is the view that besides the collection of descriptive material there is, in the present stage of economic knowledge, no useful work to be done. They protest also against the confusion of the descriptive material of a science with the science itself. As observed

---

[1] Professor Menger complains with considerable justice that the advocacy of the historical method in an extreme form does not arise out of the scientific needs of economists who are investigating the problems of their own science, but is rather forced on the science from outside. "The historians," he says, "have stepped upon the territory of our science like foreign conquerors, in order to force upon us their language and their customs, their terminology and their methods, and to fight intolerantly every branch of enquiry which does not correspond with their special method" (*Die Irrthümer des His-torismus in der Deutschen Nationalökonomie*, Preface).

[2] *Zur Litteraturgeschichte der Staats- und Sozialwissenschaften*, p. 279.

by Professor Sax, it cannot but be regarded as a thoroughly wrong idea to bid our age renounce the vocation of obtaining a satisfactory theory of political economy until such time as an incalculable number of investigations in the sphere of economic history shall have been completed[1].

Taking our stand simply on the necessity for scientific division of labour, it is better that those who are working in the field of economic theory should do what they can with the materials already available, rather than that they should occupy their time with researches that belong to the province of pure historians. The more thoroughly the historical enquiries are carried out the better; for thorough work in any department of economic study will be an assistance, not a hindrance, to workers in other departments. But there is work of more than one kind to be done.

Over and above any dispute, however, as to the most fruitful direction of enquiry in the particular stage of development that political economy has now reached, there is involved in the ultra-historical view an exaggerated idea of the sufficiency of the part that historical material can ever play in the building up of the science, and of the extent to which, without the aid of explicit theory, the historian can assign to phenomena their causal connexions. It has been already shewn that economic history itself needs to be interpreted by theory. Moderate advocates of the historical method, such as Arnold Toynbee, have clearly recognised that "without the help of deduction, this method can serve only to accumulate a mass of unconnected and

---

[1] *Das Wesen und die Aufgaben der Nationalökonomie*, p. 3.

unserviceable facts."[1] It follows that to postpone considerations of theory until an indefinite number of facts have already been collected is, even from the historical point of view, a mistake.

The case against the supremacy of the historical method in economics is all the stronger, if we regard the method as literally confining itself to the facts of past times. For the purely historical method is obviously much narrower than the inductive; and it will hardly be denied that the facts which are essential to the economist are to a very great extent obtained from contemporary observations or from records so recent that they have hardly yet passed into what we understand by economic history. Moreover, inferences based on historical research, as distinguished from observation of the present order of events, labour under special disadvantages. Often there is more or less uncertainty concerning the facts themselves. "History has suffered to drop from her pages, perhaps has never recorded, much of the information which would now be most precious to us"[2]; and an incomplete record may be even worse than no information at all, so far as affording a basis for theoretical conclusions is concerned. We see the past as it were through a mist; and we cannot "cross-examine its facts" as we often can the facts of the present time[3].

---

[1] F. C. Montague, *Arnold Toynbee* (Johns Hopkins University Studies in Historical and Political Science, Seventh Series, i. p. 33).

[2] Richard Jones, *Literary Remains*, p. 570.

[3] Compare Marshall, *Present Position of Economics*, § 17. Wagner also calls attention to the special caution that has to be exercised in appealing to historical evidence, just because the historical method "cannot grant a premeditated, to say nothing of an experimental,

It is still more important to observe that just because of the evolution of industrial systems, and the shifting character of economic conditions, upon which the historical school of economists so much insist, the study of the past is rendered the less serviceable for the solution of present-day problems. Upon many of these problems extremely little light is thrown by economic history that relates to an earlier period than the nineteenth century. How indeed can generalizations based upon one set of circumstances be safely applied to quite another set of circumstances? Not only may the problems calling for solution be novel in their character; there may even arise new industrial classes. With what classes in the fourteenth century, for example, are we to compare the modern factory operative and the modern capitalist employer? If, therefore, for no other reason than that institutions and habits and conditions change, another method of investigation than the historical must for very much of our economic work be essential. Political economy can never become a specifically historical science.

isolation of causes" (*Grundlegung der politischen Oekonomie*, vol. I., p. 223).

CHAPTER X.

ON POLITICAL ECONOMY AND STATISTICS.

§ 1. *The claims of statistics to be regarded as a distinct science.*—A leading German statistician has gone so far as to say that there are almost as many different views of the nature and province of statistics, as there are writers who have occupied themselves with the subject. Many different definitions of the term *statistics* have also been proposed; a list of 180, more or less differing from one another, was drawn up by Quetelet as long ago as 1869. Even the etymology of the term, or at all events the mode of its derivation from the Latin *status*, has been a matter of dispute[1].

---

[1] The correct account of the derivation of *statistics* seems to be that it came through the Italian *stato*, which was in the fifteenth century first used in the signification of territory, or "state" in the political sense. See Rümelin, article *Statistik* in Schönberg's *Hand-buch*, § 2; and Wappäus, *Einleitung in das Studium der Statistik*, p. 7. "Achenwall," says Professor Wappäus, "never in his writings explained the origin of the name *statistics*, but it comes out in his lecture-notes. His explanation is as follows. The Italians were the first to form a science of the State, and called it *Ragione di Stato*. From this—in Latin writings, and lectures given in Latin—arose *Ratio status*, or *Disciplina de ratione status*, or *Disciplina de statu*.

Only two or three views, however, such as are most
broadly distinguished from one another, need be noticed
here.

Gottfried Achenwall, professor of law and politics at
Göttingen about the middle of the eighteenth century,
though not the originator of the Latin adjective *statisticus*, appears to have been the first to use the German
substantive *Statistik*, and he is usually regarded as
the founder of statistics considered as a special branch
of knowledge[1]. He meant by statistics a collection of
noteworthy facts concerning States—the historical and
descriptive material upon which political science, as we
now understand it, is largely dependent. It is to be
added that as treated by the school of statisticians to
which Achenwall belonged—the so-called "descriptive"
school—statistics was not essentially numerical or
quantitative. Verbal description took the first place,
and figures were used merely as accessory thereto.

Since the time of Achenwall the term, as ordinarily
used, has changed its meaning, and the distinguishing

There being in classical Latin no simple expression for 'state' in our
sense, the word *status* was used with this meaning. The Italians at
the same time gave to any one learned in the above science or art
the name *statista*. German scholars adopted the word *statista* into
Latin, and formed the adjective *statisticus*."

[1] This view is not strictly correct, as Achenwall had predecessors
at the German universities (Conring, Schmeitzel, and others) whose
subject-matter and method resembled his own. His treatment was,
however, more thorough than theirs, and attracted more attention.

mark of statistics is considered to be the employment of numerical data[1]. Moreover, regarded as a science, statistics is not content to be merely descriptive, but claims to be theoretical and speculative. The principal question at issue is whether statistics can legitimately be regarded as constituting a distinct science at all. This question is complicated by the fact that, in addition to Achenwall's view, two very different conceptions of statistics as a science have been formed.

Statistical science is, according to Dr Mouat, "a special science of methods from which, and by which

[1] Statistics in this sense may be traced back to the "Political Arithmetick" of Sir William Petty, and other English writers of the seventeenth and eighteenth centuries; and the influence of Quetelet and Knies was important about the middle of the nineteenth century in favour of the arithmetical, as opposed to the descriptive, school. The latter still has some, though not many, adherents. The late Professor Wappäus of Göttingen, for example, in his *Einleitung in das Studium der Statistik*, published after his death in 1881, defends Achenwall's conception. He recognises that quantitative data have assumed a greater relative importance than formerly, but he ascribes this simply to the fact that they are now more easily procurable. "The increased facilities for obtaining numerical facts have," he says, "necessarily affected the method of statistics. We now have two equally important resources: description, and numerical expression. The two methods supplement one another, and it is a mistake to try to make two separate branches of science out of them. Misunderstandings have arisen about statistics, because demands have been made upon it, which cannot be fulfilled—demands only to be satisfied by a purely philosophical branch of study, which statistics is not. Statistics is a positive science, an aggregate of knowledge brought together for a practical end, namely, the knowledge of the concrete State. This is a very simple definition, and justified by the genesis and history of the science" (pp. 32—4).

alone, the natural laws can be deduced which govern most of the conditions of man, and many of those of the animal and vegetable kingdoms." "There is not," Dr Mouat adds, "a branch of human knowledge to which the science of statistics is not closely allied, and for the correct understanding of which the scientific marshalling of figures, and observation of aggregate facts, is not more or less necessary. That the laws deduced from them fall into the ranks of the branches of knowledge to which they belong when they are fairly established does not, in my humble judgment, invalidate the scientific claim of the agency to which they owe their existence."[1]

The concluding portion of the above statement would probably meet with universal acceptance. A method or an agency may, however, be scientific without thereby becoming itself a science. Statistics, or statistical method, as understood by Dr Mouat, is a very important means whereby human knowledge is extended; but as such it is to be regarded as a scientific instrument, rather than as an independent body of doctrine constituting a distinct science.

It is, indeed, necessary to recognise a theory of statistics, dealing with what may be called the technique of the statistical method, that is to say, the

[1] *History of the Statistical Science of London* (Jubilee volume of the *Statistical Journal*), p. 47.

conditions that statistical data must fulfil, the modes in which they are to be ascertained and collected, the manner of their arrangement and employment for purposes of reasoning, the criteria determining the validity of arguments based upon them, and the logical character of the conclusions established by their aid. But all this is really antecedent to the actual use of statistics for any particular purpose. The whole discussion constitutes, not a separate science, but a special branch or department of inductive logic or methodology—that is, of the science or art which treats of scientific method in general.

It is, however, in quite a different sense from the above that the existence of an independent science of statistics is affirmed by the majority of Continental statisticians, and also by some English writers[1]. Statistical science is regarded, not as an abstract science of methods dealing with phenomena of very various kinds under a distinctive aspect, but as a concrete science with a distinctive subject-matter. A distinction is clearly drawn between statistics as a method and

[1] Compare Mr Wynnard Hooper's paper on the *Method of Statistical Analysis* in the *Statistical Journal* for March, 1881; and the same writer's article on *Statistics* in the ninth edition of the *Encyclopaedia Britannica*. Mr Hooper himself takes the view advocated in the text, namely, that there is no independent science of statistics. The two views are sometimes spoken of as the English and the Continental respectively. There is not, however, universal agreement amongst Continental, any more than amongst English, writers on the subject.

statistics as a science. It is recognised that the method has a very wide application; but the science is described as studying exclusively man's social life.

As thus interpreted, statistical science becomes practically equivalent to sociology, with the implication that the sole means whereby sociological, including economic, knowledge can be attained is the systematic collection and inductive interpretation of social pheno- mena. There is the further implication that the data are mainly, if not exclusively, numerical.

Dr Mayr, taking this view, defines the science of statistics as "the systematic statement and explanation of actual events, and of the laws of man's social life that may be deduced from these, on the basis of the quantitative observation of aggregates."[1]

If it is asked why the quantitative observation of social aggregates should constitute a distinct science, while no similar claim is made in regard to the obser- vation of purely physical aggregates, the reply given is that in the determination of the laws of social life statistical enquiry is "the only possible mode of investigation," and not—as in the case of the physical sciences—a merely secondary or supplementary method.

---

[1] This definition is given in Dr Mayr's *Die Gesetzmässigkeit im Gesellschaftsleben*, an abridged translation of which will be found in the *Statistical Journal* for September, 1883 For definitions given by English statisticians, who take a similar view, see *Statistical Journal*, December, 1865, p. 492; and Jubilee volume, p. 8.

Social science and political economy are spoken of as branches or departments of the science of statistics, a science which studies social and economic phenomena in the only satisfactory way, namely, by the accumulation of facts and generalization from them. It will be observed that the doctrine here set forth is even narrower than that which regards induction as the sole valid method of economic enquiry. For we are now limited to *quantitative* induction; qualitative induction, whether historical or comparative, is out of place as well as the deductive method.

Our grounds for rejecting this view have been given in a previous chapter, and to pursue the discussion here would merely carry us back to a class of considerations that have been already sufficiently insisted upon. It may, however, be added that for the general science of society we have at any rate another name—sociology or social science—which does not beg the question as to method, and which is free from the ambiguity that at best must attach to the term statistics. For it has to be allowed that by this term is also meant a method of analysis having an indefinitely wide range of application outside the science of man in society. Thus we speak of moral and intellectual statistics, of vital and medical statistics, of astronomical and meteorological statistics, of physical and physiological statistics, as well as of economic and political statistics. It can hardly be said that there is any concrete department of enquiry, in which statistics as a method may not find a place; and it is upon this character of universality that the claim of statistical research to public recognition and encouragement is frequently based.

If a less extreme view than that above described is taken, and statistics is considered to be a distinct science, but nevertheless not to include the whole of social science or of economics, then it becomes a part which is only differentiated from the remainder by the employment of a particular method. Professor R. Mayo-Smith explicitly recognises statistical science as "a branch of social science employing a specific method, and devoting itself to those problems of life in society which can best be solved by that method."[1] It seems, however, both unusual and undesirable to differentiate sciences by their method as distinguished from their subject-matter. We might equally well identify other scientific methods with those particular sciences in the development of which they happen to be of special importance. At any rate the question now becomes little more than a verbal one. There need be no fundamental disagreement between those who take the view just indicated, and those who prefer to treat

[1] *Statistics and Economics* (Publications of the American Economic Association, vol. 3), p. 118. Professor Mayo-Smith divides social statistics into population statistics, economic statistics, and statistics of vice and crime.

statistics simply as a particular method or instrument of scientific enquiry, which is not peculiar to the study of social facts, although it may be of much greater relative importance in connexion with that study than in other departments of knowledge.

There seems, however, to be an idea that if the claim of statistics to recognition as a science be not admitted, then the statistician becomes a mere drudge, who is denied the luxury of opinions, and whose sole function is to collect materials for others to reason about and base theories upon. Professor Mayo-Smith's main ground for calling statistics a science is that this is the only way of rescuing the study from "the barrenness which results from viewing its object as simply the collection of masses of figures, with which the statistician has nothing further to do." He regards the question whether statistics is or is not a science as not a merely verbal one, because the answer to it determines "the position of the statistician and the authority with which he speaks."

By another writer it is said that if statistics is not a science, then the statistician is merely as one who binds up sheaves of wheat for others to thresh out[1]. But this by no means follows. There is, indeed, special risk of error when statistics are used by others than those who have prepared them. For, as Mr Hooper

[1] Dr Guy in the *Statistical Journal*, 1865, p. 483.

remarks, "there are usually 'pitfalls' even in the simplest statistical statement, the position and nature of which are known only to the persons who have actually handled what may be called the 'raw material' of the statistics in question." Hence the statistician rightly, and even necessarily, performs the function of interpreting results. But in so doing he becomes the economic statistician, the political statistician, the medical statistician, the physical statistician, as the case may be. He applies his statistics, that is to say, within the domain of some particular science; and it may be added that unless he has an adequate knowledge of that science, not only will he probably go astray in his interpretation, but the very facts themselves are not likely to be suitably selected or arranged.

But all this, it is clear, applies to medical and physical and other statistics, just as much as to social statistics; and no one would maintain that we have a distinct science, wherever we have a branch of knowledge in which statistics may be usefully employed. Hence if we go out of our way to recognise a science of statistics which is concerned with social phenomena alone, we seem thereby to cast an undeserved slur upon statistics used in other departments of enquiry. We may, on the other hand, refuse to recognise a distinct statistical science in any sense, without lowering the standard of what is required from statisticians, or in the slightest degree underrating the importance of the functions which they perform.

§ 2. *Statistics regarded as a method.*—In seeking to define statistics regarded as a method, it is convenient to adopt the somewhat clumsy phrase already quoted from Dr Mayr, and say that it is a scientific method based on the *quantitative observation of aggregates*. It is, in the first place, a method based on *observation*. It goes direct to facts, which it collects and systematically arranges. It is, in the second place, based on an observation of *quantities*. It deals with phenomena that are measurable, and hence capable of numerical expression. It is, in the third place, concerned with *aggregates*, as distinguished from individuals or units. Series of isolated numerical facts are popularly called statistics, and they may be of use simply as information or as means of description or illustration, but they are of little or no value as a scientific instrument. In the scientific use of statistics the observations must be made in the mass, they must involve a certain degree of continuity, and the resulting figures must be carefully and systematically grouped[1].

---

[1] The term *statistics*, when used as a singular noun, signifies the method above described, or—if we recognise such a science—the science of statistics (German, *die Statistik*; French, *la statistique*). In English, however, the term is generally used as a plural noun, and it then signifies the numerical data which constitute the basis of the statistical method.

By the aid of statistics, thus understood, we are enabled to employ the method of concomitant variations. In this way, quantitative inductions are established, and the laws of the variations of phenomena determined.

There is a close connexion between the statistical method and the doctrine of chances. On the basis of the quantitative observation of aggregates, the influence exerted in individual cases by accidental causes may be eliminated. For when instances are taken in the mass, it is often a fair assumption that accidental causes will operate so as to neutralise one another. The effects of agencies exerting a permanent influence on phenomena of a certain description can in this way be calculated, even though in any given individual case their influence may be slight and uncertain. The manner in which aggregate regularity is found to emerge out of individual irregularity, when instances are taken in sufficient number, has been one of the most striking results of statistical research. It was this fact that excited the enthusiasm of the Belgian mathematician Quetelet; and to his influence may be ascribed the impetus given to the study of statistics in the second quarter of the nineteenth century.

In the use of statistics, considerable assistance may often be derived from the employment of diagrams. The graphic method is not only useful for the popular

exposition of statistics, enabling the mind more accurately to realise numerical comparisons; but it has also
a genuine scientific value.   Thus by means of graphic
representation we may employ the special method of
quantitative induction called by Whewell the *method
of curves*[1].   The relative positions of curves can be

[1] The graphic method takes different forms.   Straight lines of
different lengths, for example, are sometimes used, and rectangles, or
triangles, or other geometrical figures, the relative size of which can
easily be compared.   Maps are also very serviceable as a popular
method of illustration, where the statistics relate to different geographical divisions.   Statistical maps are sometimes called cartograms, cartography being defined as "the employment of maps
for the graphic illustration of statistics."   The above forms have
not, however, the scientific value that belongs to the use of curves,
so drawn as to represent the manner in which the variations of
some given quantity are related to the variations of some other
quantity.   Whewell defines the method of curves as follows: "The
Method of Curves consists in drawing a curve, of which the
observed quantities are the Ordinates, the quantity on which the
change of these quantities depends being the Abscissa.   The efficacy
of this Method depends upon the faculty which the eye possesses, of
readily detecting regularity and irregularity in forms.   The Method
may be used to detect the Laws which the observed quantities follow;
and also, when the Observations are inexact, it may be used to correct
these Observations, so as to obtain data more true than the observed
facts themselves" (*Novum Organon Renovatum*, Aphorism xliv).   On
the graphic method of statistics in general, see a paper by Professor
Marshall in the Jubilee volume of the *Statistical Journal*; also
Dr D. R. Dewey's *Elementary Notes on Graphic Statistics*, Mr Bowley's
Elements of Statistics, Part I., Chapter 7, and the article on *Graphic
Method* by Mr A. W. Flux in Mr Palgrave's *Dictionary of Political
Economy*.   Practical examples of the employment of this method will be
found in Jevons's *Investigations in Currency and Finance*.   The use of
diagrams for statistical purposes should be clearly distinguished from
their employment in economic theory as discussed in a previous chapter.

more easily compared than columns of figures; and correspondences may thus be observed, and empirical laws suggested, that would otherwise have escaped attention. This is especially true when there are more than two series of phenomena whose mutual relations are made the subject of investigation. The mere saving of space may be a matter of importance. Several distinct curves can be placed in a single chart, and it thus becomes possible to grasp at one and the same moment a greater multiplicity of detail[1].

The use of curves also renders us less liable to be distracted by movements of a partial or temporary character. There are indeed cases, as pointed out both by Whewell and by Jevons, where diagrams to a certain extent supersede the taking of averages; for we may apprehend intuitively the *general course* of a curve, neglecting individual irregularities. A similar apprehension would generally speaking not be possible, or at any rate not equally reliable, were we limited to mere columns of figures[2].

[1] Care must be taken to render it easy to follow the course of the different curves without risk of their being confused one with another. They may be distinguished by form as well as by colour. Thus one curve may consist of an unbroken line, another of a broken line, another of a succession of dots, another of dots and dashes alternately, and so on.

[2] It should be added that whilst the graphic method of statistics is—for the reasons above stated—scientifically important, certain precautions are necessary in order to prevent the comparison of

§ 3. *The functions of statistics in economic enquiries.*—Cairnes lays it down that "the relation of statistics to political economy is in no respect different from that in which they stand to other sciences which have reached the deductive stage."[1] But this summary dismissal of the question cannot be accepted. In the first place, notwithstanding the importance of deduction in economics, the science cannot be regarded as having reached the deductive stage in the same definitive manner as those sciences with which an analogy is here suggested—for instance, physics and astronomy. Its premisses are less determinate than theirs, and greater prominence needs to be assigned to empirical confirmation and criticism. In the second place, although statistics ought not to be identified with sociology, the quantitative observation of aggregates is certainly of far greater relative importance in the social sciences than it is in the great majority of the physical sciences. In the latter—for instance, in optics or in electricity—so far as conclusions rest on an inductive

curves from proving deceptive. This is especially the case when we represent by curves the progress of phenomena, with a view to comparing their proportional rates of progress. Professor Marshall indicates the nature of the needful precautions in the paper referred to in the note on p. 340.

[1] *Logical Method of Political Economy*, p. 86. While the above is given as summing up Cairnes's view of the relation between statistics and political economy, some of his incidental remarks on the subject seem to indicate a less extreme position.

basis, it is usually a basis of experiment. Individual cases can be treated as typical; and where a repetition of trials is necessary, it is only in order to guard against error. The statistical method is important in special instances, *e.g.*, in meteorology, but generally speaking it occupies a subordinate position. In the social sciences, on the other hand, there is little room for experiment, while statistics play a part for which no substitute can be found. Political economy, in particular—being concerned pre-eminently with quantities, and with groups as distinguished from individuals —has a special tendency to become on its inductive side statistical, just as on its deductive side it tends to become mathematical.

To begin with, statistics are of paramount importance in economic enquiries in respect of their merely descriptive functions. For example, statistics of production and of wages and prices are essential elements in any complete description of the social condition of a community; statistics of exports and imports in the description of its foreign trade and intercourse with other nations; statistics of taxation and of national indebtedness in the description of its financial condition. This point is, however, so obvious that we need not dwell upon it, but may pass on to consider further uses of statistics in economic enquiries.

The functions of statistics in economic theory are,

first, to suggest empirical laws, which may or may not be capable of subsequent deductive explanation; and, secondly, to supplement deductive reasoning by checking its results, and submitting them to the test of experience. Statistics play a still more important part in the applications of economic science to the elucidation and interpretation of particular concrete phenomena.

We have seen that there are certain departments of economics in which we are compelled to content ourselves with empirical laws. In such cases we are usually concerned with aggregates, and can make little or nothing of individual phenomena taken by themselves. Our main reliance must, therefore, be placed upon statistics, which may be either historical or contemporary. An illustration is once more afforded by the Malthusian doctrine of population. Malthus himself made elaborate statistical enquiries concerning the proportion of yearly marriages to population; the fruitfulness of marriages in different countries; the effects of epidemics on births, deaths, and marriages; and so forth. He hence inferred that in favourable circumstances population tends to double itself in twenty-five years; and on a similar basis he estimated the effects of the various checks to population operating in the less civilised parts of the world, and in past times, as well as in the different States of modern Europe.

In this connexion it is once more necessary to point out the characteristic weakness of empirical generalizations. They may be true of a given state of society, but with the changes incident to the progress of time may become false. It is necessary, therefore, to keep as it were a watch upon them, and from time to time bring up to date the statistics upon which they are based. It is no exaggeration to say, as Sir Robert Giffen has said, that Malthus's statistical enquiries remain as valuable as ever. At the same time, further experience gained during the present century suggests certain qualifications in the statement of the Malthusian doctrine, and in some degree modifies the practical conclusions drawn from it.

Empirical laws need not, however, always remain such. Statistical investigations may suggest laws which can subsequently be established on a more or less satisfactory deductive basis. In other words, the observed uniformities may be referred to causes which are adequate to account for them, and which are shewn to be in operation. Thus the tendency of financial crises to recur at periodical intervals was not first worked out theoretically; it was disclosed by statistical observations, and theories to account for the cyclical movement were afterwards propounded. Another simple illustration is to be found in the autumnal drain on the Money Market.

Besides affording absolute additions to economic knowledge, statistics are of great value in enabling the deductive economist on the one hand to test and where necessary modify his premisses, and on the other hand to check and verify his conclusions. By means of statistics, also, he may sometimes roughly measure the force exerted by disturbing agencies.

Thus, Mr Bagehot appeals to statistics to test the legitimacy of the postulate that in modern industrial communities there tends to be a movement of labour from the worse paid to the better paid localities. He holds that patent statistical facts shew what may be called "the tides" of the people, the set of labour being steadily and rapidly from the counties where there is only agriculture and little to be made of new labour, towards those where there are many employ-ments and where much is to be made of it[1]. Statistics may, again, be called in to determine how far in a given state of society this tendency does actually result in an equality of wages, or how far there are other strong forces in operation which succeed in more or less counteracting it.

Another illustration is afforded by the functions of statistics in the controversy between free traders and protectionists. Statistics cannot by themselves decide this controversy, but they are of assistance in supple-

[1] *Economic Studies*, p. 22.

menting more abstract reasoning. The free trader, whilst basing his conclusions mainly on a deductive process, is bound to deal with all available statistics, shewing in what respects they bear out his theory, and in what ways any apparent inconsistencies may be accounted for[1].

Attention may especially be called to the part capable of being played by statistics in the solution of problems that are left theoretically indeterminate. Let us assume, for example, that, so far as theoretical considerations are concerned, it is left an open question whether temporary protection is desirable in order to establish in a country a new industry; that is to say, theory shews that such protection may under certain conditions be advantageous, but that it is not necessarily so. Statistics relating to protected industries in new countries may help us in dealing with this question generally, by shewing how far the conditions telling in favour of protection have as a matter of fact been

---

[1] Compare Lord Farrer, *Free Trade versus Fair Trade*, and Sir R. Giffen on the *Use of Import and Export Statistics* (*Essays in Finance*, Second Series). "Statistics," Sir Robert Giffen remarks, "though they cannot logically prove the affirmative in the direct issue between free trade and protection, from the difficulty of finding exactly parallel cases and eliminating other causes, may be used to prove negatively that there is nothing in the apparent facts to help the protectionist" (p. 223). In other of Sir R. Giffen's essays there are excellent instances of the mutual bearing on one another of statistics and deductive reasoning.

frequently realised, and in particular how far the protection has justified itself by its continuance being rendered after a certain stage unnecessary. Statistics may also help us specifically if we are considering the problem in relation to some particular case in which the adoption of a policy of temporary protection is contemplated[1]. There are many other cases in various departments of economics in which theory takes us up to a certain point, but in which the theoretical discussion needs to be supplemented by statistics if we are to reach a determinate conclusion.

If from considering how general theorems are to be established and tested we pass on to enquire how particular concrete problems are to be solved, we find that the aid to be derived from statistics is relatively even greater. There are many important problems of fact—especially where a comparison is instituted between different times or places, though not in this case alone—which are statistical in their very nature: for example, the enquiry whether during a certain period of years there has or has not been an appreciation in the value of gold; the comparison between the position of the labouring classes at different times; the analysis and explanation of a given depression of trade; the investigation of the relative

---

[1] Compare an article by Sir R. Giffen on *Protection for Manufactures in New Countries* (*Economic Journal*, March 1898, page 3).

pressure of taxation, under existing conditions, upon different classes of the community. A sound knowledge of theory is requisite for a satisfactory treatment of problems of this kind. Theory guides us in our selection of statistics, and teaches us how to turn them to the best account. But the data for the solution of the problems must necessarily be numerical.

In the majority of cases, moreover, aggregate regularity has to be evolved out of individual irregularity, and hence a special reason why we must deal with phenomena in the mass, and not individually. Thus— again taking as our examples the enquiries above referred to—if we compare prices now with prices at an earlier period, some will be found to have fallen, some to have risen; similarly if we compare wages now with wages a number of years ago; even in a year of depression some trades are found to be flourishing; the pressure of taxation varies in the case of different individuals in the same class. Averages must, therefore, be taken[1]; and it is clear that the essential conditions for the right solution of the problems are reliable statistics, and ability to use the statistics in a sound manner.

The right use of statistics is, indeed, far from being

[1] The importance of the taking of averages in statistical investigations cannot be exaggerated. This is so fully realised by some writers that one of the definitions proposed for statistics is the "science of averages."

a simple matter. Statistics, it is often said, can be made to prove anything. And if they are used without special knowledge, or grouped simply with the object of establishing a foregone conclusion, the charge is well founded. As against ignorant or prejudiced statisticians, or against the casual employment of a few figures picked up at random and regardless of what may be called their context, it is not difficult to defend the paradox that there is nothing more misleading than facts—except figures. For reasoning from statistics, in addition to the dangers which it has in common with all empirical reasoning, is subject to difficulties and dangers peculiar to itself[1]. If, however, the limitations of statistics are clearly recognised, if they are accurately collected over an adequate range, if they are employed without prejudice and after full enquiry into their true significance, and if they are fairly and properly grouped, then their value is unique, and the statistical method easily makes good its claim to rank as a most effective and reliable instrument of science.

[1] The nature of these difficulties and dangers is briefly indicated in the note following this chapter.

NOTE TO CHAPTER X.

On some of the Precautions requisite in the Use of Statistics in Economic Reasonings.

§ 1. *Conditions of the reliability of statistical data.*—
If arguments based on statistics are to be of any value,
particular attention must be paid to the following points:
(a) the sources from which the statistics are obtained,
with special reference to their reliability; (b) their true
meaning and significance; (c) their completeness or incompleteness as covering the whole range of the phenomena to
which they relate; (d) the manner of their grouping, with
special reference to the taking of averages. Each of these
points may be briefly considered in turn[1].

The initial difficulty in the use of statistics is the
possible inaccuracy of the original data. Statistics may be
obtained and published officially, or they may be collected
through private channels. Under the former of these conditions, the accuracy of the figures is sometimes practically

---

[1] In what follows I am specially indebted to Sir R. Giffen's *Essays
in Finance,* First and Second Series; to papers on Statistics by Pro-
fessor R. Mayo-Smith in the *Political Science Quarterly,* the *Quarterly
Journal of Economics,* and the *Publications of the American Economic
Association;* and to various papers in the *Journal of the Statistical
Society.*

unquestionable; as, for example, in the case of railway
traffic receipts. But this is by no means the universal
rule, even when official statistics are forthcoming. Thus
up to 1854 the values of imports into this country were
calculated at the prices of the end of the seventeenth
century. From 1854 to 1870 they were officially computed
according to the best information obtainable. At the
present time both imports and exports are in this country
valued according to the declarations of the importers and
exporters. The returns are of course checked by the officers
compiling the statistics; but still their accuracy depends to
a considerable extent upon the good faith and carefulness
of the consignees and exporting agents, who it is said are
often insufficiently instructed by their principals. The
chance of error is greater in some cases than in others. For
example, when goods are sent into the country to be sold
on commission, there is no available invoice of the same
definite character as when they are sent to order. Again,
the check exercised by the customs' officers is likely to be
more effective in the case of goods that are subject to a
duty than in the case of those that are non-dutiable.

The uncertainty attaching to the accuracy of statistics
is still greater when they are collected through private
channels. Wages statistics may be taken as a special
example. If they are obtained by the simple process of
writing to some individual in each district under investigation, and asking him to give the best information in his
power, they can hardly be of much practical value, unless
the sources of the informant's own knowledge are fully set
forth and are themselves capable of being tested. Both
employers and workmen are in danger of being more or

less unconsciously biassed by class prejudice or by consideration of the uses to which the information they afford may be put. Probably the best sources of information are the actual ledgers and pay-rolls of large establishments if recourse can be had to them, or records kept by trade societies primarily with a view to the enlightenment of their own members. When two or more sources of information are available, they will serve mutually to check one another.

It is of importance that access should be had to the ultimate data themselves, and not merely to calculations based upon them. For instance, knowledge of the actual wages paid to individuals, and the number of men employed at each rate, is of much greater value to the statistician than ready-made averages provided either by employers or workmen. This of course applies not only to wage-statistics, but to all statistics.

Where the statistics are obtained by the issue of blank forms of enquiry to be filled in by a large number of individuals, as in the case of census returns, the way in which the forms are drawn up may have a material effect on the accuracy of the answers. From this point of view the enquiries should be as simple as possible, and should be accompanied by clear instructions, so as to minimise the chance of unintentional or perverse mistakes on the part of those who have to answer them[1]. They should also be

---

[1] The chance of such mistakes is greater than would be imagined à priori. Thus, in the *General Report on the Census of* 1891, it is stated that the enquiry as to whether individuals were employers, employed, or working on their own account, was answered so imperfectly and often in so contradictory a way as to make the returns on this point quite untrustworthy.

framed in such a way as not to appear inquisitorial, and so as not to raise the idea that the information asked for may be used to the advantage or the detriment of the person making the return. Unless these conditions are satisfied the answers may be intentionally erroneous or incomplete It should be added that the answers to enquiries circulated in this way have to be tabulated and arranged before they properly constitute statistics, and that their value will very much depend on the method of tabulation adopted[1].

A distinction may be drawn between the *absolute* accuracy of statistical data, and their *relative* accuracy In some cases, while absolute accuracy may be unattainable, it may nevertheless be possible to institute quite reliable comparisons; and it is in the comparisons they enable us to make, not in the figures considered absolutely, that the value of statistics generally consists. In such cases relative accuracy is essential; the statistics should be collected on the same method, and in similar circumstances. If these conditions are fulfilled, error within certain limits need not be seriously misleading; for, in accordance with the doctrine of chances, it may be a legitimate assumption that the error will exert approximately the same proportional influence on each side of the comparison.

It follows that in comparing statistics of any kind for consecutive years, what is specially important is that no change shall have been made in the mode or circumstances of their collection or estimation[2]. For example, in com-

---

[1] For detailed illustrations of methods of collecting and tabulating statistics, compare Bowley, *Elements of Statistics*, pp. 23 to 106.

[2] Reference has been already made to the change in the mode of

paring income tax returns at different periods, it may be necessary to make allowance for improvements in the means adopted for preventing false returns. It should also be remembered that in consequence of changes in the rate of the tax, inducements to falsify statements of income may be increased or diminished.

In the case of official statistics, it is most desirable that on the occurrence of any change in methods of collection, the old method should for a few years be carried on alongside of the new. It can then be approximately calculated what allowance must be made for the change in comparisons involving periods before and after it.

A similar difficulty frequently arises when statistics of different nations are compared. There is, for instance, the greatest variety in the methods by which the values of exports and imports are calculated in different countries. It has already been mentioned that in England the practice is for values to be declared by exporters and importers. In most foreign countries, however, values are computed according to tables of prices officially drawn up[1]. With a

---

estimating the values of imports into this country that occurred in 1854, and striking instances could be quoted of errors due to ignorance or forgetfulness of this change.

[1] Again, "as regards the basis of valuation most European countries adopt the practice of valuing imports as they lie in the port of arrival, *i.e.*, including cost of freight, and exports at their value at the port of export, *i.e.*, excluding cost of freight. The United States, however, presents an exception to this practice as regards imports, which are valued according to the invoice values declared by the importers at the port of shipment, *i.e.*, excluding the cost of freight." Further difficulties are caused by the divergent methods of classifying articles of import and export which are adopted by different countries. See a paper on the *Comparability*

view to international comparisons, statisticians are exerting all the influence they can command in the direction of bringing about uniformity in methods of collecting statistics in different places.

Where complete accuracy is unattainable, it is important to be able to calculate the limits of the possible inaccuracy. If we know the exact conditions under which the data were collected, and the precautions taken to ensure correctness, then to calculate such limits may be within our power, and due allowance for error can be made. It may be added that if, when statistics are being collected, the use that is to be made of them is known and borne in mind, then—although it may be necessary to make some allowance for the possible effects of bias—they are more likely to be valuable for their purpose.

§ 2. *The interpretation of simple statistics.*—Apart from any inaccuracy in the actual figures, there is a constant danger of reading into statistics what—when properly interpreted and analysed—they cannot be shewn to imply. For in the phenomena to which they relate there may be differences, of which the mere figures taken by themselves yield no indication. A few simple illustrations may be given of the kinds of error likely to result, if heterogeneous and incommensurable quantities are treated as though they were homogeneous and commensurable.

In the comparison of price-lists, and in many other enquiries, constant guard must be kept against overlooking differences in quality. This applies even to raw materials. The quality of corn. for example, as well as the yield of the harvest, varies with the season; so that the Gazette average of wheat may itself be misleading. The fact of variation in the quality of raw materials is clearly recognised by Professor Rogers in his *History of Agriculture and Prices*. He purposely omits all notice of inferior grain, and in calculating the average price of cattle neglects such quotations as evidently relate to animals much below the average quality. Similar omissions are made in the case of wool; and it is pointed out that in this case the difficulty is increased by the fact that even among the various kinds of best wool, there is so large a difference in value as to suggest a difference of breeds in different districts. It is clear that under such conditions as these, the most careful judgment in the selection and manipulation of figures is essential. The task of comparing prices, simple as it may at first sight appear, is found to be one that needs for its adequate performance, not only freedom from bias, but also wide experience, and sagacity of a high order[1].

[1] "As regards agricultural production, the initial difficulty of all the statistics is the different value of the units which go by the same name. The wheat, oats, and barley of one country, though called by the same names, are not the same as the wheat, oats, and barley of another country. There are the very greatest differences in quality, as any price list of London or other market, where grain from every part of the world is sold, would shew. Yet nothing is so common as comparisons of the world's production of wheat, for instance, in which this difference of quality is ignored, and fine reasonings are indulged in where this difference of quality might seriously affect the result. What is true of grain is as true, if not more true, of live stock. There are sheep and sheep, cattle and cattle, horses and horses; in truth the agricultural live stock of any two countries, instead of being susceptible of ready comparison, can hardly be compared directly at all. The point is notoriously of great importance in historical investigations. In comparing England of the present

When we pass from raw matérials to manufactured goods, the difficulty is enormously increased. There is room for wide divergence in quality, when only one kind of material enters into the composition of the commodity in question; and when materials are mixed, the proportion of the more valuable to the less valuable may in some cases vary almost indefinitely. The same names may even in course of time come to denote things that are practically different in kind.

One or two instances may help to illustrate the point under discussion. It might have been anticipated that during the extraordinary inflation in the price of tin in the early part of 1888, the exports of tin-plates would decrease. As a matter of fact, however, they shewed a slight increase; and the explanation of the apparent anomaly seems to be that a large proportion of the goods classed as tin-plates in the Board of Trade returns have little or no tin in their composition. During the period when the price of tin was so high, the shipment of these thin iron plates largely predominated over those more thickly coated with tin[1].

Another example is afforded by an instance in which

day with the England of previous centuries the difference of the average weight and qualities of the live stock called by the same names has always to be considered. In nothing in recent years, as I understand, have some continental countries such as France made more remarkable improvement than in the quality of their live stock, so that with no increase in numbers, or little increase, there has been an enormous advance in real production. The point is of equal importance in international comparisons" (Giffen *on International Statistical Comparisons* in the *Economic Journal* for June 1892, p. 225). Many other valuable illustrations of points mentioned in the text will be found in this article.

[1] See the *Economist*, 30 June 1888, p. 823.

the value given for a consignment of shirtings to New
Zealand was challenged as being so low as to be obviously
incorrect. Invoices were accordingly produced, and they
proved both that the figures were rightly quoted, and that
the goods were really described as shirtings. Further
enquiry, however, brought out the fact that their object
was to serve as shrouds for the carcases of sheep sent to
Europe in refrigerating chambers. It need hardly be added
that for this purpose an article much inferior in quality and
price to those ordinarily classed as shirtings was required[1].

In some cases the differences in quality are now in one
direction, now in the other, so that over any fairly large
area they practically cancel one another. Error may then
be avoided by simply taking averages. But no such resource is available where the changes tend to be all in one
direction, as in the improvement in the quality of some
manufactured goods, and in house accommodation. In
certain cases, as already indicated, there is a progressive
change of quality even in raw materials. "An ox or a
sheep," Professor Marshall remarks, "weighs now more
than twice as much as it used to; of that weight a larger
percentage is meat, of the meat a larger percentage is
prime meat, and of all the meat a larger percentage is solid
food, and a smaller percentage is water."[2]

An instance of a somewhat different kind may be
added, in which mere price-lists are likely to mislead those
who have not special knowledge of the trades in which
the lists are used. Where the price of the raw material is
subject to considerable fluctuations, it is not unusual for

[1] *British Association Report* for 1885, p. 870.
[2] *Contemporary Review*, March, 1887, p. 375.

the nominal wholesale price of finished goods to remain unchanged—that is to say, there is no alteration in the published price-lists—while there is, nevertheless, an actual alteration in prices through a modification of discounts and in other ways. For reasons of this kind, price-lists may sometimes be even worse than useless, unless supplemented by additional information.

Another obvious case in which care is necessary in the interpretation of statistics need be touched upon only briefly. Whenever there are changes in the prices of commodities, it is clear that values, say of exports or imports, afford no adequate measure of amounts. For instance, in 1872 we exported iron and steel to the value of £35,996,167, and cotton yarn to the value of £16,697,426; while in 1882 the figures had fallen to £31,598,306, and £12,864,711. The amounts were, however, only 3,382,762 tons and 212,327,972 lbs. in the former year; while they were 4,353,552 tons and 238,254,700 lbs. in the latter. Here then is a further reason why all statistics involving prices need to be interpreted with caution. It is now generally recognised that between distant periods any bare comparison of prices is worthless; we are practically more in danger of being led astray in the comparison of statistics over a long series of consecutive years.

Passing to statistics of wages, it is to be observed that the figures themselves usually give nothing more than nominal time wages, and hence afford a very uncertain criterion both of real wages and of task wages. Other variables are involved in the determination of both of these, and supplementary statistics are therefore required if a comparison is to be made either of the well-being of the working classes, or of the cost of labour, at different periods or in different localities. Account must, for instance, be taken, not only of variations in the prices of those commodities upon which wages are habitually spent, but also of variations in their quality, thus again introducing the difficulties to which reference has already been made. We need not dwell upon the importance of also taking into consideration variations in hours of labour, intensity of labour, continuity of employment, and so on. The necessity of having regard to such points as these shews, however, the difficulty attending arguments from wage-statistics to the condition and progress of the working classes. Any argument bearing upon this problem should if possible be cumulative, the same result being obtained from different points of view and from quite independent figures.

In other questions relating to wages it may be necessary to take account of the quality of the work done; and the neglect of this consideration may equally vitiate an argument from statistics. Professor Cliffe Leslie, in seeking to controvert the doctrine that wages tend to an equality, remarks that "Dorsetshire, Somersetshire, and Devonshire labourers have for the last fifty years been earning less than half what the same men might have earned in Northumberland." Granting, however, that, during the period referred to, agricultural wages in Northumberland were twice those of the south-western counties, it does not follow that the same men, who earned ten shillings a week in Devonshire, would have been able to earn twenty shillings if they had migrated to the north; for the very fact that the northern labourers had for two or three generations been earning higher wages would be likely to make them more efficient workers and more valuable to their employers.

A further difficulty arises from the fact that in the course of time the character of the work itself may change; so that men who are called by the same name are not necessarily doing the same work. For instance, the rates of pay of postmen in India have increased considerably in recent years. The work required of them is, however, found to be of a different character, involving greater responsibility, and demanding a better education and a higher degree of intelligence. In 1855 they had only to deliver letters, and many of them could not even read their own vernacular. Now they have to pay money orders, and some of them are expected to read English as well as the vernacular language of the district[1].

From what has been said in this and the preceding section it follows that if a collection of statistics is to be of scientific value, it should not be a mere list of figures. The method of collection and the principle of compilation should be carefully explained; and, if possible, notes should be added touching on any peculiar influences that have affected the phenomena themselves, or the accuracy of the returns, during the period over which the statistics extend. There should in particular be evidence that any apparent anomalies have been made the subject of special investigation, so as to exclude the possibility of their being simply due to error of some kind. The more experienced the statistician, the more scepticism he shews about all statistics which have not been compiled in accordance with the above conditions.

[1] See Barbour, *Theory of Bimetallism*, p. 125.

§ 3. *The range of statistics.*—Another danger to be guarded against in the use of statistics is that of basing conclusions upon an incomplete survey. It need hardly be said that if we are seeking empirically to determine the effects of any cause, either our facts and figures should be gathered from the whole area or period over which the operation of that cause is felt, or we should at least have adequate grounds for believing that those statistics to which we confine our attention are typical and representative. A similar precaution is necessary when by the aid of statistics we investigate the course or progress of economic phenomena.

From this point of view it is necessary again to refer to the importance of considering the manner in which statistics are collected. The individual statistics may be perfectly correct, but they may be unrepresentative. It is, for instance, unsatisfactory to obtain statistics of wages by means of circular letters forwarded to workmen with the request that they will fill in various details. Only a few send answers, and these are likely to be the better off and the more intelligent. There is, therefore, no guarantee that the statistics so obtained are really typical.

Another point to notice in connexion with wage-statistics is that in comparing wages in different occupations and at different times, average yearly earnings constitute the only satisfactory unit. The regularity of employment varies enormously in different trades and at different periods; and a mere record of the daily or weekly wages earned by those who succeed in getting work may, therefore, be misleading, in so far as it gives no indication of the extent to which workmen are liable to be temporarily unemployed.

Professor Thorold Rogers's view that the fifteenth century and the first quarter of the sixteenth may be regarded as "the golden age of the English labourer" has from this standpoint been criticized by Dr Cunningham and others, on the ground that it rests not only upon the interpretation of prices, but also upon the assumption that the labourer's income is fairly represented by three hundred times his daily wages.

Turning to a different department of economic enquiry, it is unsatisfactory, in seeking to investigate the effects of gold discoveries on prices, to attend only to statistics of prices in a few principal markets. Cliffe Leslie adduces evidence to shew that the gold discoveries of 1850 coincided with the opening up of backward places through improvements in means of communication. This tended to bring about—what there had not previously been—a level of prices between the hitherto backward places and the great centres of commerce and industry; and the new gold enabled the process to be carried out by a levelling-up instead of a levelling-down, *i.e.*, it was made possible for prices to be raised in the former localities without their being at the same time lowered in the latter. It was, accordingly, in backward places—for example, on the new lines of railway in the inland parts of Ireland and Scotland, and similarly in many countries of Europe—that the effect of the gold discoveries in raising prices was most apparent; it could not be properly estimated by merely considering prices in great towns such as London and Paris[1].

Considerations of a somewhat similar kind are pertinent

---

[1] *Essays in Political and Moral Philosophy*, 1888, pp. 282, ff.

in relation to the effects of diminished gold supplies. Professor Nicholson holds that a falling off in the supplies of·gold is likely to exert its primary influence in countries on the margin of the commercial world, in which credit is comparatively little developed; and that we cannot, therefore, properly investigate the operation of the diminished production of bullion by simply attending to statistics of gold reserves, and movements of the precious metals, in the great centres of commerce.

§ 4. *The grouping of statistics.*—While our statistics must not be partial, we must also seek to fulfil the more difficult requirement of so grouping or "weighting" them, as to bring out correctly their relative importance. In studying the course of prices, for instance, while careful not to overlook any markets occupying a unique position or affected by peculiar influences, we must also be careful not to assign the same relative weight to small as to large markets.

A simple example will serve to indicate what is here meant. Suppose that on two successive days the price of corn in any market is thirty-two shillings and thirty-six shillings a quarter; then a bare consideration of these figures gives thirty-four shillings as the average price for the two days. But suppose further that three times as much corn is bought and sold on the first day as on the second, then for most purposes it would be more correct to say that the average is thirty-three shillings. Speaking more generally, if amounts a, b, c are on different occasions sold at prices x, y, z respectively, we weight our price returns accordingly, and take as our average not $\dfrac{x + y + z}{3}$, but $\dfrac{ar + by + cz}{a + b + c}$. Where data for the determination of a, b, c are not available, it is usually impossible to ensure that our averages are not sometimes unduly enhanced, and sometimes unduly depressed, by reason of an exaggerated importance being assigned to small transactions of an exceptional character. In such a problem as that of measuring changes in the general purchasing power of money, the task of assigning varying weights to our primary figures becomes at the same time of increasing importance and increasing difficulty[1].

In taking the average of a series of averages there is a special risk of error, somewhat analogous to that just discussed. Thus, if there is a relative increase in the number of workers in more highly paid occupations, the average wages of all labour may rise much faster than the average of representative wages in each trade, or may even rise while the latter is stationary or falling. To quote an illustration given by Professor Marshall,—"If there are 500 men in grade A earning 12s. a week, 400 in grade B earning 25s., and 100 in grade C earning 40s., the average wages of the 1000 men are 20s. If after a time 300 from grade A have passed on to grade B, and 300 from grade B to grade C, the wages in each grade remaining stationary, then the average wages of the whole thousand men will be 28s. 6d. And even if the rate of wages in each grade had meanwhile fallen 10 per cent., the average wages of all

---

[1] The need for a "weighted index-number" is, however, diminished, if the number of commodities taken as the basis of the calculation is made very large indeed.

would still be about 25s. 6d., that is, would have risen more than 25 per cent."[1]

The taking of averages is thus frequently complicated by the fact that an equal significance ought not to be attached to all the figures; and the difficulty of the problem is still further increased when some kind of average less easy of calculation than the arithmetical is appropriate. In the great majority of economic investigations the arithmetical average is, indeed, the most suitable as well as the simplest; but there are some exceptions. For instance, if population doubles itself in twenty-five years, it is obviously

---

[1] *Principles of Economics*, vol. i., 3rd edition, p. 772 *note*. Similarly Sir Robert Giffen, in the article referred to in the note on p. 358, points out that "it is quite conceivable that in one of two countries the earnings may be higher than in the other in every single employment which can be enumerated and compared, and yet the average earnings of the average wage earning man may be higher in the latter country than in the former, the reason being the different distribution of the people according to earnings." The correctness of the above statement is shewn by a theoretical comparison as follows. Take first a community of 1000 wage-earners distributed amongst employments A, B, C, D, E, the annual wages in these employments being respectively £50, £60, £70, £80, £90, and the numbers of men employed in them being respectively 500, 200, 100, 100, 100. Then take another community also of 1000 wage-earners in which the corresponding wages are £40, £50, £60, £70, £80 and the numbers employed 100, 100, 100, 200, 500. The average wages per head will be found to be in the first case £61, and in the second case £69. "In a comparison of rates of wages merely according to the nature of the employment, the wages in the first community would obviously appear higher than in the second, and this would be strictly true in a sense; but the inference would be untrue that the average earnings of the wage-earning classes in the first community, striking a true average, would be higher."

incorrect to say that the average annual increase is four per cent.[1]

There are some cases in which to take an average at all may be misleading. If, for instance, we take an average of men's wages and children's wages, or of the earnings of professional men and manual labourers, or of house-rents in Whitechapel and in the neighbourhood of Hyde Park, we are averaging things that belong to different categories, neither of which is really represented in the result. Even if such an average can be of service for any special purpose, it will become delusive when used in ignorance of the diverse nature of the data on which it is based[2].

If there is continuity in our data, so that—although the extremes are far removed from one another—we pass between them gradually and through all intermediate grades, then it is a different matter. But in any case the value of an average is enormously increased if at the same time the range of the variations on both sides is clearly stated. The truth is that an average from its very nature lets drop a considerable amount of information. In itself it tells nothing as to the manner in which the data from which it

[1] On the different kinds of averages, and on the subject of averages in general, see Venn, *Logic of Chance*, 1888, Chapters 18, 19; also Bowley, *Elements of Statistics*, pp. 107, ff.

[2] It has been said, *e.g.*, by Mr Longe, that there is no such thing as an average or general rate of wages. In one sense this admits of easy disproof, since we can take the arithmetical mean of any series of quantities whatever. What is meant, however, is that wages in different occupations are unrelated to one another and disparate, so that their average is a mere number and has no practical signification or importance. This view, although it may be rejected, will serve to illustrate the meaning of what is said above in the text.

is obtained are grouped. It may, therefore, advantageously be accompanied by a supplementary statement on this point, giving not only the extreme deviations from the average as above suggested, but also the average deviation[1].

This leads to the remark that in treating of fluctuations from an average, considerable importance attaches to the particular range over which the average has been calculated. In dealing, for instance, with the statistics of some phenomenon over a term of years, we may seek to establish a periodicity in the movements towards and away from the average; but the average, if taken for successive periods of years, may itself be subject to progressive variations, and unless these are correctly calculated and due allowance made for them, our conclusions may be seriously vitiated. Thus what has been called the "par" of trade, that is, the level which indicates neither prosperity nor depression, is itself ever gradually shifting its position. The exports and imports of any given year, the railway traffic receipts, the production of iron and the like, must not be compared simply with the corresponding statistics of some former period; for they may all shew an increase, and yet—because the normal level has itself risen in the interval—the later date may coincide with the lowest tide of depression, whilst the earlier coincided with the highest tide of prosperity[2]. On the other hand, if we are studying the secular movements, it is equally necessary to have analysed the periodic variations. Averages of terms of years have to be

---

[1] Compare Venn, *Logic of Chance*, pp. 444, ff.

[2] If we merely compare a single year at one period with a single year at another, we are practically committing the fallacy referred to in the preceding section, namely, of arguing from partial data.

compared, and the periods over which these averages are taken should be such as to eliminate as far as possible interferences caused by the periodic movements[1].

It is not intended to give here a systematic discussion of the technique of the statistical method; and enough has now been said to indicate the nature of the difficulties to which the treatment of statistics may give rise. The theory of statistics, which investigates in detail both the principles in accordance with which statistics should in the first instance be collected and arranged, and also the right methods of taking averages and dealing with fluctuations, is, as we have already pointed out, a department of applied logic or methodology. As such, it demands a distinctive treatment, though it seems hardly appropriate to speak of it as an independent science.

---

[1] Compare Jevons, *Investigations in Currency and Finance,* pp. 34, ff.

INDEX.

378 INDEX.

Method of political economy, 30.
Mill, James, on the consumption of wealth, 106 *n.*, 107 *n.*, 108 *n.*, 110.
Mill, J. S., on the scope and method of political economy, 11 *sqq.*; on the distribution of wealth, 42 *n.*; on the rule of *laisser faire*, 74; on export duties, 77; on political economy as a psychological science, 90: on capital, 103 *n.*; on the consumption of wealth, 110 *n.*; on political economy as an abstract science, 116 *sqq.*; on socialism, 132, 3; on the problem of sociology, 141; on the 'statics' and 'dynamics' of political economy, 146; on definitions, 155; on the method of difference, 192, 198 *n.*; on peasant proprietorship, 206, 7; on the method of simple observation, 210, 11; on the deductive method, 216; on the verification of deductive reasoning, 233; on international values, 246, 7; his use of mathematical conceptions, 253; his use of numerical illustrations, 256 *n.*; on the applicability of mathematical principles, 256, 7; his treatment of variables as constants, 263; on economic progress, 284.
Mobility of labour, 132; 310; 361.
Money, definition of, 168; 170; value of, 162 *n.*
Monopoly, 68; 241.
Montague, F. C., 326 *n.*

Moral forces, operation of, 40—5.
Moral science, 87.
Mouat, F. J., on statistical science, 330, 1.
Mutual dependence of economic phenomena, 211; 264.

Narrative economics, 174, 5.
National economy, 100.
National economy, art of, 78.
Natural liberty, maxim of, 71.
New South Wales and Victoria, 193, 4; 196—8.
Nicholson, J. S., on Adam Smith, 73 *n.*; on the definition of wealth, 96 *n.*; on the use of an historical method of definition, 168 *n.*; his treatise on 'Money,' 232 *n.*; on general prices, 247 *n.*, 271 *n.*; on the effects of machinery on wages, 280, 281 *n.*; on the effects of diminished gold supplies, 365.
Normal value, 224, 5.
Normative science, 34, 5.
Norway and Sweden, 191, 2; 195
Numerical premisses, 256—60.

Observation, 173 *sqq.*; 227—36.
Official statistics, 351, 2; 355.
Over-production, 107; 312.
Owen, R., 185.

Palgrave, R. H. I., *Dictionary of Political Economy*, 22 *n.*; 174 *n.*; 245 *n.*; 340 *n.*
Peasant proprietorship, 18; 206, 7.
Permissive legislation, 184.
Perpetualism of theory, 298 *n.*
Personal wealth, 99